Instant Encore 1.5

Douglas Spotted Eagle

Routledge
Taylor & Francis Group

LONDON AND NEW YORK

First published 2004 by CMP Books, an imprint of CMP Media LLC
This edition published 2013
by Focal Press

Published 2021 by Routledge
2 Park Square, Milton Park, Abingdon, Oxon OX14 4RN
605 Third Avenue, New York, NY 10017

Routledge is an imprint of the Taylor & Francis Group, an informa business

ISBN 13: 978-1-578-20245-4 (pbk)
ISBN 13: 978-0-080-50885-6 (ebk)

DOI: 10.4324/9780080508856

Table of Contents

With Gratitude

Each and every book is different. The words in this book are my responsibility, but lots of people have gone into making it possible through their help, kind words, criticisms, pointers, tutorials, and other forms of encouragement and commitment. It's rare readers ever see or hear from the people that really drive this video industry; I hope to point a small amount of recognition to those that are a big part of the industry as a whole.

First and foremost, I need to thank Linda for always being there, making sure that everything is organized, and that my life runs as smoothly as it can for someone running on seven cylinders.

Second, Mannie Frances, my partner in VASST, who keeps the business side of everything organized. Mannie, thanks for being part of realizing this dream of our own book series. We finally did it, partner!

To Wes Howell, my tech editor, friend, and inspiration on this project. Your points on this book were right on, your words were masterful, and without you, there is no way this book would have been put into a form that readers could comprehend. Thanks a lot, man! I'm looking forward to our being on the Encore road and training folks on using this great tool.

Of course, ultimately the book wouldn't be in anyone's hands if it weren't for Paul Temme and Dorothy Cox at CMP. I can't express my appreciation for you two in seeing the dream and understanding the complex world of VASST. Thank you for taking the risk in creating a new book series. We know we won't let you down. Gail, thanks for making sure we said our words in the correct format.

To the crew at Adobe, folks like David Trescot, Kristin Chan, Marc Coates, Erik Lundblade, Kendall Eckman, Bruce Bowman, Hart Schafer, Kelly Lynn, Jason Levine, Richard Townhill, Tina Eckman, Daniel Brown, and Adobe evangelists like Mike Downey, Tim Kolb, Mike Gunter, Graham Shanks, and, of course, Wes—thanks for all the support and encouragement.

To the folks at Echo, Canopus, ADS Technology, Contour Shuttle Pro, Matrox, Ulead, Artbeats, Canon, Sony, B&H, Mackie, M-Audio, Videoguys, Pixelan, DMN, DVInfo.net, DV.com, thanks for supporting what VASST is. To Ron, whose words of discouragement became my motivation, and to Michelle, whose positive critiques became my improvement. As the song says, "We're Still Here!"

Phil, Julie, Wanda, Bob, and everyone at Artbeats: thank you so much for providing us with great footage to work with in the VASST series books.

Chris Hurd, thanks for your constant support. Earl Foote, Jerry Lonn, Rudy Sarzo, Jeffrey Fisher, Richard Harrington, Ron Dabbs, Mark Dileo: damn, who'da thunk VASST would grow this much in just a few years? Thanks to Lou, Frank, and Michael, for helping us stand tall. Lawrence, Cindy, thank you for all the Asian support of VASST.

Dave H, Dave C, Curtis P, Michael B, Gary R, Caleb P, Dennis A, Richard K, you guys have been an amazing uplifting force in my education as a videographer. Amanda, thanks for teaching me that with faith, we can survive tragedy and go on to be better human beings.

The VASST attendees over the years have inspired this book series, we hope we meet and exceed the benchmarks that we've set with our live and DVD training products.

Finally, I have to thank the music. The music elevated me to a level of being creative with video. Thanks to the folks at Windham Hill and later Virgin who inspired me to do my own music videos. Thanks to the folks at PBS, BET, CNN, and other networks who have run my work. If it weren't for the music, I'd never have learned I had a video side to my brain. The music drives me, but the video is a wonderful extension of that, so thank you to all my fans who have helped me keep making the music, and given me support.

Tech Editor's Notes

This book is about helping people get up to speed quickly with the Encore; smoothing the learning curve and giving the reader the opportunity to glean knowledge and experience from someone that's walked a mile in their shoes. As many of you already know, Douglas Spotted Eagle is an accomplished musician, author, videographer, renowned presenter and all around digital video guru. You've picked a great book, and most impressively, an even better author. Not every Emmy or Grammy winner is willing to sit down and share their knowledge with others.

As an author myself, I can honestly say that Douglas is one of those people that possess an uncanny knack for empowering people with the right amount of information at the right time; not too much, not too little, and not too technical either. It's all about getting the job done. That's the point of this book. One of the book's greatest strengths is its ability to provide quick access to the most relevant information. Learn what you need to know when you need to know it.

I also believe it's fair to say that there are a few areas of Encore that may be challenging to learn for some users. Fortunately there aren't very many of these hurdles to clear. Once a few key points are absorbed, everything comes together very nicely. That was the greatest challenge of editing the technical sides of this book, trying to determine exactly what the reader needs to comprehend without intimidating the eye with a thick tome.

Getting to the point where you understand Encore is a very satisfying experience, and one you're certain to appreciate as you read through this book.

Wes Howell
Associate Producer/Trainer
Sundance Media Group
www.vasst.com

Introduction

Welcome to DVD authoring with Encore 1.5, brought to you by Adobe, the leader in desktop graphics.

DVDs have taken over the video world as a means of distributable, navigable, and interactive-experienced video presentations, and Adobe's Encore 1.5 allows users to create DVD projects that rival anything coming out of Hollywood today.

DVDs are part of the revival of all sorts of older movies, musical projects, television series, and the new delivery mechanism for your family home videos, slideshows, or "this is your life" videos. DVDs also allow a one-man show look like a major production studio with good DVD authoring tools and creative skills. Encore is a great DVD authoring tool, and this book will teach you how to use it. Through consistent and constant use of the application, close observation of DVDs from the big name studios, and a little perspiration, you should be able to develop a creative skillset in a short period of time.

Encore isn't the highest-end tool available, but it is many levels above the typical consumerware that's available.

This book isn't written to impress you with lots of fancy methods of using Encore DVD 1.5. It is written with sound workflows in mind, to teach you how to use the software quickly, efficiently, and correctly. This book is also written to give you some tricks to finding faster means of accomplishing seemingly complex tasks. One caveat: Adobe's Encore 1.5 is a powerful standalone application, but it's strongly recommended that you have Adobe's Photoshop on hand if you are interested in creating deep, high-end menus. Encore is tightly integrated with Photoshop, and files may be opened directly in Photoshop from the Encore interface. This book does not go deeply into the Encore/Photoshop relationship. That alone is entirely another book.

The VASST philosophy is to give you information you need to get started and then provide more information to get you inspired. Developing the chops that make you unique as an editor are your own responsibility. VASST merely opens the door for you.

In order to use Encore at its best, you'll need a fairly powerful computer. Encoding to MPEG is one of the toughest tasks you'll throw at your CPU; so the faster, the better. While Adobe requires only a Pentium III 800 and 256MB of RAM, I recommend you look at a Pentium 4 with at least 1GB of RAM to optimally use the application.

Make sure you have plenty of hard drive space. Chances are if you are already editing video, you've got a good amount of storage already, but it's a great idea to have at least two drives. Never store video, audio, or graphics files on the boot drive unless absolutely necessary. It slows down the entire process.

If you are authoring DVDs containing surround, have a good set of surround sound monitors and a decent sound card. While a Soundblaster or similar PCI card will suffice, it barely will pass muster. A higher quality card like an Echo, M-Audio, or similar product will provide a much better monitoring experience.

I highly recommend dual video monitors. Encore has a lot of palettes and workspaces, and dual monitors make it much easier to work with when you can spread the application out over two views. Dual-head video cards are available from many vendors. Here at Sundance Media, we use the Matrox Parhelia and Matrox Millenium products.

Of course, you'll need a DVD burner to burn your final project, and if you intend on using Macrovision, CSS, or long-form projects exceeding 90 minutes in length, you'll need a DLT machine. Because DLTs are very expensive, consider finding a facility that can take an ISO file or an Encore project from a hard drive and write it to a DLT for you.

Another great tool to have in the arsenal is the Adobe Audition sound editing application. This product comes with audio files known as "loops," which allow you to create looping audio for your menus. Seamless looping of audio is a wonderful feature of a DVD menu. Audition, Sony's ACID libraries, or downloaded looping files may all be used to enhance most any DVD menu.

The technical standard for DVDs specifies the video compression scheme known as MPEG-2. You'll read a lot about MPEG in this book, but it should be said that using the templates in your NLE for MPEG rendering is usually a good idea for folks just starting out. MPEG is somewhat finicky, and playing with the render settings of an NLE's encoding process can potentially make the DVD not playable. If you want to know more about MPEG encoding, some references are available in the back of this book in the bibliography. The more you know, the more your skills will grow.

Check out websites like DV.com, DVInfo.net, and DMNforums.com for more information and access to community-based discussions on MPEG authoring, tips and tricks for Encore, and menu-creation techniques. On the VASST.com site, you'll also find more tutorials from the author and other VASST trainers for Encore, MPEG authoring, and general DV and MPEG information.

Don't forget to check in to us at the VASST.com website!

Keep in mind that to use Encore, you don't need to have all the technical information down. You just need your video content, a little time, some motivation, and of course, this book.

And now...On with the show! Or rather, Encore, Encore!!

Chapter 1

Welcome to Encore

If you haven't already loaded Encore, please do so, to assure you are able to follow along with the various instructions found in this book. Insert the disk into your CD or DVD drive and install the application, following along with the screen prompts.

Be sure to register the application as Adobe is very good about notifying registered users of upgrades, special deals, and other materials available as a benefit to registered users.

Before you start authoring, it's going to take a little while to get familiar with the application, how it functions, and how it appears. If you already use other Adobe products, the interface will look very familiar. Grab a soda or cup of coffee, launch the application on your computer screen, and let's get into Encore!

The Interface

As you assemble your project, you will use several windows, tabs, and palettes. It is important to understand the function of each window in the application in order to get the most out of Encore.

The Project Window

The Project window is the master window providing instant access to all parts of a project. It contains four main tabs representing the major aspects of a project.

The Project tab displays all the files used in a project: assets, menus, and timelines.

The Menu tab shows all the menus in a project. When a menu is selected, the lowest pane shows all the buttons in the menu.

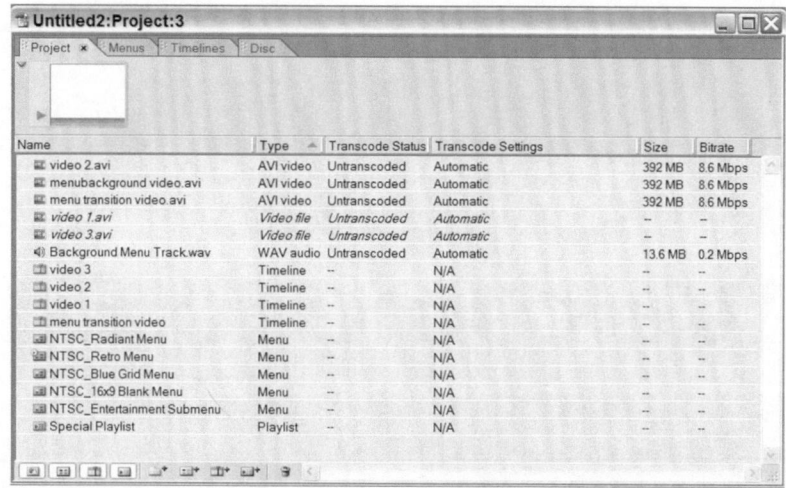

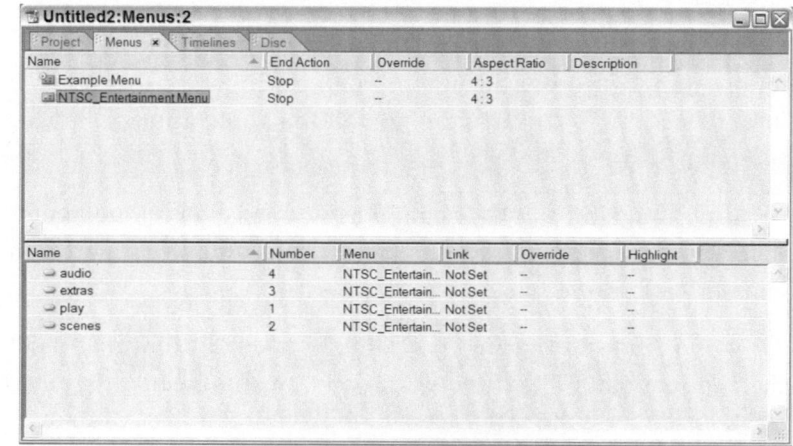

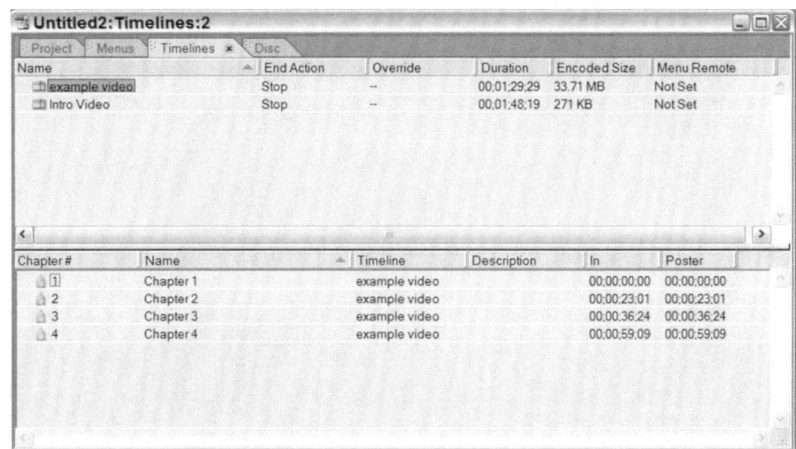

The Timelines tab displays all the timelines in a project. If a timeline is selected, its chapter points are displayed in the lowest pane.

The Disc tab is used in the final stages of a project. It presents options when building a final project.

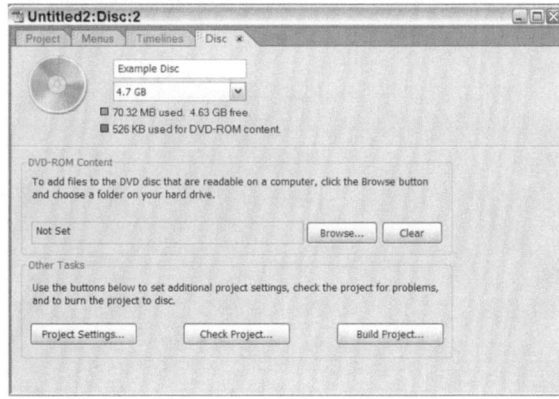

The Palette Window

The Palette window is a collection of the most essential tools in Encore.

The Properties palette is the most frequently used palette in Encore. It displays the properties of selected items.

The Library palette stores frequently used graphics, buttons, menu backgrounds and menu templates.

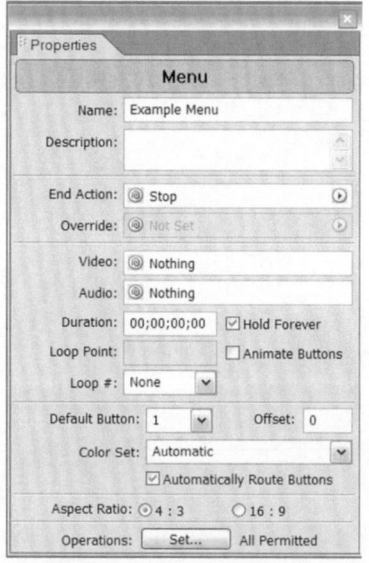

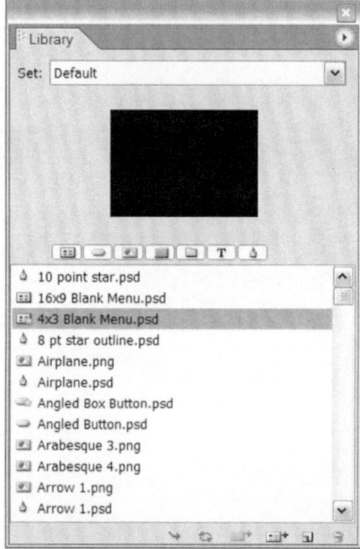

The Layers palette gives a look into the structure of menus and buttons.

The Character palette provides several options for customizing text in a menu and for subtitles.

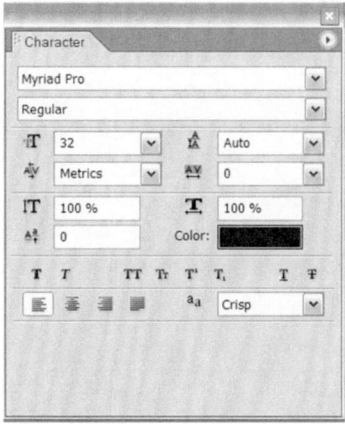

The Menu Editor

You can create menus in the Menu Editor. This is where you can adapt templates for a project. If there are several menus, users can toggle between menus using tabs positioned at the top of the window.

The Timeline Window

The Timeline window is where audio and video for the main content is assmebled. Chapter points, subtitle tracks, and slideshows may also be created using this window.

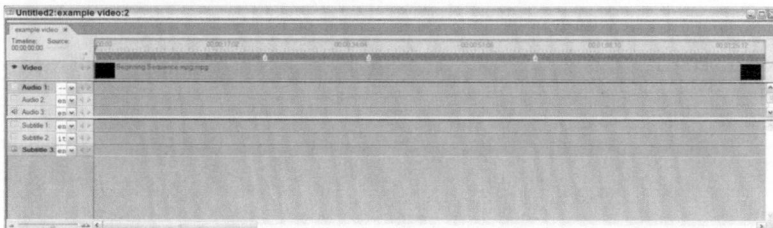

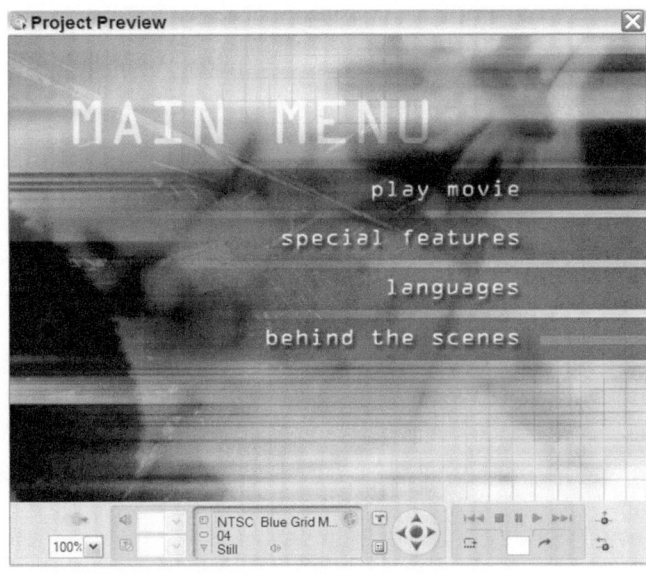

The Monitor window previews content in timelines and can also be used to navigate between and to create subtitles.

The Toolbar

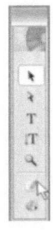

The Toolbar provides access to selection, text, and zoom tools. Version 1.5 adds two icons. The first is used for previewing projects; the second provides quick access to the Edit in Photoshop function.

The Preview Window

The Preview window behaves like a DVD player simulator. It provides navigation controls that emulate the remote control on a set top player. This window is typically used to preview projects, double check links and navigation, and insure that menus are working properly.

The Workspace

During a project, you will use multiple windows, which may possibly crowd the work area. To get the most out of Encore, it is important to maintain an effective workspace. A cluttered workspace will slow down workflow and create unnecessary frustration. Of course, you can always use dual monitors with Encore as well. In fact, I highly recommend that you use dual monitors unless you are working on a laptop or if cost is a large barrier. Dual LCD monitors are quite reasonable these days.

It's a good idea to minimize windows that are not in use. Some windows can be resized by clicking on the lower-right corners and dragging them to an appropriate size. In Encore 1.0 several

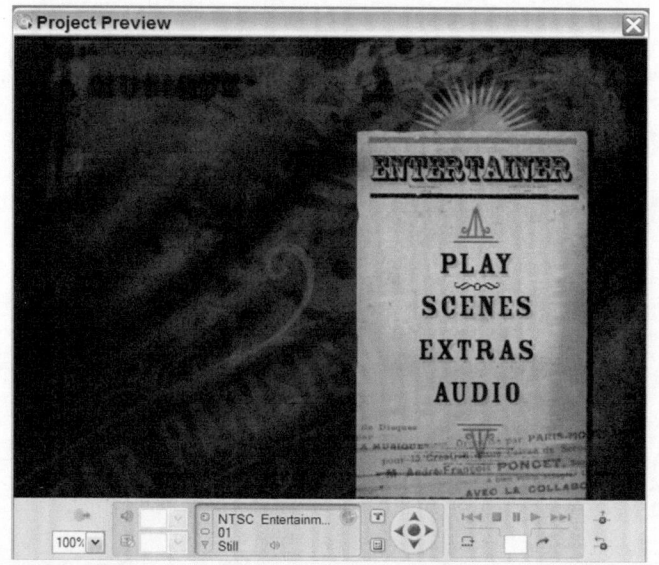

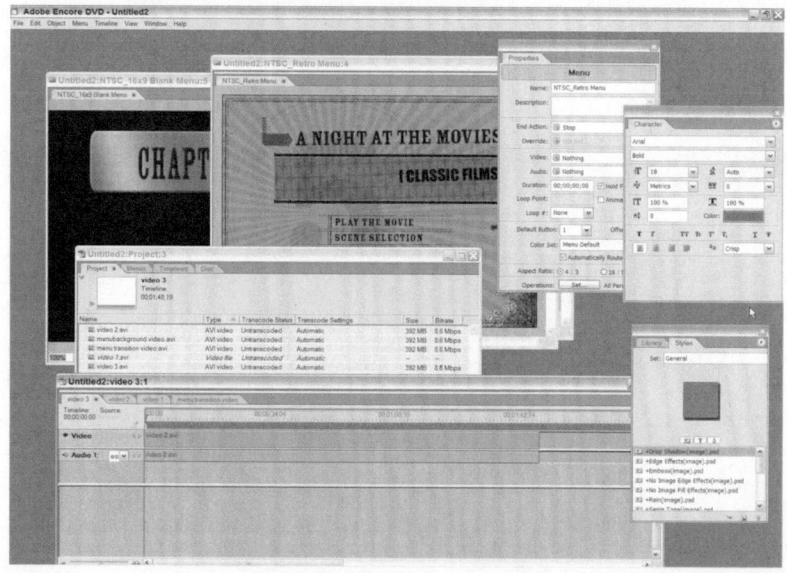

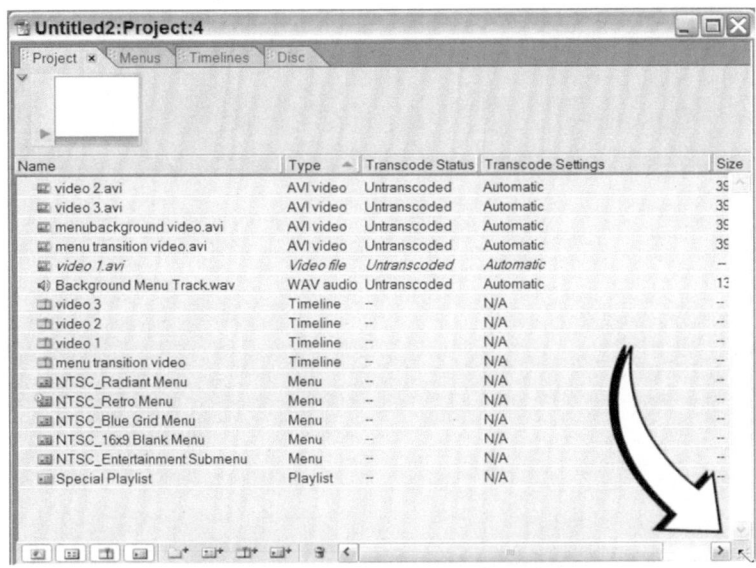

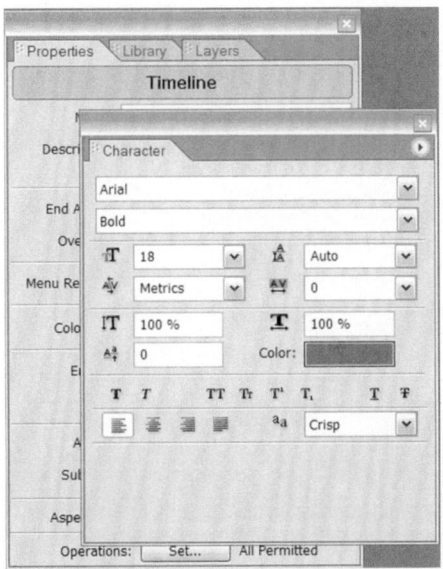

palettes could not be resized. Encore 1.5 has a more flexible workspace allowing you to resize most of the different palettes.

Palettes and tabs can be removed from their parent windows by clicking on the upper tab and dragging them outside the parent window. They can be recombined in the same way. A palette or tab can only be placed in the parent windows in which they belong. Therefore, a palette cannot be placed in the Project window, and a menu from the Menu Editor can't be placed in the Timelines window.

The properties window will be used to access and set properties for all aspects of a DVD project. Place the properties palette in a visible portion of the screen, and make sure it doesn't get covered by other palettes or windows.

The palettes will always remain on top. Move them over to the corner of the screen.

In the majority of tasks, the Properties palette is used. Make sure to place this palette in an accessible portion of the workspace.

Once a project is closed in Encore 1.5, the window locations are not preserved. The palette locations can be returned to their default places during a project.

To reset the palette locations:

Go to Window>Reset Palette Locations.

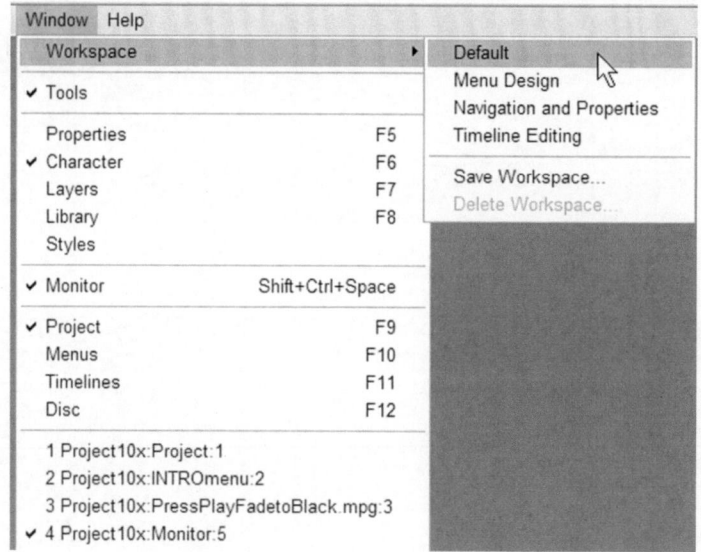

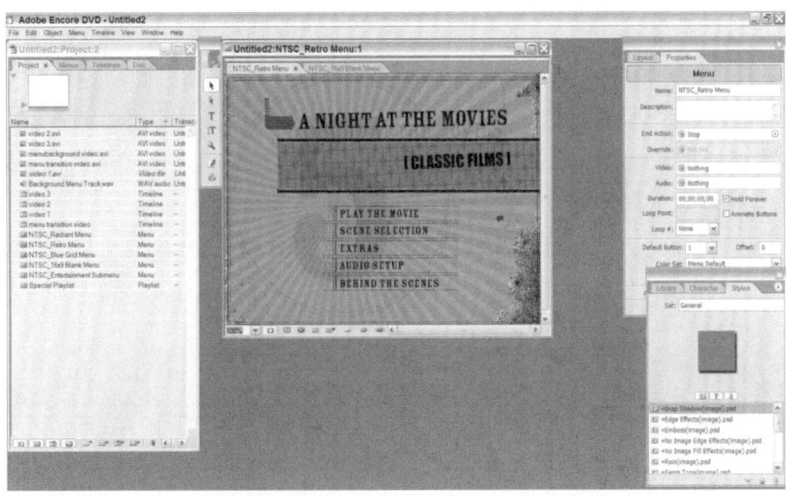

Custom Workspaces
(Encore 1.5 only)

After sizing and arranging palettes and windows, the configuration may be saved as a custom workspace.

Encore saves the palette arrangement including which ones are open, their size, and their location. Encore also remembers the position of the Menu Editor, Timeline, and Monitor windows. This allows the user to build custom workspaces that cater to specific tasks and workflows.

To create a custom workspace:

Arrange and size windows the way you want.

Choose Window > Workspace > Save Workspace.

Type a name for the workspace, and click Save.

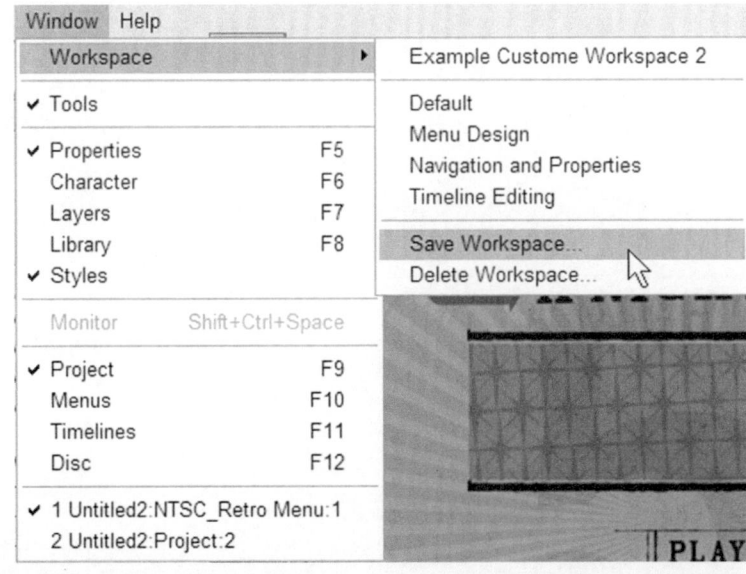

To use a workspace:

Choose Window > Workspace, and choose a workspace.

To delete a custom workspace:

Choose Window > Workspace > Delete Workspace, choose a name, and click Delete.

The First Project:

When using Encore for the first time, the interface is empty until a new project is created or opening an existing project takes place.

To open a new project:

Go to File>New Project

Or use the keyboard shortcut Ctrl+N.

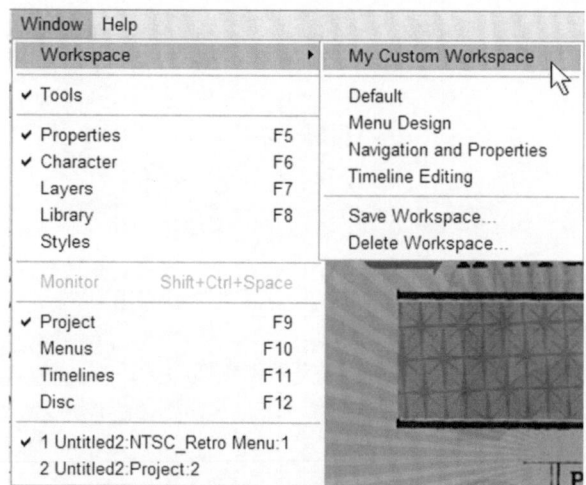

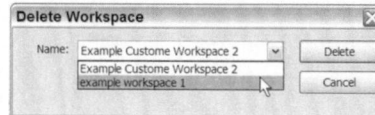

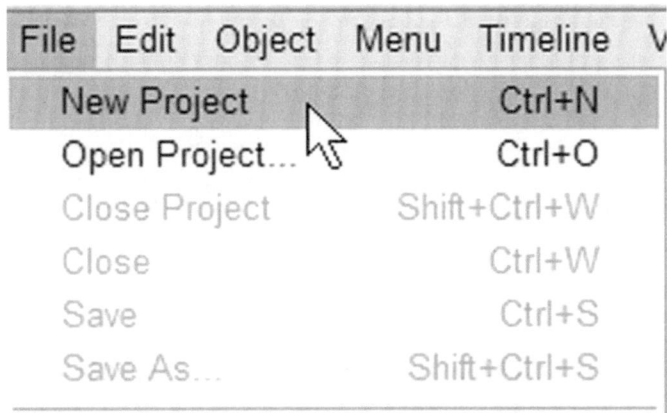

At this point Encore opens the New Project Settings dialog. This dialog determines the television standard on which the DVD will be played.

Choose NTSC for North America.

Choose PAL For Asia and Europe.

Click OK.

When you open a new project, the Project window is displayed. At this time, Encore is ready to import assets.

Turn On/Off the Prompt for TV Standard

When you open a new project, the Don't Prompt for TV Standard option is given in the Project TV Standard dialog. If you check this box before clicking OK, the next time you open a new project, it will immediately use the TV standard you chose earlier.

You can turn the Prompt for Television Standard back on for new projects, even if the "Don't Prompt" box was checked in the New Project settings. This is done by accessing the General Preferences settings. However, if you open a project under one particular TV standard, reactivating the prompt does not change the TV standard for the present project.

An "Asset" is any video, graphic, audio, or other element to be used in the creation of the DVD. Manage your assets carefully for the most efficient use of your time and the Encore application.

To access the General Preferences:

Go to Edit>Preferences>General

Or use the keyboard shortcut Ctrl+K.

This opens the Preferences settings for new projects. Also Tool Tips and Beep When Done can be turned and off using this window.

To turn the Prompt for TV Standard on or off:

Check the Prompt for TV Standard box.

Click OK.

To change the default TV standard without prompting for a TV standard:

Select NTSC or PAL and leave the Prompt for TV Standard unchecked.

Click OK.

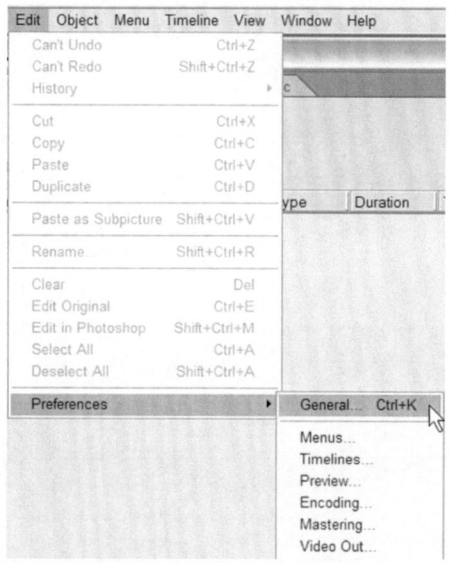

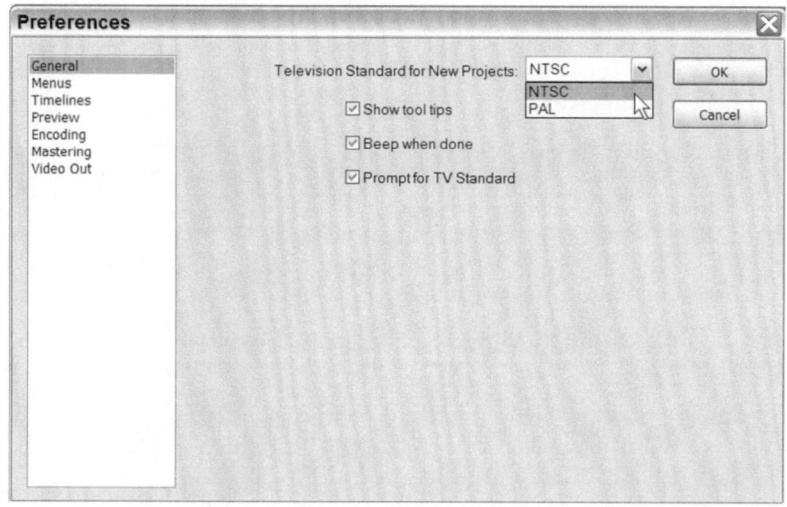

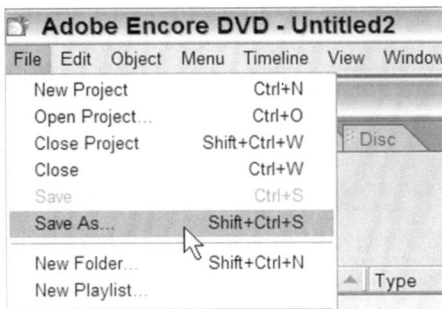

Save and Recall the Project

When you close Encore or a project, a Save Project prompt opens. However, Encore does not use timed backups. In the case of a power failure or computer crash, all unsaved work will be lost. So during the course of a project, it is important to save often.

To save a project for the first time:

Go to File>Save As.

Or use the keyboard shortcut Ctrl-Shift-S.

This opens the Save As dialog.

All projects are saved as Untitled-1,-2, and so on by default.

Choose a desired file location.

Type the name of the project in the File Name field.

Click Save.

Saving to the desktop is a convenient place to save the project files, but it is best to create a new folder on the desktop and save into that folder. This is because Encore creates two file folders and a project preferences file, in addition to the main project file. Creating a separate folder will help reduce clutter on the desktop and prevent accidental deletion.

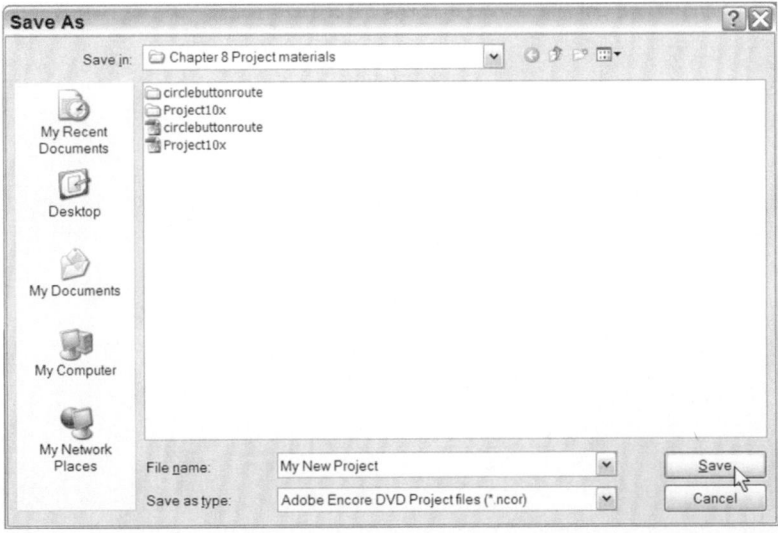

After a project has been saved, Encore allows two options for saving: Save and Save As.

To save a project:

Go to File>Save

Or use the keyboard shortcut Ctrl-S.

Choosing Save updates the previously saved file without prompting for a file name.

To save a project under a new file name:

Go to File>Save As.

Type a new file name for the project.

Click Save.

Choosing Save As opens the Save As dialog. Saving under a new file name saves the project in a different file without saving over the original project file.

You can open projects in one of three ways.

1. Open projects in Windows Explorer by double-clicking on the project (.ncor) icon.

File	Edit	Object	Menu	Timeline	V
New Project				Ctrl+N	
Open Project...				Ctrl+O	
Close Project			Shift+Ctrl+W		
Close				Ctrl+W	
Save				Ctrl+S	
Save As...			Shift+Ctrl+S		
New Folder...			Shift+Ctrl+N		
New Playlist...					
Import as Asset...				Ctrl+I	
Import as Menu...			Shift+Ctrl+I		
Import as Timeline...		Shift+Ctrl+T			
Replace Asset...				Ctrl+H	
Locate Asset...			Shift+Ctrl+H		
Interpret Footage...					

My New Project
Adobe Encore DVD Project
195 KB

Type: Adobe Encore DVD Project
Date Modified: 2/23/2004 3:27 AM
Size: 194 KB

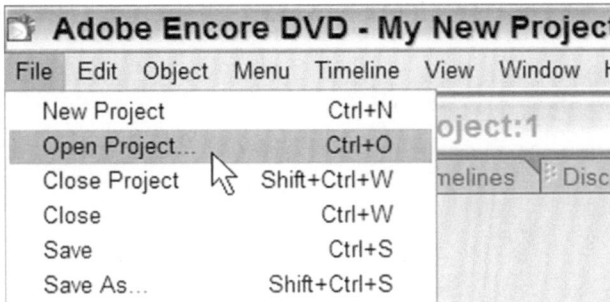

2. Use the Open command in the File menu. This is best for new project files that have been imported from another computer or have not been opened recently.

To open a project file:

Go to File>Open

Or use the keyboard shortcut Ctrl-O.

This opens the Open Project dialog.

Highlight the desired project file.

Click Open.

3. Encore offers yet another choice for opening files. Like many applications, Encore keeps a list of recently used project files for quick access.

To open a recently used project file:

Go to File.

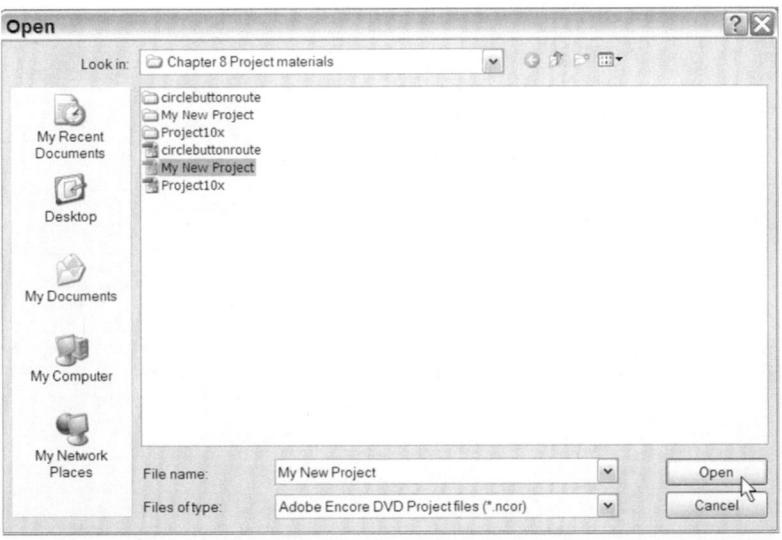

In the lowest portion of the File pull-down menu is a list of files.

Click on the desired file.

Encore now directly opens the project.

Importing Video Assets

An asset is anything imported to the project to use within the project. Nearly all DVDs have motion video as their main content, except in the case of slideshow discs. Encore 1.0 will import most Direct Show compatible video formats, with the exception of QuickTime.(.mov or .qt). QuickTime files are supported in Version 1.5. For DVD authors, MPEG-2 (.mpg, .m2v, .mpv) and AVI are the two most commonly used formats.

There are also restrictions depending on the television standard of the project.

NTSC video must have a frame size of 720¥480, 720¥486, or 704¥480, and must have a frame rate of 23.976, 24, or 29.97 frames per second (fps).

PAL video must have a frame size of 720¥576 or 704¥576, and must have a frame rate of 25 fps.

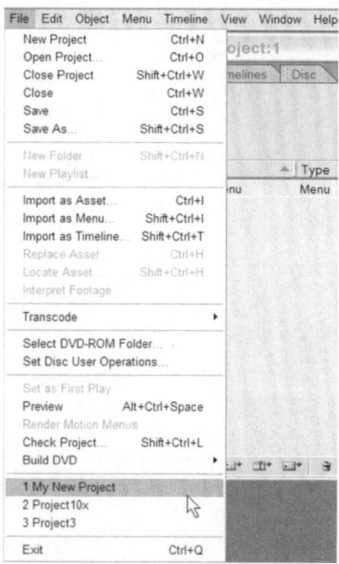

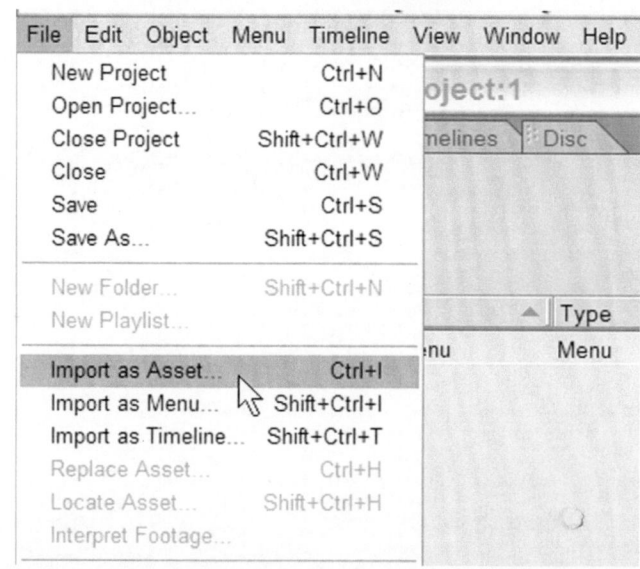

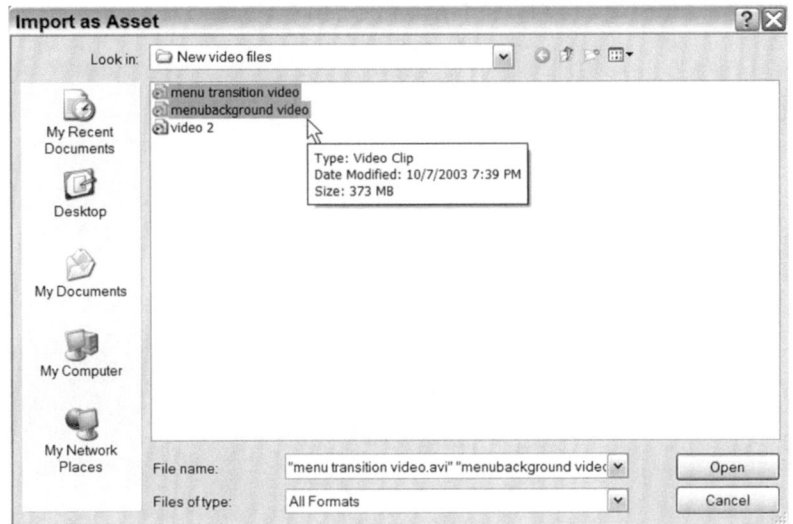

There are three ways to import video assets:

Using the File menu

Using the Project window

Dragging from Windows Explorer

To import video assets using the File menu:

Go to File>Import as Asset

Or use the keyboard shortcut Ctrl-I.

This opens the Import as Asset dialog.

Locate and select the video file(s).

Holding Ctrl while you click on files selects multiple files for import.

Click Open.

The files are imported into the Project window. Any unsupported files will not be imported.

The Project tab in the Project window lists all the major components of the project, such as menus, timelines, and assets. It provides a spreadsheet view of the materials, showing important information such as file size and type of file.

To import video assets using the Project tab:

Right-click inside the Project tab.

Select Import as Asset.

This opens the Import as Asset dialog.

Select the desired file(s).

Click Open.

The video assets now have been imported into the Project tab.

To import video assets using Windows Explorer:

In Windows, open the folder containing the video file(s).

With the Encore Project tab in view, left-click and hold on the file.

Drag the mouse cursor into the Project tab.

Release the left mouse button.

The file(s) have now been imported into the Project tab.

If dragging and dropping files into the Project window is your favorite method, you'll notice that dragging Photoshop files into the Project window always imports them as assets. To change this behavior and to import menus, hold alt while dragging and the Photoshop file will be imported as a menu rather than an asset.

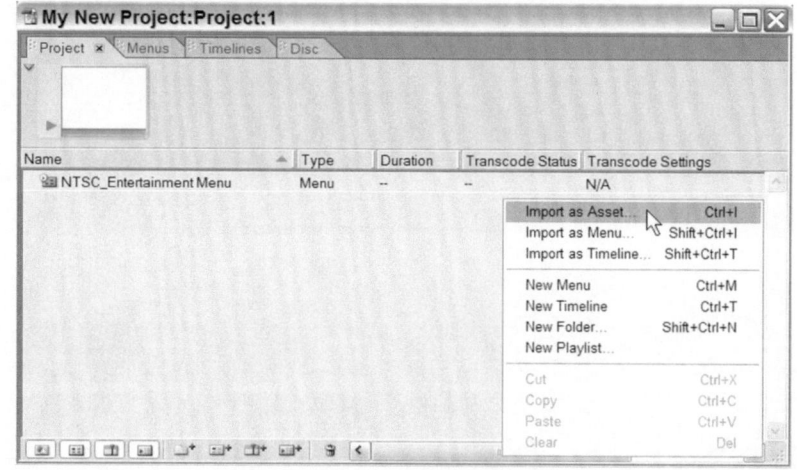

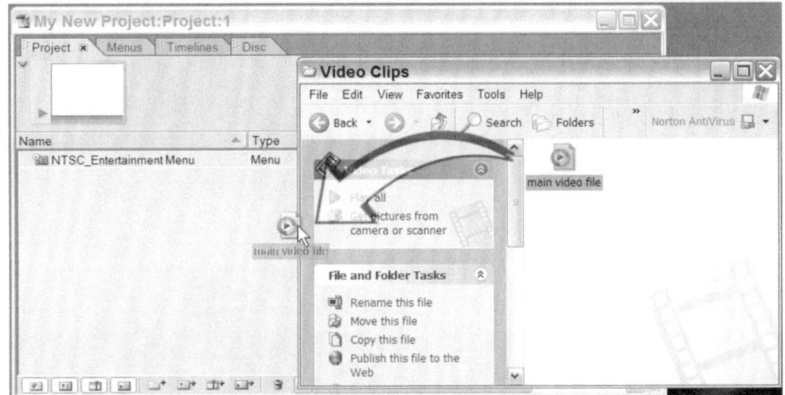

AVI vs. MPEG-2 Source File Considerations

One of the decisions DVD authors will make is whether to use AVI or MPEG-2 source files to build their DVD projects.

Audio Video Interleave, or AVI, is usually a source format used in Windows. AVI source files are typically very large, because, they contain much of the original source data. AVIs are easier to edit in an NLE than MPEG-2. However AVI is not a DVD video–compliant format. All AVI files imported into Encore are automatically transcoded into MPEG-2.

The Motion Picture Experts Group Codec 2, or MPEG-2, is a delivery codec. It compresses large source files, such as AVI, into relatively small files. Most DVDs use MPEG-2 files for this reason. The compression works by discarding or compressing redundant information in a frame and across frames (over time).

When using AVIs in Encore, Encore will automatically handle the encode to MPEG-2 when building the disc. Encore and Premeire use the same MPEG-2 Encoder. Either application can be used to prepare DVD legal content.

Using MPEG-2 as the source file allows Encore to skip the extra step of compressing the file when building the disc. This workflow accomodates other external applications or source material that has already been compressed to MPEG-2.

Import PCM Audio Files

PCM audio, or Pulse Code Modulation, is a common uncompressed audio format. It offers lossless fidelity to the original source. However, its file size is typically much too large for economical DVD authoring. When PCM is imported into Encore, by default it will automatically transcode the audio file into Dolby Digital AC-3 when building the disc. By doing this Encore creates more space for video assets.

To import a PCM audio file:

Right-click in the Project tab and select Import as Asset

Or use the keyboard shortcut Ctrl-I.

This opens the Import as Assets dialog.

Locate and select the PCM File(s).

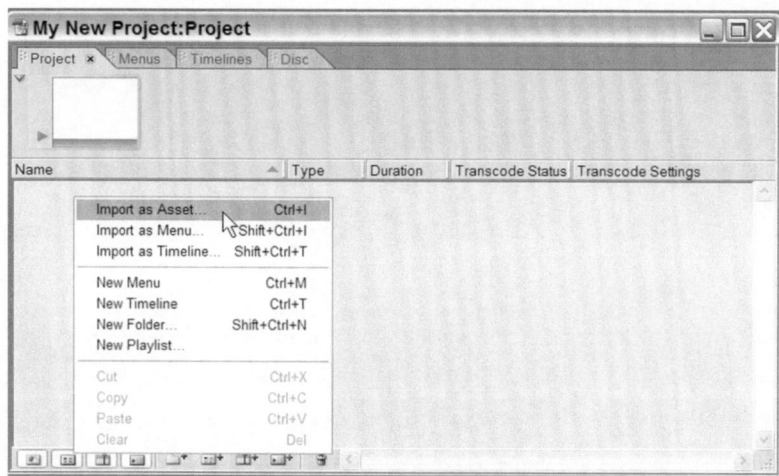

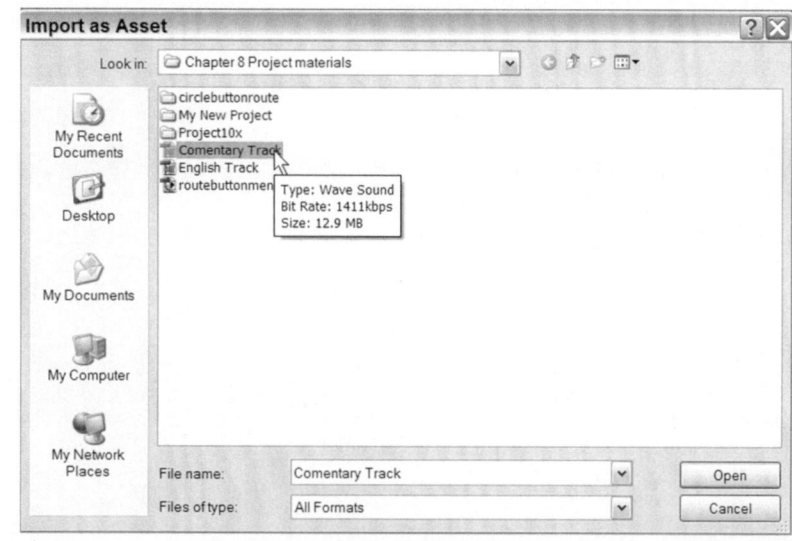

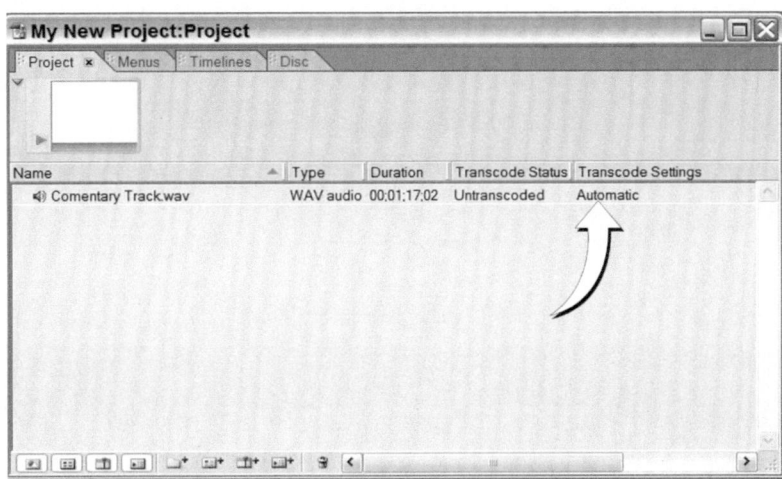

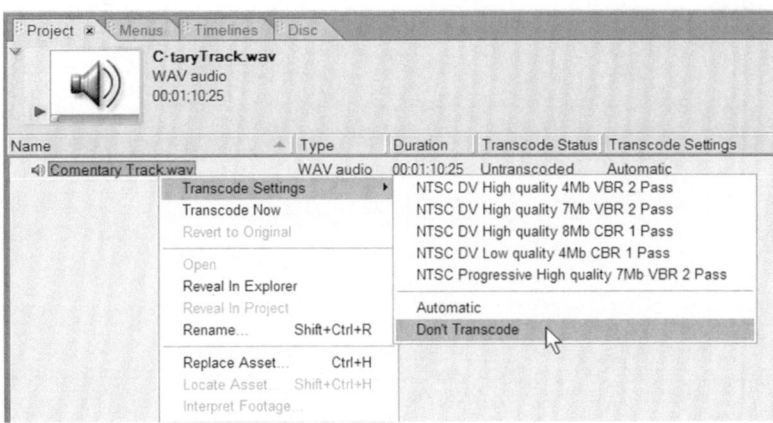

You can select multiple files by holding the Ctrl key while clicking.

Click Open.

The audio files have now been imported into the Project tab.

Some older set-top DVD players will not properly play back PCM audio files.

As mentioned before, PCM files are transcoded to AC-3 files by default. This is recommended because it compresses the audio file and allows the author to devote more available disc capacity to video. If you want the PCM format in the final product, then set the process to Don't Transcode. PCM files are DVD-legal and can be burned directly to disc without additional transcoding.

Important: The PCM file must be 48kHz and at 16- or 24-bit sample rate. Otherwise this option is not available.

To retain PCM audio in the final disc:

Right-click on the audio file.

Go to Transcode Settings>Don't Transcode.

The PCM file is now set to Don't Transcode, which will be retained on the final disc.

Import AC-3 Audio Files

AC-3 is a Dolby Digital format for Audio. It offers an efficent and economical encoding for multichannel audio content. AC-3 is also the format to which Encore transcodes other audio file formats. If AC-3 Dolby Digital 5.1 content has been prepared in another application for a project, it may be imported directly into Encore and will be preserved "as is" when burned to disc.

To import AC-3 files:

Right-click in the Project tab.

Select Import as Assets.

This opens the Import as Assets File dialog.

Locate and Select the AC-3 audio file(s) for import.

Click Open.

The AC-3 file has now been imported into Encore. Notice that the Transcode Setting for the AC-3 file is set to Don't Transcode.

PCM files are similar to .wav files. Both formats use uncompressed audio, however, .wav files must be converted to PCM when the disc is encoded.

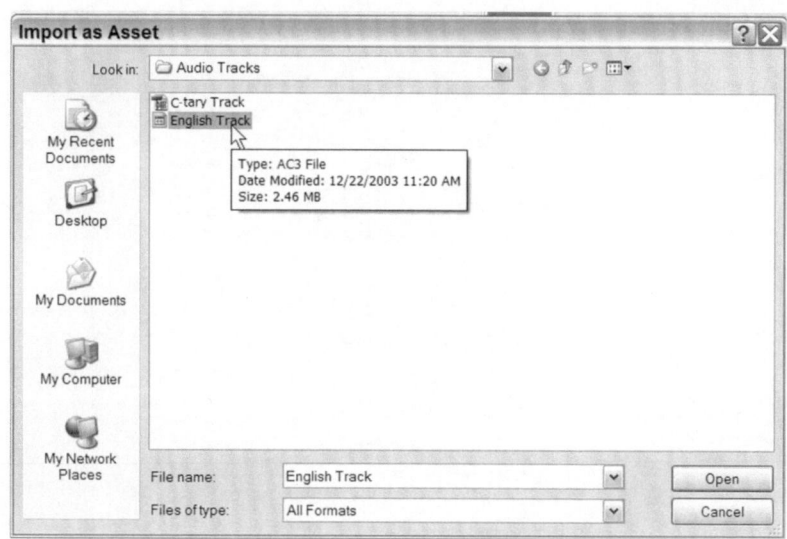

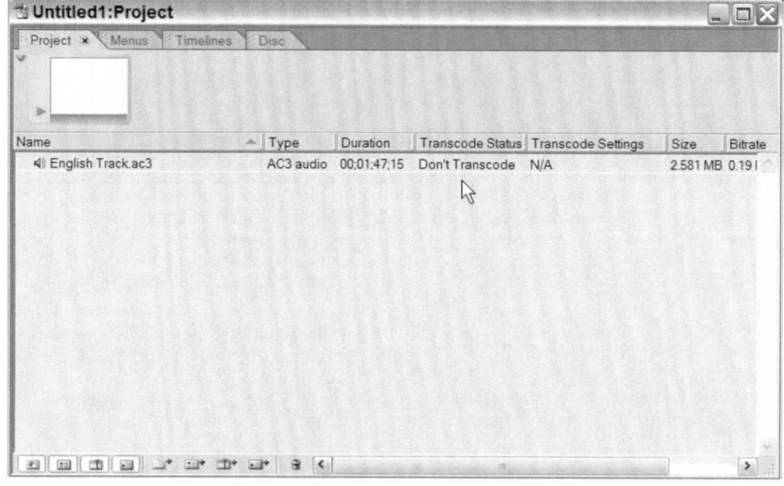

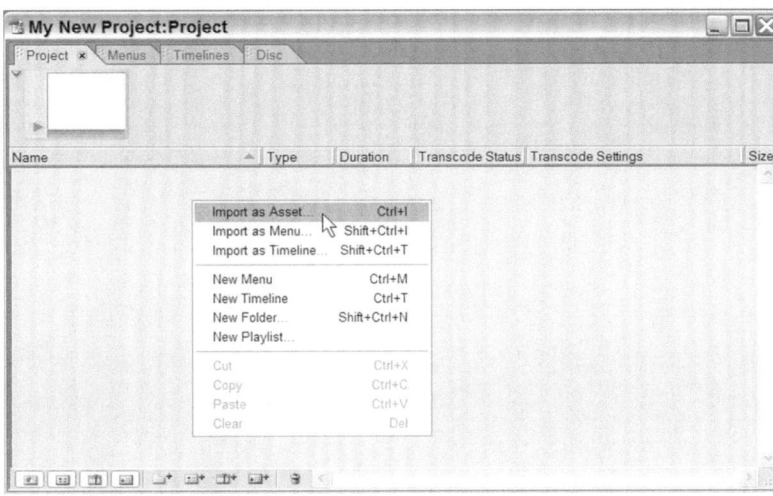

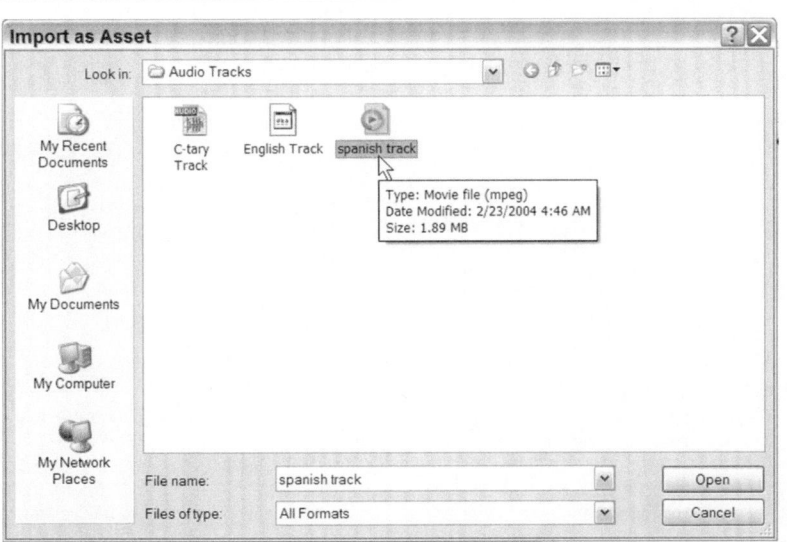

Import MPEG-1 Layer II Audio Files

MPEG-1 Layer II audio files can also be used, but this format is not widely supported by NTSC DVD players. If MPEG- 1 files are imported into an NTSC project, they will be automatically transcoded to a NTSC DVD compliant AC-3 audio file. AC-3 is the best choice for player compatibility.

To import an MPEG-1 Layer II audio file:

Right-click in the Project tab.

Select Import as Asset.

The keyboard shortcut Ctrl-I may also be used.

This opens the Import as Asset dialog.

Locate and select the desired MPEG-1 audio file(s).

Click Open.

The MPEG-1 audio file has now been imported into the Project tab. Notice it has been set to Automatically Transcode.

If this is a PAL project, the Transcode Settings can be set to Don't Transcode.

AC-3 is almost always a better choice than MPEG-1 audio, unless the known target audience only has very old equipment to play back the project. All computers less than four years old that contain DVD players will play back AC-3 files.

Important: This setting can be changed on an NTSC project, but most NTSC DVD players do not support MPEG-1 Layer II audio.

To retain MPEG-1 Layer II audio on a PAL DVD project:

Right-click on the MPEG audio file.

Go to Transcode Settings>Don't Transcode.

The MPEG-1 Layer II audio file will now be preserved on the final DVD.

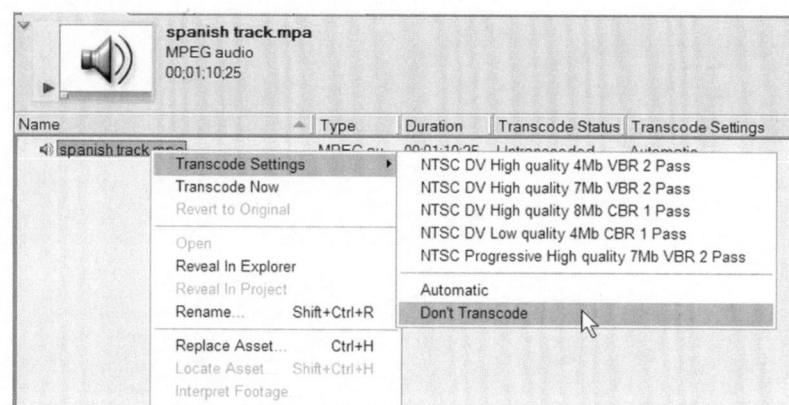

Change the Default Audio Encoding Scheme

By default, Encore encodes non-Dolby Digital Audio into the Dolby Digital AC-3 format. Imported AC-3 files are automatically set to Don't Transcode. The AC-3 format is widely supported and is recommended for all projects. However this default scheme can be modified to PCM or MPEG-1 Layer II audio.

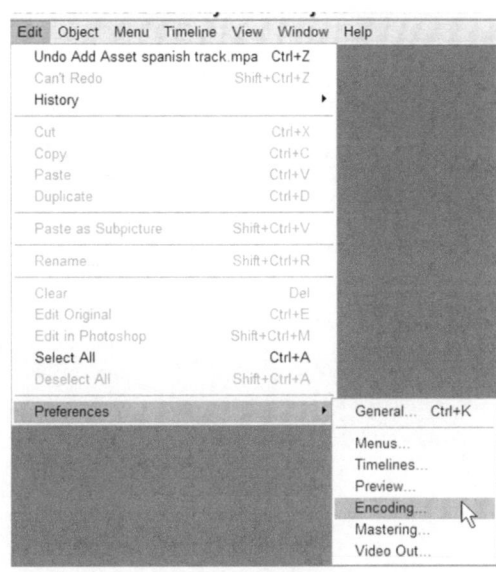

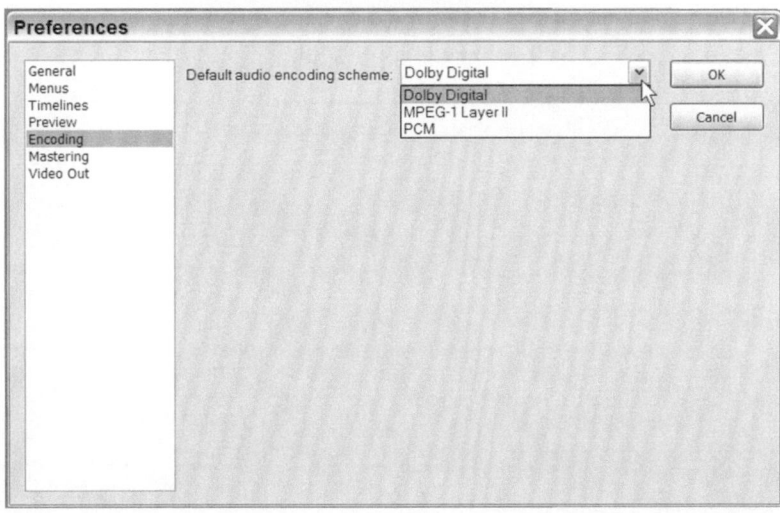

Changing the default audio encoding scheme only applies to audio files imported. after the scheme has been changed.

To change the default audio encoding scheme:

Go to Edit>Preferences>Encoding.

Click on the arrow next to the Default Audio Encoding Scheme.

Select the desired default audio format.

Click OK.

Now all audio files imported into Encore will be transcoded to new default audio format.

Import Files as Graphics

Encore will import of a wide variety of graphic formats. These graphics may be used in a slideshow, become a part of a menu, or both.

Remember that files may also be dragged and dropped directly into the Project window.

Encore supports BMP, MPEG, TIFF, GIF, JPEG, PNG, EXIF, and PSD. When Quick-Time is installed, it also supports TGA and PICT.

Note: Importing a PSD file as a graphic discards the layers.

To import a file as a graphic:

Right-click inside the Project tab.

Select Import as Asset.

This opens the Import as Asset dialog.

Locate and select the graphic file(s).

Holding Ctrl while clicking selects multiple files.

Click Open.

The graphics have now been imported into the Project tab.

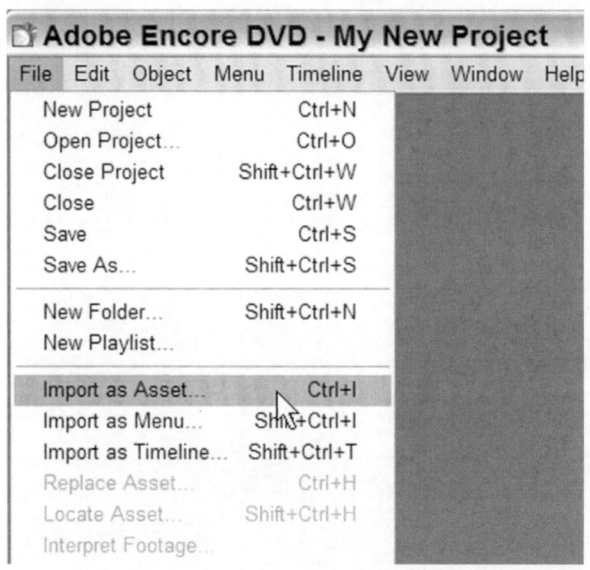

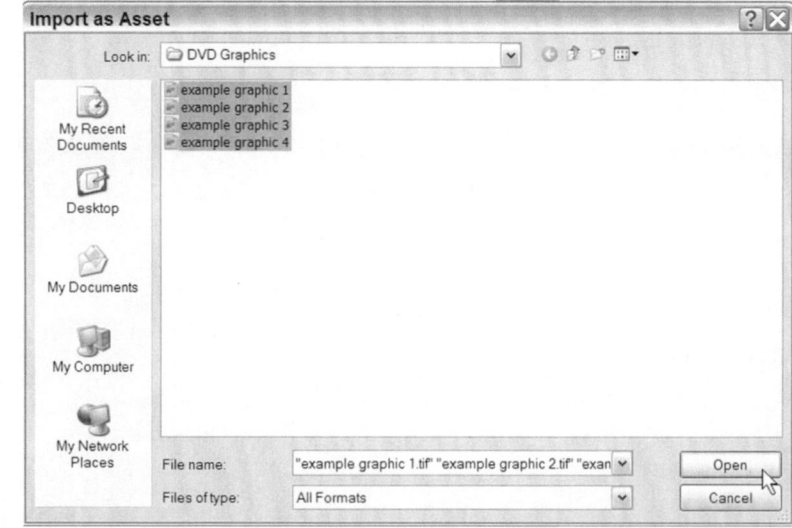

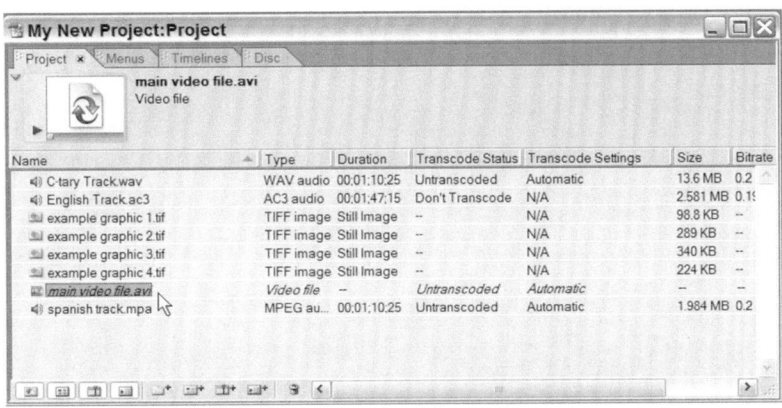

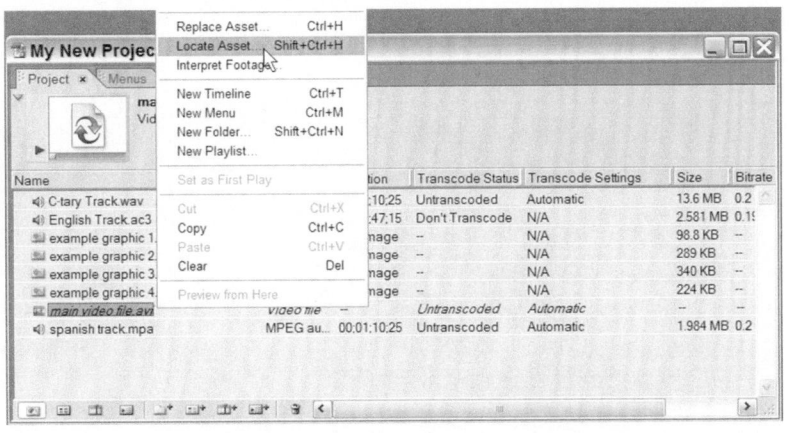

Find Missing Files (Assets)

While Encore is open, it keeps track of assets and checks for them upon opening. During the course of a project, files might get moved to another drive, the drive containing those files may be disconnected, or the files may be renamed or deleted. In these cases, Encore cannot track the file.

If Encore cannot locate an asset, it will put the file name in italics in the Project tab.

Instead of reimporting the missing asset and starting over, Encore allows the user to locate the asset.

Note: This function is only available for missing assets.

To locate a missing asset:

Right-click on the asset in italics.

Select Locate Missing Asset.

This opens the Locate Missing Asset dialog.

Locate the asset's new location or filename.

Click Open.

When the asset is located, its file name appears in normal type.

Important: The name of the original file is preserved when using Locate Asset, even if this is not the filename of the located file.

Replace Assets

Many hours are spent creating a project and sometimes the only difference between two projects is the content. Instead of creating a whole new project, Encore can simply replace the assets in an old project.

The Replace Assets command is very similar to the Locate Assets command. However instead of keeping the original filename, Replace Assets uses the new asset's filename.

To replace an asset:

In the Project tab, right-click on the asset to be replaced.

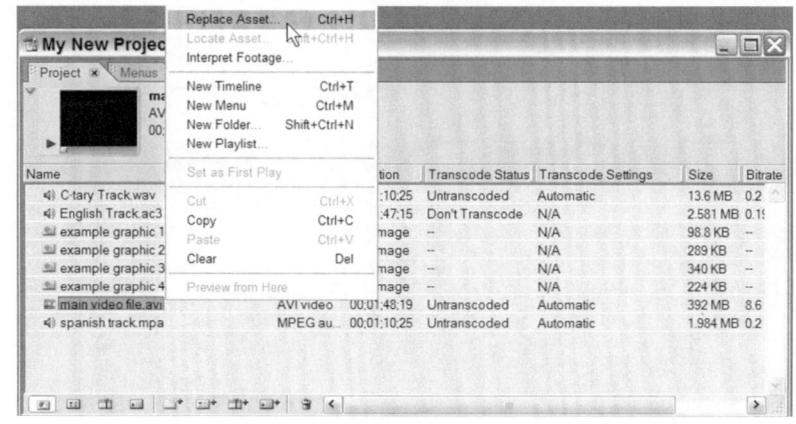

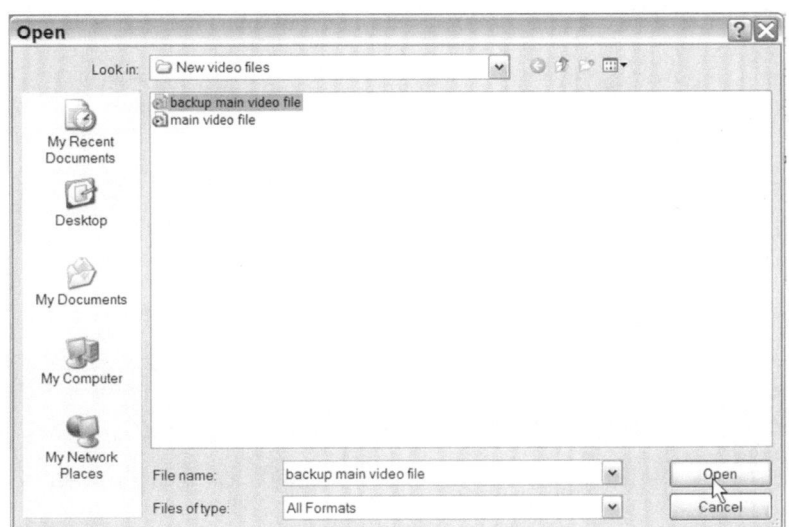

Select Replace Asset.

This opens the Replace Asset dialog.

Locate and select the new asset.

Click Open.

The old asset has now been replaced in the Project tab.

When replacing video assets associated with timelines and chapter points, it's important to check the chapter point locations and adjust them if necessary.

Get Organized!

Large projects typically have multiple menus, assets, and timelines. If for example, a project has a number of slideshows with multiple graphics in each slideshow, the Project tab's list could be too long to use effectively. A small measure of organization can save a great deal of time down the road.

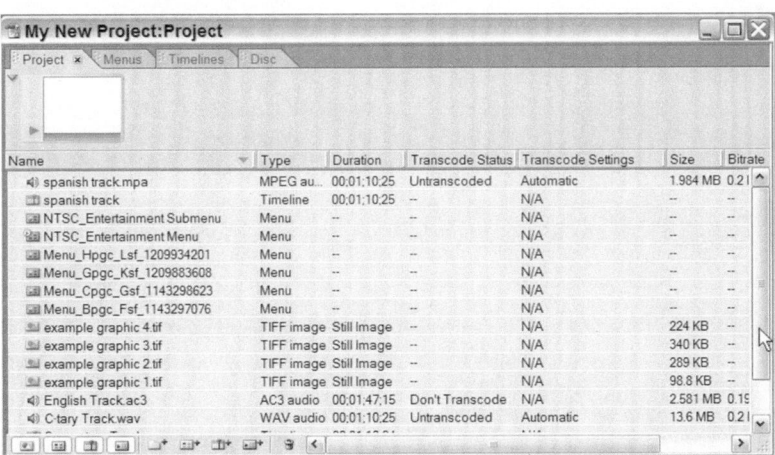

Encore's Project tab offers the ability to organize files into separate file folders.

To create a new folder:

Right-click in the Project tab.

Select New Folder or

Click the New Folder icon located at the bottom of the Project tab.

This opens the New Folder Name dialog.

Enter a name for the new folder.

Click OK.

The new folder now appears in the Project tab. The next step is to add files to the folder.

To add files to a folder:

Click and hold the mouse button on the file.

Drag the file into the new folder.

The file is now added to the new folder.

Several files can be moved at the same time by using the Ctrl and Shift keys. Hold Shift to select a range of files. Hold Ctrl while clicking to select several non-contiguous files.

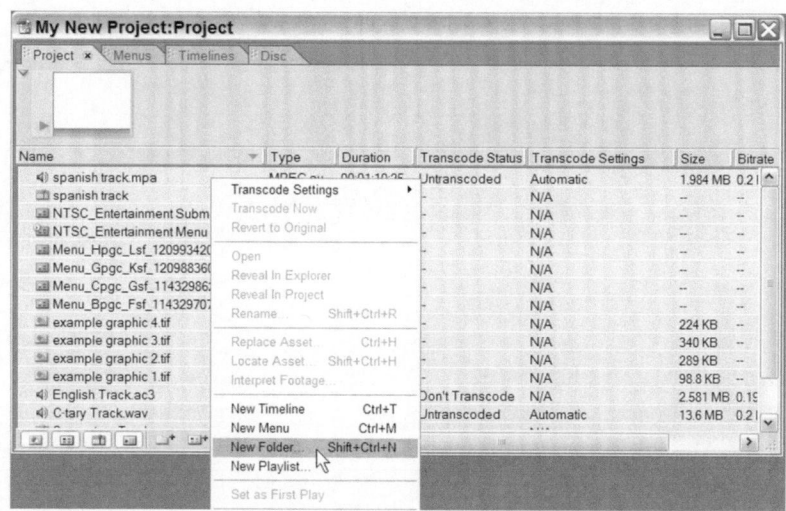

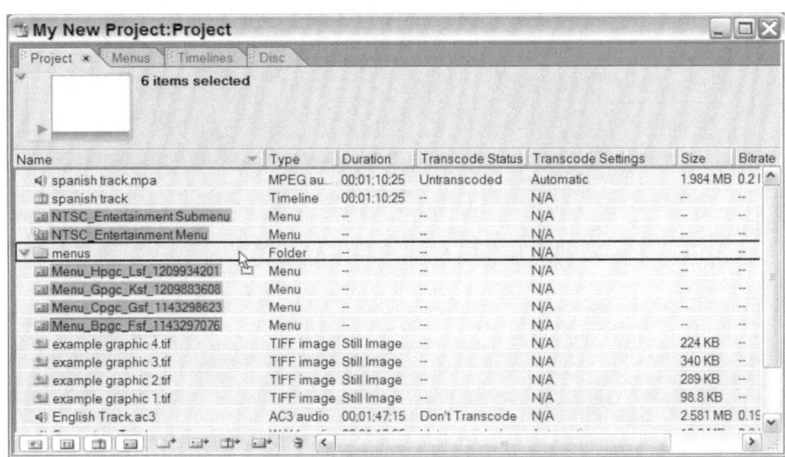

Plan the DVD Project Using a Flowchart

While organization is not only essential during the use of using Encore, it is important to be organized before ever turning on the computer. DVDs use a system of links and actions that put all the aspects of the project together. The trick to mastering DVD authoring is starting with a simple flowchart that outlines the organization of the project. Pencils and paper are useful in this process.

Start by listing all the different features of a project such as menus and timelines. Will it have an introductory video (stinger) that plays when the DVD is inserted? Will it have special features or a submenu that accesses individual chapter points?

Then decide how each feature will link together and create a flow chart.

Projects large and small will benefit from a flowchart.

When all assets are listed in a flowchart, it can also be used to keep track of size and number of assets. Doing so will be helpful when determining bitrate.

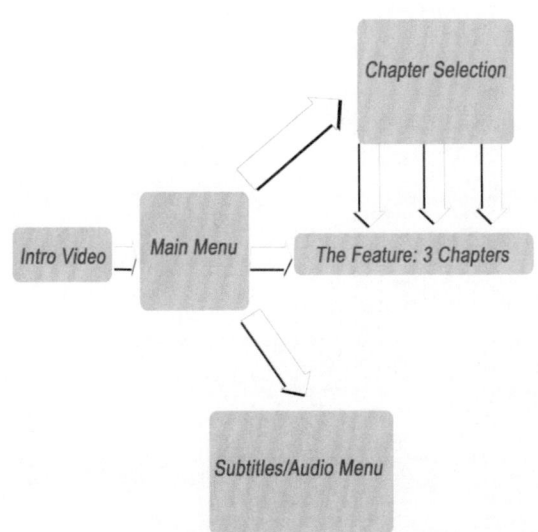

View Specific File Types in the Project Tab

Sometimes during a project, it helps to see only one kind of a file at a time, such as the menus or assets. Encore's Project tab can show or hide file types.

By default, all file types are shown.

To hide a file type:

In the Project tab, go to the bottom of the window.

Click to deselect the icon and hide those file types.

Now the file type unselected will no longer show up in the Project tab.

To show only one file type:

In the Project tab, go to the bottom of the window.

Click to deselect and hide the other two file types.

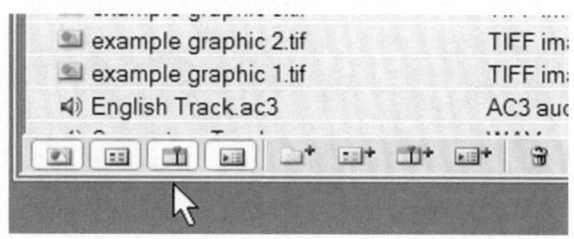

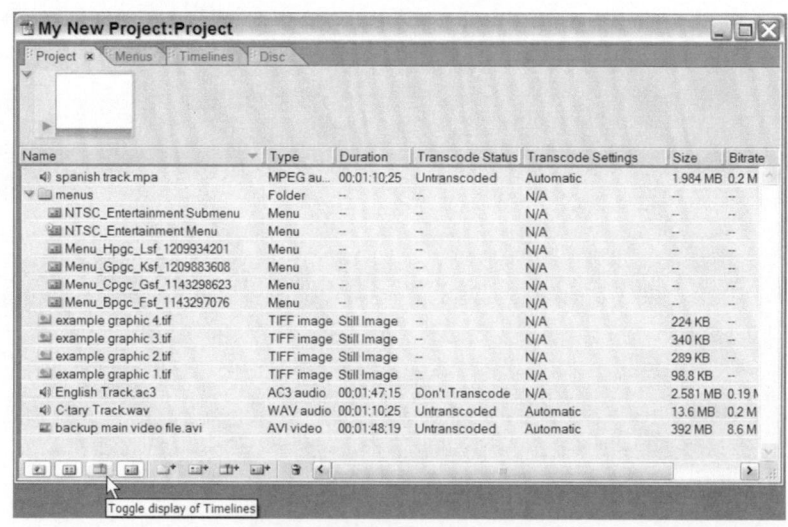

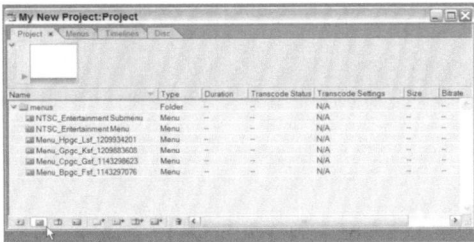

If files appear to be "missing" in the Project tab, often it is because the file type has been set to hide.

Change the Transcode Settings for Video.

Encore, by default, automatically transcodes non-DVD compliant video into MPEG-2 video. In addition to this, Encore automatically sets the bitrate and encoding scheme for the video that best matches project material and the destination format. If you do not have experience with setting video codecs or don't need a specific aspect ratio, it is best to leave these settings alone.

Encore supplies a number of transcode presets. If NTSC was chosen for the TV standard, then only NTSC compatible transcode presets are available. This is true for PAL as well.

To specify a transcode preset for a video file:

Right-click on the file.

Go to Transcode Presets.

Select the desired transcode preset.

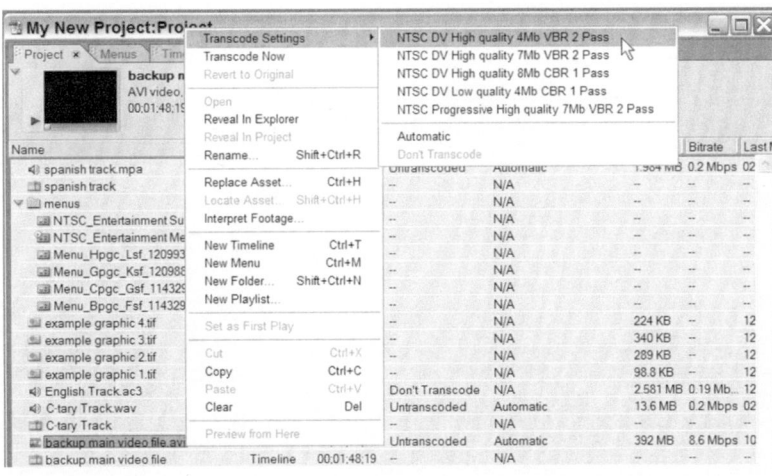

The video will now be transcoded according to the settings in the preset.

Note: The presets have audio encoding settings. Any audio that is multiplexed with a video file will be transcoded according to the audio settings in that preset.

Custom Transcode Presets for Video

Advanced DVD authors with experience in MPEG-2 encoding will appreciate the ability to adjust the transcode by creating new presets. Again, Encore does a fine job of transcoding assets and creating new presets may result in a low quality or unusable MPEG-2 if done incorrectly.

Encore uses the same Main Concept Encoder that is included with Adobe Premiere, however, the Premiere encoder offers additional advanced options.

Again, this is for advanced users.

To create a new custom Transcode Preset:

Go to File>Transcode Settings>Edit Transcode Presets.

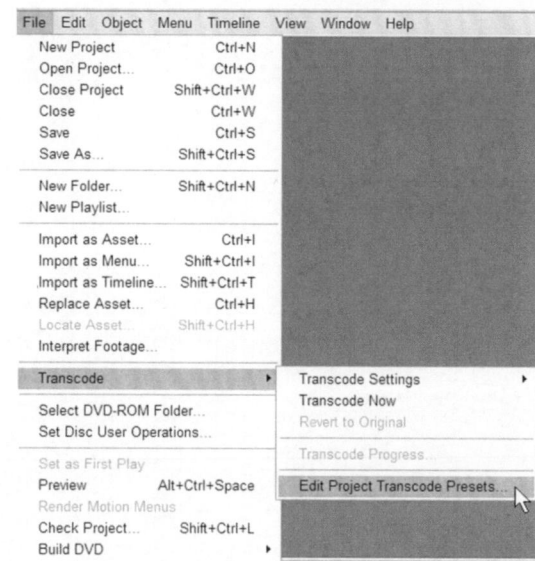

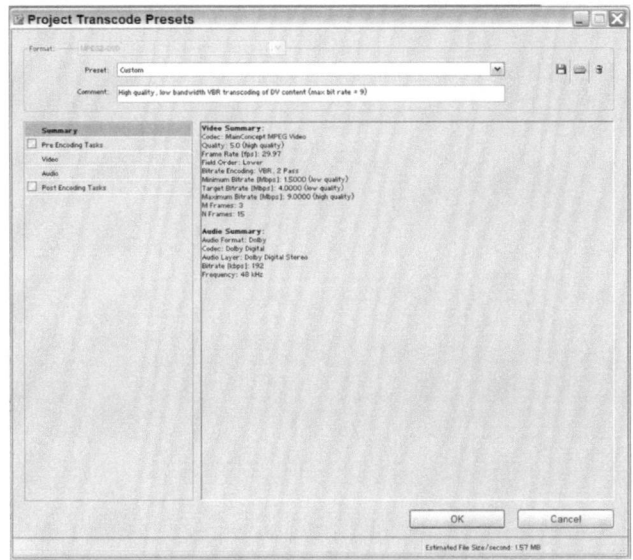

This opens the Edit Transcode Preset Settings dialog. An existing preset can be edited to create a new preset or a custom preset can be created from scratch. If a preset is created from an existing preset, the original preset will not be affected.

It is faster to create a new preset by editing an existing preset that best matches the desired settings. Editing the custom preset requires more adjustments because all the settings are set to the highest possible levels.

Select a preexisting preset or choose Custom from the pulldown menu.

In the lower-left pane, click Video.

This opens the Video settings for the preset.

Adjust the sliders and options for the transcode.

Quality Slider: Adjusts overall quality from 1 to 5, five being the highest. Higher quality will result in a longer encode.

Aspect Ratio: 4:3 or 16:9. This defines the output Aspect Ratio.

Frame Rate: Defines the frames per second. Not adjustable in NTSC.

Program Sequence: Interlaced or Progressive. Determines the scan mode of the MPEG-2 video.

Field Order: Only available for an Interlaced Program Sequence. Determines which part of the field is scanned first, upper or lower.

Bitrate Encoding: CBR (Constant Bit Rate) or VBR (Variable Bit Rate). VBR is the best choice for quality, because bits are allocated when needed most. CBR will encode at one bitrate, and quality may suffer if the bit rate is set too low.

M Frames: Sets the number of B frames between I and P frames.

N Frames: This number of frames between I frames must be a multiple of the M frames number.

Bitrate: This is only an option if a Constant Bit Rate is selected. Determines the megabits per second.

Encoding Passes: Only available in Variable Bit Rate mode. Specify one

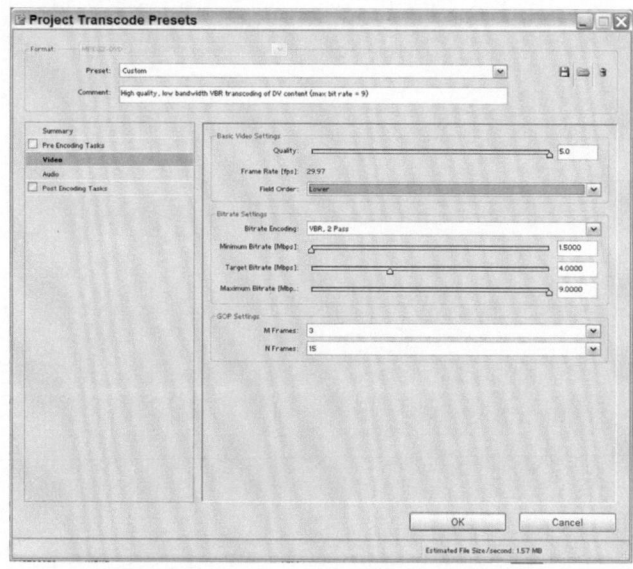

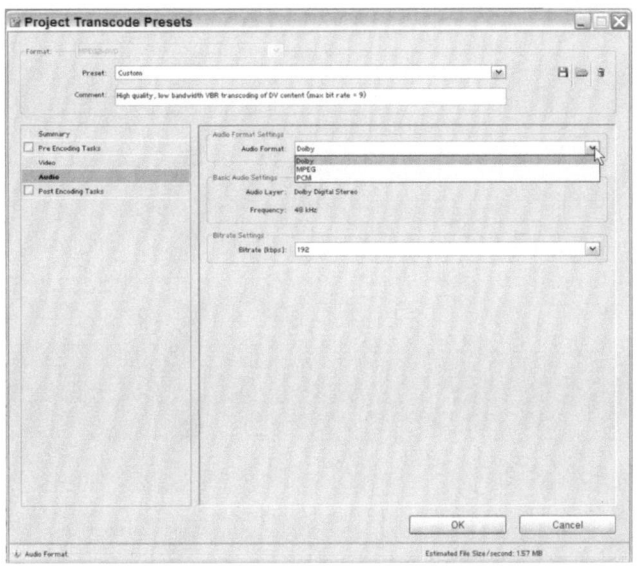

or two encoding passes. Two passes will give the best quality but will take twice as long to encode.

Target Bitrate: Set the slider to the average bitrate desired for the file.

Maximum Bitrate: 9.8 Mbps is the maximum bitrate allowed.

Minimum Bitrate: Must be at least 1.5Mbps, but this is not a recommended minimum bitrate.

Insert pic 1.65 The Encoder Settings for video.

At this time adjustments can be made to the audio that accompanies the video. By default, a 192 kbps 2-Channel, AC-3 Dolby Digital audio format is used.

Click the Audio button in the left pane.

Make any necessary adjustments to audio format or bitrate.

Audio Format: Dolby Digital Stereo, MPEG- 1 Layer II, and PCM. Dolby Digital is recommended because it is widely supported by DVD players.

Bitrate: Not available for PCM. Determines the kilobits per second of the final audio. A higher number means a higher quality sound, but at the expense of disc space. The default 192 kbps for Dolby Digital is a good balance of bitrate and quality. The same is true for 220 kbps for MPEG-1.

Click the Save icon.

Encore will prompt for a name for the new preset.

Type a name for the preset, and then click OK.

In the Transcode Presets dialog, click OK.

The custom preset is now ready to be applied to the individual assets. It is still necessary to change the Transcode Preset for each asset in the Project tab.

Preprocess Video in a Nonlinear Editor for Best Encode

When it comes to DVD production, there is no replacement for a capable NLE, or nonlinear editor. A program such as Premiere Pro is ideal for preparing assets, creating motion menus, mastering audio, and even transcoding assets to MPEG-2.

If cuts need to be made, graphics are

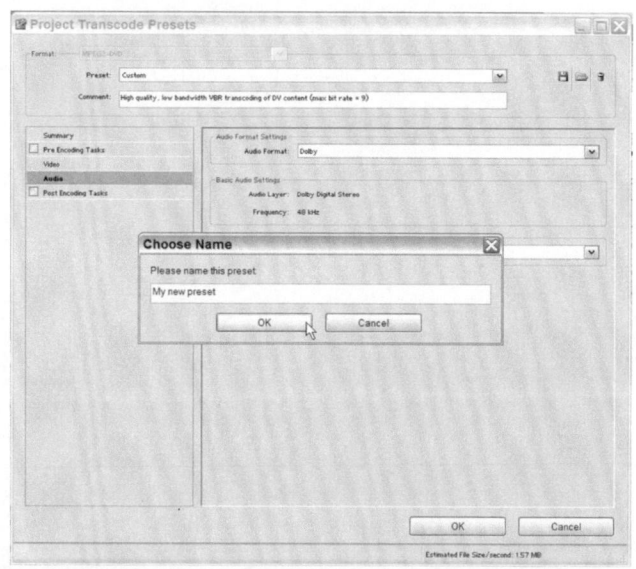

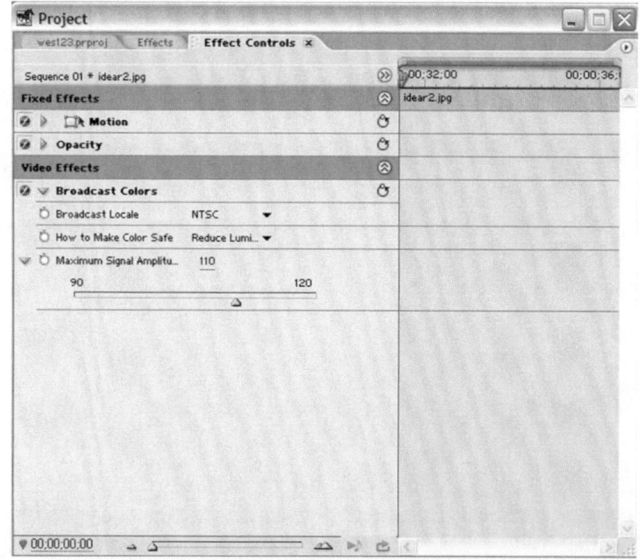

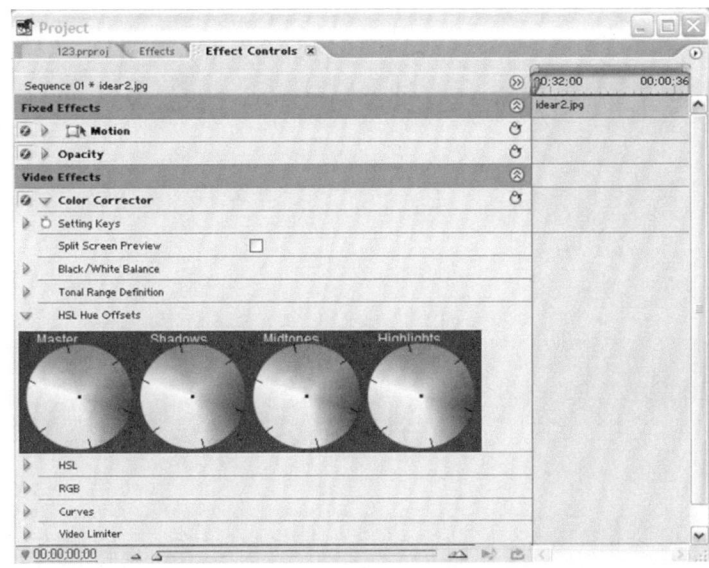

desired, or video needs to be color corrected, a nonlinear editor will become an important part of your toolset.

When working with computer generated media, it's a good idea to make sure your graphics are color safe. This is especially true when working on content that will be broadcast.

Video can also be color corrected to maintain continuity between different clips or add creativity for stylistic effect.

Premiere Pro also offers an Encoder nearly identical to the one that is included with Encore. You can also use Premiere Pro to export sections of a sequence to individual MPEG-2 files as well as to join multiple clips together in order to create a larger, seamless timeline.

Pros know that reducing color saturation is beneficial to most good encodes, particularly in high-motion video. Cropping off the edges of video frames that originated in DV is usually another good practice, because DV cameras typically have "fringing" or video noise on the right and left edges of the frame. The MPEG encoder sees this information as video and tries to encode it correctly. Another good practice is to "crush the blacks," removing gradations of black and having as few variants of black as possible, which allows the encoder to see as much redundancy as possible.

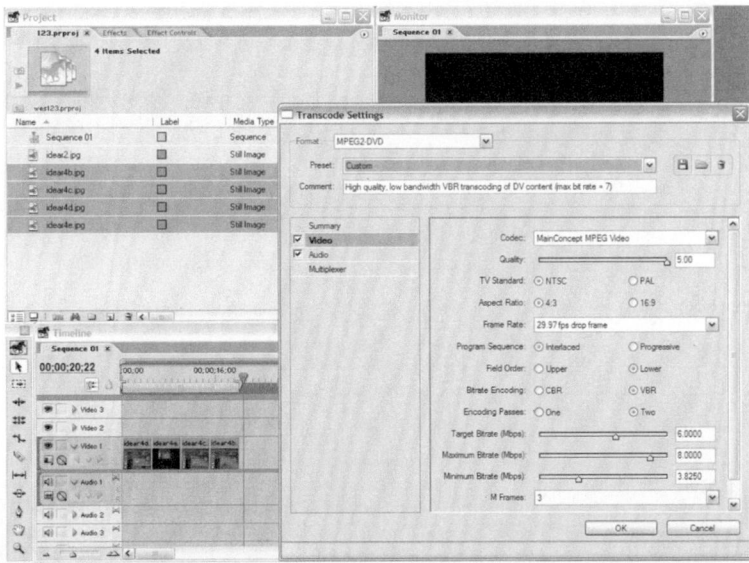

Change the Transcode Preset for Audio

Additional audio for multilingual tracks or special features, such as director's commentary, should match the quality of the main track. If a preset is used to transcode the main content, use this same preset for the other audio files.

Note: Do not transcode or use a preset for Dolby Digital 5.1 AC-3 files. Applying a preset will convert them into two-channel AC-3. By default, Encore recognizes 5.1 AC-3 files and sets them to Don't Transcode.

To apply a transcode preset to audio:

In the Project tab, right-click on the audio file.

Go to Transcode Settings.

Left-click on the appropriate Transcode Preset.

The transcode preset now applies to the audio file.

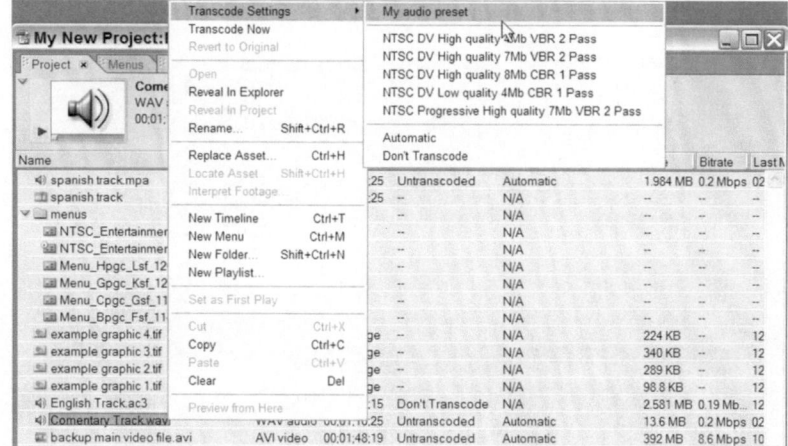

Manually Determine Bitrate

Encore by default automatically determines bitrate, but sometimes it is better to manually determine bitrate, such as in complicated projects with multiple assets. By taking control of the bit budget, less is left to chance. After all, Encore cannot know which assets require higher quality over others.

When determining video bitrate, take into account that a disc has two parts; video and non-video. The obvious non-video aspects of a DVD are menus, audio, and subtitles. In addition to these, it has a disc overhead, which accommodates for factors such as data allocated to the file structure of the disc.

Determining bitrate is as simple as taking the maximum data capacity of the disc and subtracting the non-video aspects. This magic number is what is left for encoding video. Take that number and divide it by the length in seconds of the video. The result is the maximum megabits per second (Mbps), or target bitrate.

Use a powers of 10 system when working with optical media. In other words 1kb = 103 = 1,000 bits, not 1KB = 210 = 1,024 bits, like on hard disks. (1GB = 1,000,000,000 bits)

The average DVD project has:

A 90-minute feature

2 audio tracks (AC3 2-channel)

1 subtitle track

3 still menus

It will be burned to standard 4.7GB media (37,600,000,000 bits)

To begin, subtract out the overhead. In this example, five percent of the media will be tied up in overhead. More complicated projects could potentially require more overhead.

$$5\% = 0.05, .05 \times 37,600,000,000 = 1,880,000,000 \text{ bits}$$

The next step is to subtract out the audio tracks. The sample AC3 tracks were encoded at the standard 192Kbps. Because this measurement is in kilobits per second (kpbs), we will convert it to bits per second.

$$192 \times 1000 = 192,000\text{bps}$$

Because an audio track runs the length of the feature, all that needs to be done is determine the number of seconds in the feature.

60 × 90 = 5,400 seconds

Then multiply the number of seconds by the number of bits per second.

5,400 × 192,000 = 1,036,800,000 bits

Therefore, the space consumed by two audio tracks is:

2 × 1,036,800,000 = 2,073,600,000 bits

The subtitles' use of space is:

10,000bps × 5,400 seconds = 54,000,000 bits

The three still menus won't account for much in the total disc space, so there is no need to calculate their bit usage.

When all the bits are determined for all the non-video assets and overhead, add up the bits.

1,880,000,000 + 2,073,600,000 + 54,000,000 = 4,007,600,000 bits

Now just take that sum and subtract it from the total disc capacity to figure out how much of the disc can be devoted to the video.

37,600,000,000 − 4,007,600,000 = 33,592,400,000 bits

To find the target bitrate, divide the space available by the number of seconds.

33,592,400,000 bit ∏ 5,400 seconds = 6,220,814bps

Or

6.22Mbps

This is the target bitrate.

Of course, if the video project is shorter than 90 minutes, a higher bitrate is available.

Chapter 2

Timelines, Timelines...

gimme more time!

One of the best innovations of DVD over VHS is the ability to navigate video content quickly and easily. Timelines include chapter points which allow instant access to various sections of a video. Encore allows up to 99 timelines in a DVD project. Timelines are also used to create slideshows.

Once a video asset is imported into Encore, the next step is to create a new timeline.

Note: if a video asset is intended as a background for a menu, creating a timeline is not necessary.

Start me up!

Encore offers many ways to create a timeline; use the method that best matches your workflow. Each method starts with selecting the video file.

To create a new timeline:

Select the video file.

Use the keyboard shortcut Ctrl+T

Or right-click on the video file and select New Timeline.

Or use the Create New Timeline icon in the Project tab.

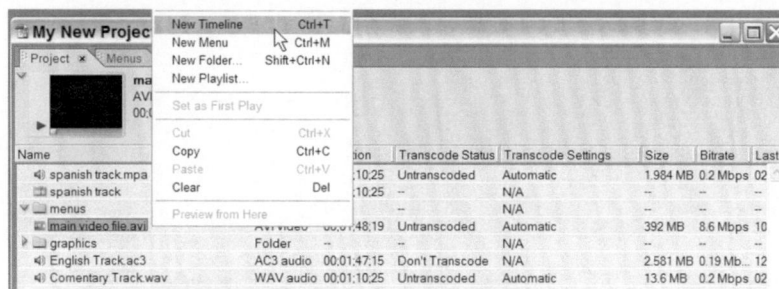

Or go to Timeline>New Timeline.

After a timeline is created, the Time-lines and the Monitor windows open.

This is a good time to reorganize the workspace to get ready to work with the timelines.

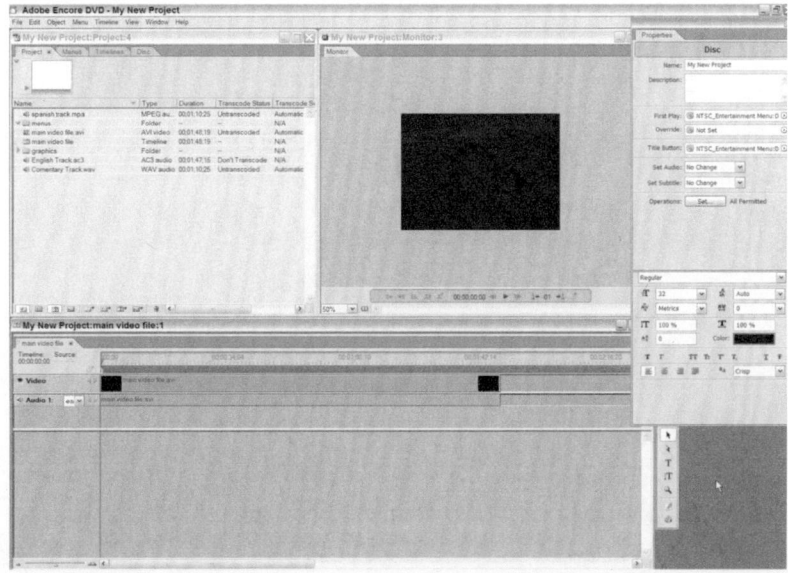

A new timeline is created with the same name as the asset. A timeline can be renamed to help identify the timeline. This is helpful when multiple timelines are created from the same asset.

Selecting a clip in the Project Window, then pressing the new timeline icon will create a timeline with the asset already added. In Version 1.5, both audio and video can be selected creating a timeline with both elements. This eliminates dragging and dropping and even names the timeline according to the asset.

To rename a timeline:

With the timeline selected in the Timelines tab, go to the Properties palette.

In the Name field, enter a new name for the timeline.

Add a short description of the timeline in the Description field.

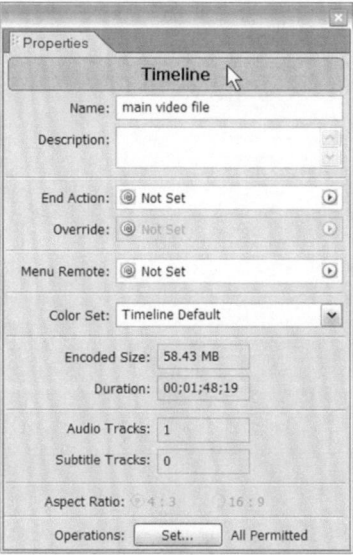

Monitor Timelines

The Monitor window is the visual extension of the Timelines window. It displays the frame where the Current Time Indicator (CTI) of the Timelines window is sitting.

To preview a timeline with the Monitor window:

Press the Play button in the Monitor window.

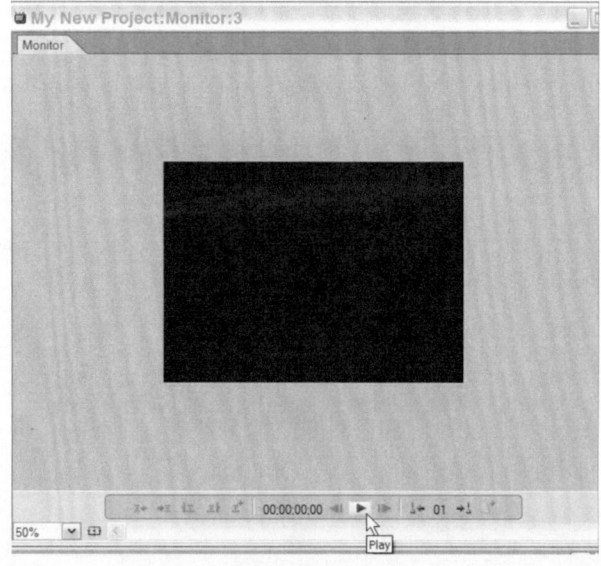

Notice that as the video plays, the CTI moves along the timeline.

Also, you can drag the CTI along the timeline.

Click and hold on the CTI drag it to the appropriate place on the timeline.

Notice that the Monitor window is controled directly by the CTI. How precisely the CTI controls the Monitor window is related to the zoom level of Timelines window. A higher zoom level provides higher precision.

To adjust the zoom level of the Timelines window:

Zoom in with Ctrl++.

Zoom out with Ctrl+–.

Press Ctrl+0 (zero) to resize the timeline to fit the window

Or at the lower-left corner of the Timelines window, use the zoom slider.

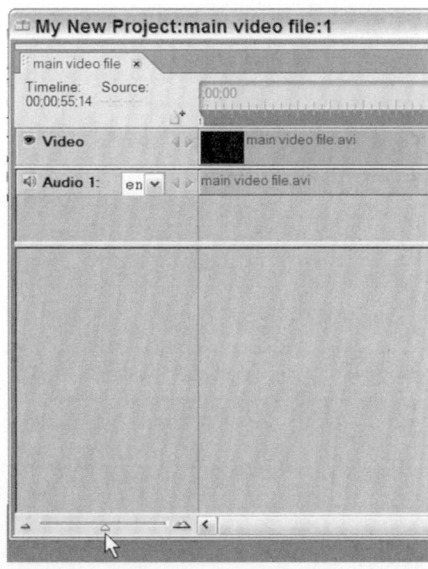

You can preview a timeline using timecode. This provides a slower, frame-by-frame preview.

Click and hold on the timecode in the Timelines window.

Drag the cursor left to move the Timecode back. Drag it right to move it forward.

If you know a specific timecode value, you can enter it directly.

Quick-click on the timecode value.

Enter a timecode.

Now the CTI jumps to the specific timecode, and the Monitor window displays the timecode's frame.

Encore 1.5 offers new icons in the Monitor window to aid subtitle creation.

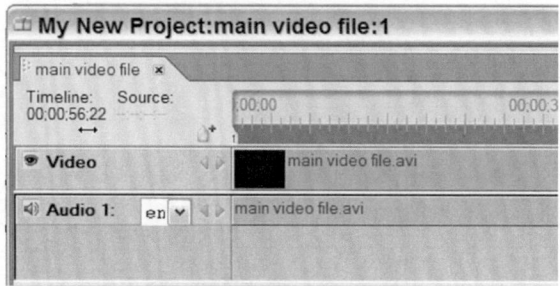

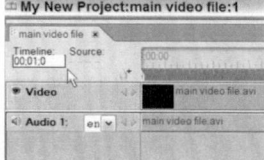

Trim Clips in the Timeline Window

Sometimes there is a bit of blank footage or other undesirable information at the beginning and/or end of a timeline. Encore allows the beginning and end of timelines to be trimmed/ edited. This does not change the asset; rather it defines the segment of the asset that the DVD player should read. Even if the timeline is trimmed to half of the original length of the asset, the entire asset is still encoded as part of the DVD.

Always import any additional audio or subtitle tracks into the timeline before trimming. If they are imported after, they must be retrimmed. If the tracks don't match up, the subtitles and audio might be mismatched with the video, or continue to play when the video is finished..

To trim clips in the Timeline window:

Hover the cursor over the beginning or end of a clip until a red bracket appears.

Click and drag the bracket to trim the timeline.

Release the mouse button when the clip is the right length.

What's the Point?

Chapter points allow viewers of your DVD to skip forward or backwards to different sections of the video. This also allows direct linking to sections of the timeline from the DVD menus. Encore automatically creates a chapter point at the beginning of a timeline; this intial chapter point cannot be moved. You can set up to 99 chapter points in one timeline.

One of the advantages to using AVI source files (instead of MPEG-2 source files) is that you can create chapter points anywhere without worrying about GOP headers and NLE chapter markers (see next two sections). However, you should place chapter points at least 15 frames apart in AVI files to insure proper playback.

Encore offers a few options when placing chapter points.

To set a chapter point using the Monitor window:

Play the video or use the CTI to set the desired place along the timeline for the chapter point.

Program streams are much easier to trim when compared with separate audio and video streams (elementary streams). Program streams contain video and audio that is linked. Inside Encore, this helps maintain sync when trimming. However, an NLE should be used for trimming whenever possible.

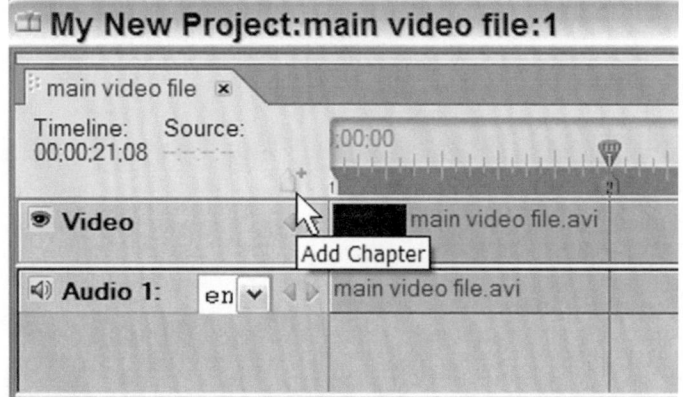

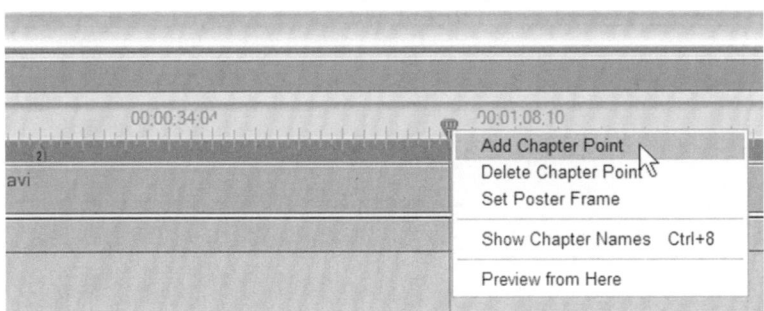

Click the Add Chapter Point icon in the Monitor window.

To set a chapter point using the Timelines window:

Set the CTI to the desired place on the timeline or input the timecode directly.

Click the Add Chapter Point icon

Or right-click on the CTI and select Add Chapter Point.

Or use the * (asterisk) key on the Num Pad to add a chapter point.

When you set a chapter point, a chapter point icon appears on the timeline. You can adjust the point by clicking on the icon and dragging it to another place.

When chapter points are added, they are automatically labeled sequentially, e.g., Chapter 1, Chapter 2, and so on. For organizational purposes, you can rename chapter points and add short descriptions to help label the chapters. This does not change how the DVD player identifies the chapter points.

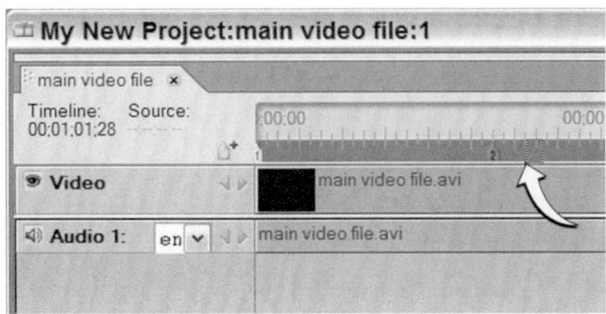

To rename a chapter point:

With the chapter point selected in the Timelines tab, go to the Properties palette.

In the Name field, rename the chapter point.

Enter a short description of the chapter in the Description field.

Set Chapter Points at GOP Headers in MPEG-2 Files

One of the disadvantages of using MPEG-2 source files is that cannot add chapter points at a specific frame. If the application allowed chapter point creation at any frame, it is likely that black frames would appear on the timeline. Chapter points must be added to the beginning of a Group Of Pictures, or GOP header for short. Only frames containing all information maybe used. These are also known as I-frames. Encore will locate them for you.

GOP headers appear as white marks along the timeline ruler when the timeline is at full zoom.

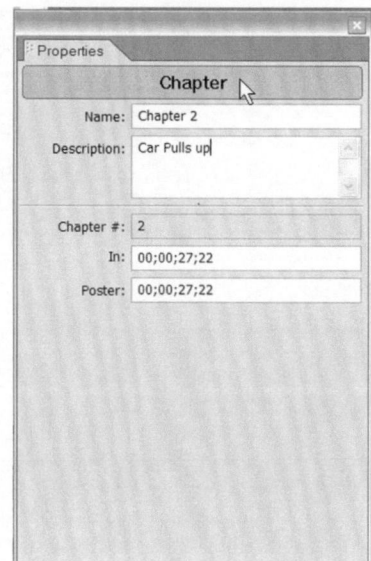

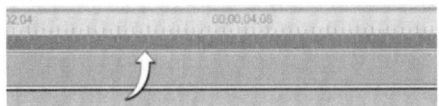

To set a chapter point in an MPEG-2 timeline:

Zoom in with Ctrl++ until the white ticks appear in the ruler.

Drag the CTI to an appropriate GOP Header indicator.

Click the Add Chapter Point icon.

Most DVDs use 15 for interlaced NTSC, 12 for progressive NTSC and 12 for Pal. Most video contains 2 GOPS for every second of content

Use Chapter Markers from a Nonlinear Editor

You can set chapter points on any desired frame when working with AVI files. However, there are some important considerations when working with clips already encoded to MPEG-2.

MPEG-2 clips arrange the video stream into small sections, called GOPs or group of pictures. This group of pictures is one of the core aspects of MPEG-2 compression. Think of them as small chunks that make up the video stream. When working with MPEG-2 clips in Encore, you can place chapter points only at the beginning of GOPs, otherwise known as the GOP header.

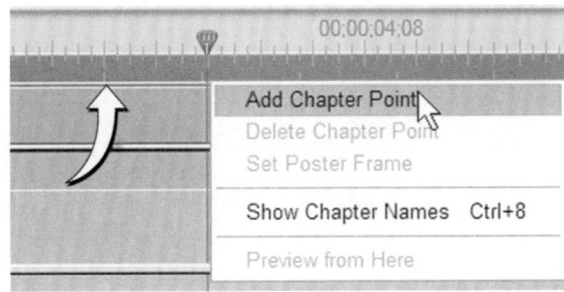

When importing MPEG-2 files, a little planning in advance is recommended.

Because you cannot change the GOP headers in Encore, you must specify them when preparing clips using an external application. Chapter markers in Premiere, for example, force a new GOP header to be created that corresponds to chapter points when compressed to MPEG-2.

When using Adobe Premiere the chapter markers must be named using the chapter field, or they will not appear in Encore.

If you use Adobe Premiere to create an MPEG-2 clip, chapter markers from the timeline can be preserved in the MPEG-2 clip. Once imported into Encore, the markers are available in the Timeline window.

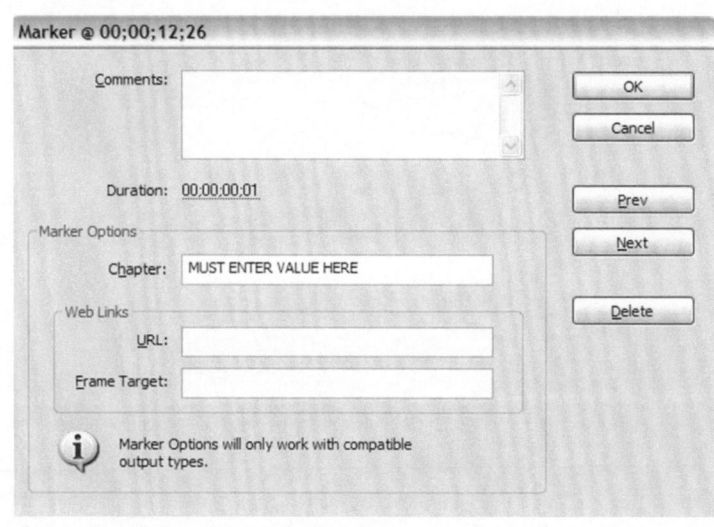

Set Poster Frames for Chapter Points

When creating still or motion thumbnail menus, it is recommended to use a frame that best represents the chapter it links to. Because many chapter points occur at frames with little action, it typically doesn't represent what is taking place in that chapter. The solution is to use poster frames.

For more information on still and motion thumbnail menus, see the chapter on Advanced DVD Menu.

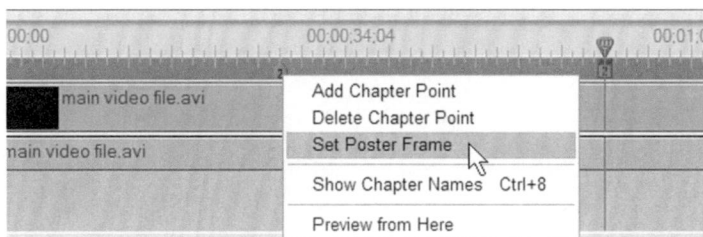

A poster frame can be any frame along a timeline. By default, Encore uses the first frame of a chapter as the poster frame. When a thumbnail is linked to a chapter point, the poster frame is displayed. In the case of motion thumbnails, it is the starting frame.

To set a poster frame for a chapter:

Within a chapter, drag the CTI to the desired frame.

Right-click on the CTI cursor and click on Set Poster Frame.

The poster frame appears on the timeline as a box with the number of the chapter it represents. Only one poster frame can be set per chapter.

If for some reason you want a poster frame before or after the chapter it represents, you can accomplish this easily.

To set a chapter point's poster frame outside the chapter:

Drag the CTI to the desired frame outside the chapter.

Right-click on the Chapter Point icon.

Encore 1.5 is also capable of importing markers from AVI files that have been created with embedded project information.

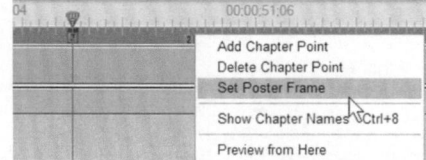

Click on Set Poster Frame.

Setting the poster frame by right-clicking on the chapter point itself allows the poster frame to be created anywhere. However, this is not recommended because it might confuse the viewer. The idea is to represent the chapter to aid in navigation.

You can set a poster frame without the Timeline window by using the Properties palette. If you know the specific timecode of the poster frame, you can use it as another way to create a poster frame.

To set a poster frame using timecode:

With the chapter point selected, go to the Properties palette.

In the Poster Frame field, enter the desired timecode.

Press Enter, or click anywhere outside the field.

Notice that a poster frame is automatically set on the timeline.

Encore 1.5 offers a new keyboard shortcut, Crtl+Alt, that you can use to easily create poster frames.

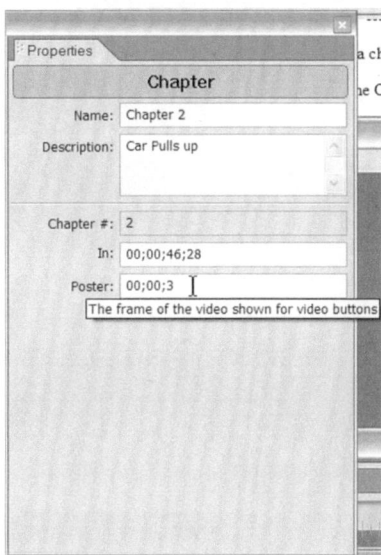

Hold down Crtl+Alt, and then click and drag on the associated chapter marker. The monitor window will display the "scrubbing" as you drag the poster frame marker to the desired frame.

Set the Remote Control Button Menu of a Timeline

Most DVD players offer a menu button on their remote controls. This allows the viewer to return to a specified menu while watching a video. This button also allows the viewer to return back to the point of the video where they initially pressed the button. Essentially it pauses and bookmarks that part of the timeline.

The Menu button and the Title button have different functions (see Title Button versus Menu Button in the last chapter).

You can set the remote control menu button destination for each timeline. The destination can be a menu or another timeline. For ease of navigation, it is best to link it to a menu.

To set the destination for the menu button:

With the timeline selected in the Timelines tab, go to the Properties palette.

In the Menu Button field, click on the arrow button.

The Menu button allows the viewer to jump directly to a related menu. If several timelines originate from the same menu, the menu button allows the viewer to pop back to the menu and easily select different content.

From the list of choices, choose the menu or timeline that the button will link to.

Now when the timeline is played, pressing menu on the remote will take the viewer to the specified menu.

Encore 1.5: Now you can set Return to Last Menu as the Menu Button link. This will take viewers back to the menu where they accessed the timeline.

Set the End Action of a Timeline

When a timeline ends, it simply ends, by default. Without an end action, the player waits for instructions. This is referred to as an Orphaned Timeline. It could be a problem if the timeline is for the introductory video (stinger or bumper clip) that preceeds the main menu of the DVD. The end action is the answer to the DVD player's question "What do we do and where do we go now?"

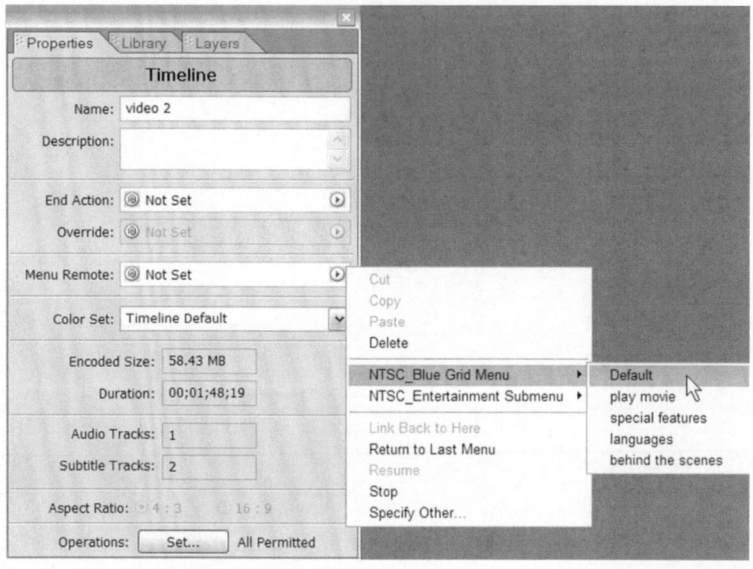

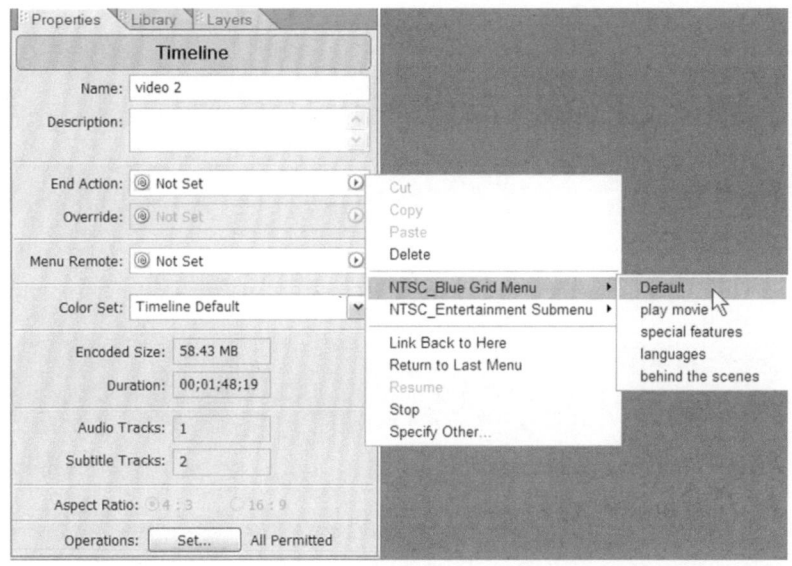

While most timeline end actions link back to the title menu, sometimes a project requires content that will loop back to the beginning of the timeline. The end action can link to anywhere on a DVD, even a specific chapter point on a timeline.

To set the end action of a timeline:

With the timeline selected in the Timelines tab, go to the Properties palette.

In the End Action field, click on the arrow button.

Choose the menu or chapter point of a timeline as the end action.

Now when the timeline ends the DVD player will go to this destination. Also notice this end action is now displayed in the Timeline tab.

The viewer can override this end action with the button that started the timeline. For instance, if the timeline was played from the chapter selection menu, the buttons in that menu can instruct the DVD player to return to the chapter selection menu instead of the main menu (see Set an Override Action of a Button).

Be certain all of your timelines have an end action set. A timeline without an end action can create a broken link ruining the navigation of the entire project.

Chapter 3

Speak the Language

Multi-Track/Multilingual Audio, Subtitles and Slideshows

One of the greatest but most overlooked features of a DVD is the capacity for multiple audio and subtitle tracks. This cuts production costs dramatically by giving one DVD a greater audience. Before DVD, companies had to release several different versions of a video in different languages. Other features such as 5.1 Dolby Digital sound, multiple audio tracks and multiple subtitle tracks take the viewer's experience to a whole new level.

In addition, a DVD offers the ability to create and display slideshows. These slideshows can display a collection of art, storyboards, or still photographs taken during production. The possiblities are limted only by your own imagination.

Import Audio into a Timeline

If you're working with AVI files or an encoder that produces program streams, the video and audio will be linked together and added to a timeline automatically. You'll have to manually add other audio tracks (elementary streams) designed to be used in conjunction with a separate video stream. This mainly applies to projects that rely on imported MPEG-2 video and a separate AC-3 audio stream.

To add audio to a timeline:

With the Timeline window in view, select the audio file in the Project tab.

Click and hold on the file with the left mouse button and drag the file into the Timeline window.

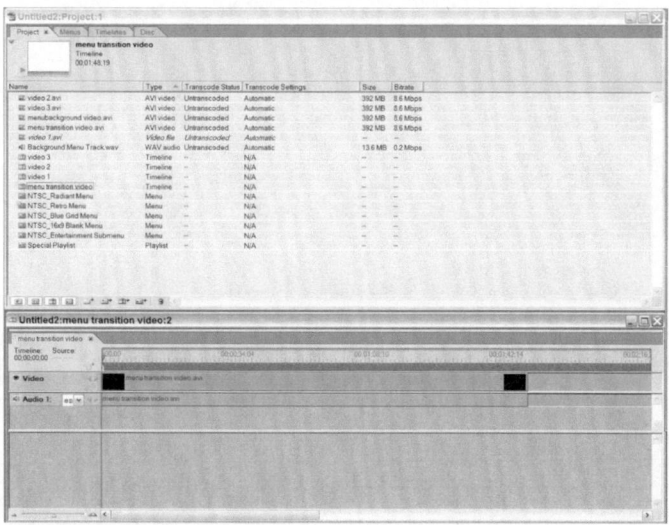

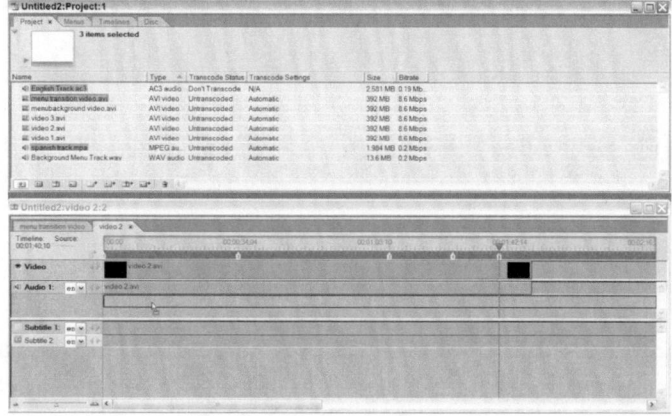

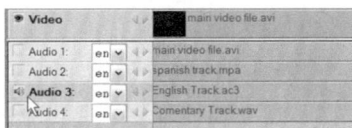

Drop (release the left mouse button) the files into the window.

The files have now been added to the timeline. Because a DVD player can window play one audio track at a time, additional audio tracks are muted.

To preview a language track:

In the Timeline window, go to the audio track to be previewed.

Click on the grey box to set the speaker icon on that track.

If for some reason the wrong file has been added to a timeline, deleting it is easy.

To delete an audio track from a timeline:

Click on the audio track.

Press Delete on the keyboard.

The audio track has now been deleted from the timeline.

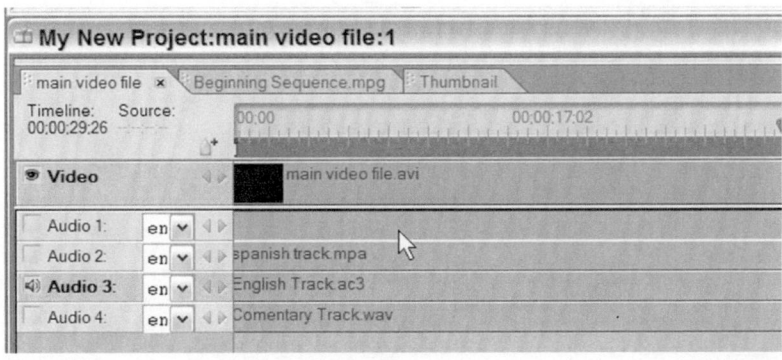

AC-3 for Me, Please?

If audio in a timeline is not AC-3, it is best to transcode it. Transcoding audio ahead of time, instead of waiting until after the content is encoded, gives an extra opportunity to preview the file in its final form.

To transcode audio:

In the Project tab, right-click on the audio file.

Select Transcode Now.

Encore, by default, will encode the audio to the AC-3 format unless the audio encoding scheme has been changed or a custom preset has been chosen.(See "Change the Default Audio Encoding Scheme" and "Create a Custom Preset" in Chapter 1.)

Also, you can have Transcoded audio revert back to the original file if the original file is still present.

To revert transcoded audio:

In the Project tab, right-click on the transcoded audio.

Select Revert to Original.

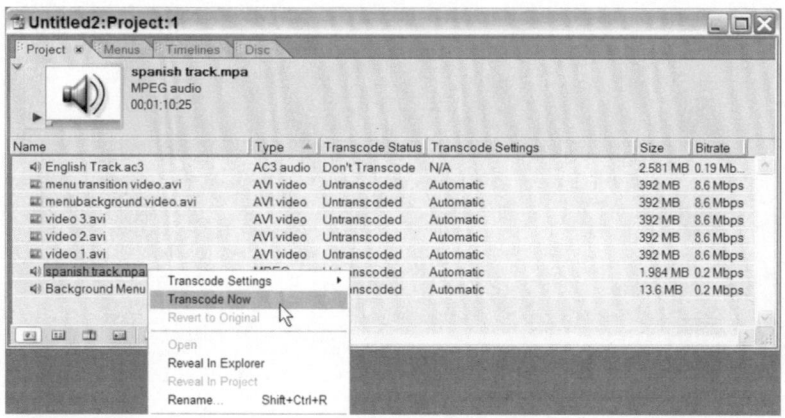

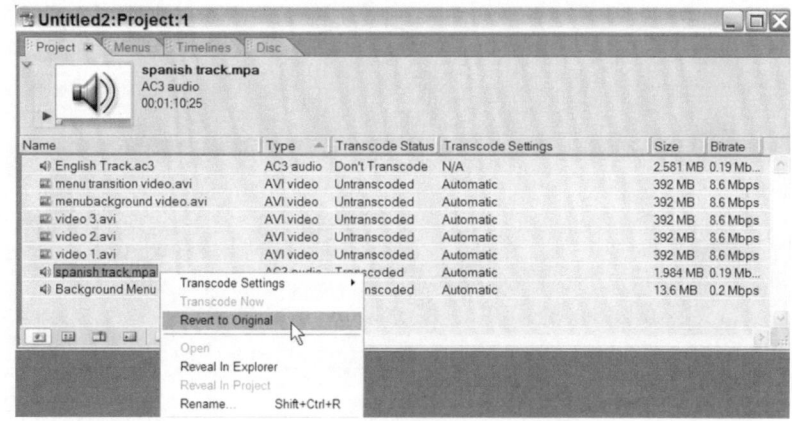

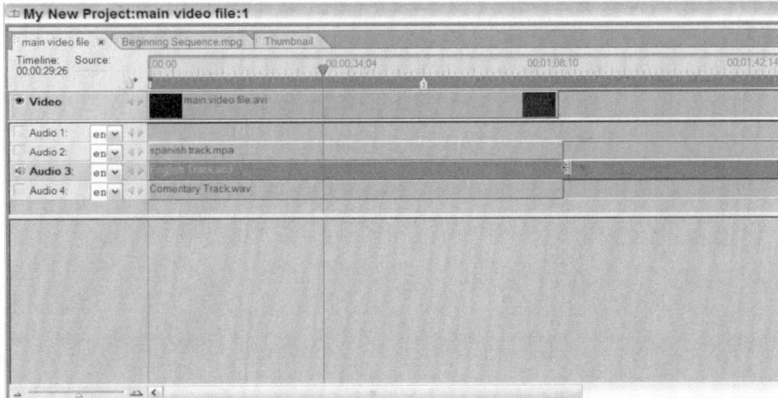

Edit Audio Clips in the Timeline Window

Audio files imported into a timeline should be the same length as the video of the timeline. You can trim the beginning and ends of audio clips to fit the video. If they are longer than the video, they will continue to play even after the video has finished.

Multiplexed audio (audio interleaved with video) cannot be trimmed shorter than the video clip.

To trim audio clips:

In the Timeline window, hover the cursor over the beginning or end of an audio clip.

When the red bracket cursor appears, left-click and hold on the clip.

Drag the clip to an appropriate size, and release the left mouse button.

Always preview your clips after trimming to assure the audio track matches the video track. Trimming the beginning of clips can cause dialog tracks to be out of sync with the video.

Specify Audio Language

DVD players are capable of recognizing the various language tracks of a DVD. Most DVD set-top players will play the language track that they've been set to play by default. For instance, most DVD players in the USA have been set to play English, but if you want, you can programm them to play a Spanish track first. If a DVD player's prefered track is not present, it will play Track 1 by default.

When using multiple language tracks, it's important to label those tracks inside Encore, including the audio track multiplexed with the video.

To specify a language track:

In the Timeline window, go to the audio track.

Click on the arrow to reveal the language codes.

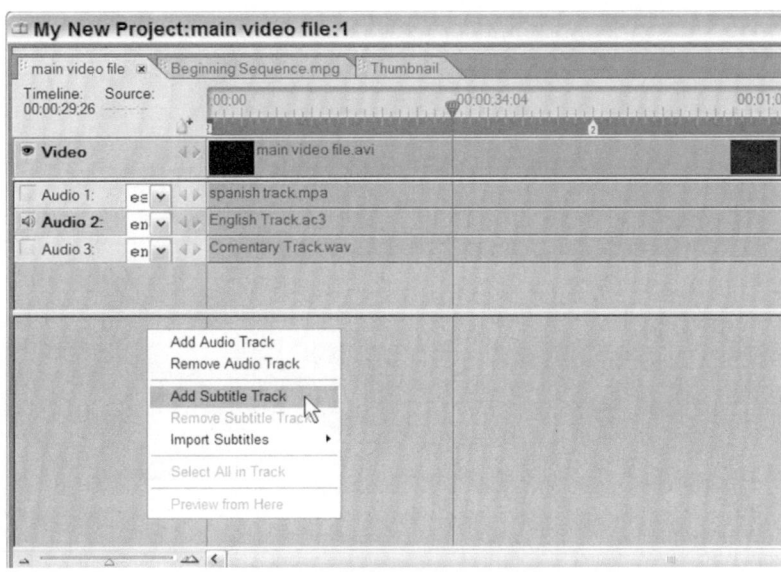

Click on the appropriate language.

Add a Subtitle Track

A DVD player must associate subtitles with a timeline. Therefore, the subtitle track must be added to a timeline.

To add a subtitle track:

In the Timeline window, right-click in the lower-left pane.

Select Add Subtitle Track.

Notice that a subtitle track has been added to the lowest pane of the Timeline window. Unlike the video and audio tracks, it appears blank at first. You can import text from a subtitle program or directly enter it in the Monitor window.

To delete/remove a subtitle track:

Right-click in the lower-left pane of the Timeline window.

Select Remove Subtitle Track.

If you have two tracks in the same language, such as a 5.1 track and a normal two-channel track, set them both to the correct language. Their order on the timeline determines which is played first.

Comprehending Subtitles

A subtitle is text that appears on the screen during a feature. Usually it is a translation of the spoken language. Subtitles are a great way of creating a multilingual disc without requiring an additional audio track for the desired language. Often DVDs have a subtitle track that displays captions for the movie, an important feature for the hearing impaired.

Subtitles should be readable but nonintrustive. Therefore, setting an appropriate length and position is important. Encore allows up to three colors to be used for subtitles. So if a scene is dialog- intensive, you can use colors to represent who said what.

The subtitle track is a stream of information that the DVD player turns into text on the screen at specific points along the timeline. DVD players are capable of generating crude two-bit overlays offering a limited number of colors that can be displayed. Avoid fonts with serifs or complicated curves. However, you can use the three available colors to antialias the text.

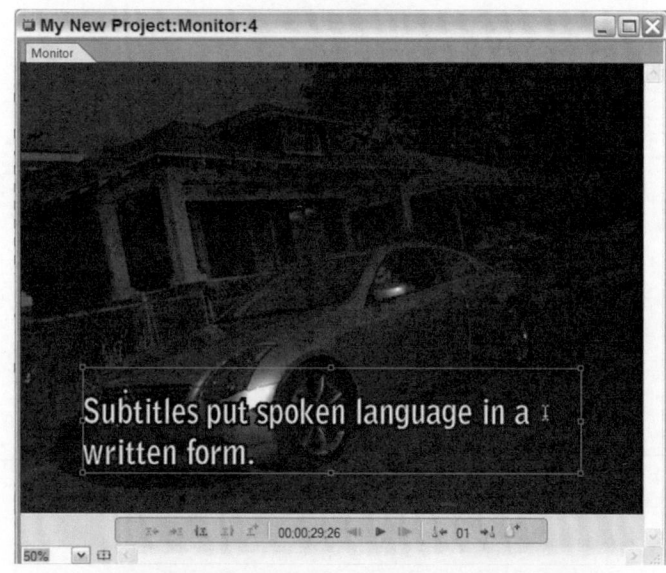

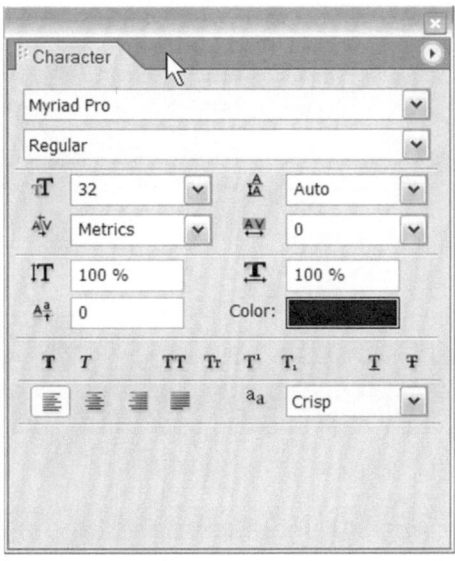

Use the Character Palette for Subtitle Fonts

Before you add the first subtitle to a project, you need to select the font and font size. Encore's Character palette offers a myriad of typesets and fonts, along with point sizes and character spacing. Find the best look and size of the subtitle font before starting, because it's difficult to redo each individual subtitle clip.

To choose a character style for subtitles:

With the subtitle track selected, go to the Character palette in the palette window.

Adjust the settings appropriately.

Font: Several fonts are available, but choose a font without serifs or complex curves. The straighter the typeface, the better it will appear on the screen. Remember that the DVD player creates the text with crude and blocky two-bit pixels. Accomodate this limitation.

Font Style: Choose either regular or bold, and use italics sparingly.

Font Size: Measured in points. Typically you should use 16- or 18-point fonts. The bigger the font, the easier it is to read, but if it's too big, it will crowd the frame and less text can be comfortably added.

Font Color: Irrelevant. The Font Color for subtitles is controlled by color sets.

The other features of the Character palette are best left alone for subtitles. Typically these other features can fine tune the presentation of certain troublesome subtitles, but the default settings are recommended. Experiment with these settings when appropriate.

Add Subtitles in the Monitor Window

Encore allows subtitles to be typed directly into the Monitor window. The first step in this process is to adjust the workspace.

To adjust the workspace for best subtitling:

Minimize the Project window.

In the Monitor window, set the Display Size to 100 percent.

Resize the Monitor window to fit the new size.

Click the Safe Areas icon, located next to the Display Size.

This displays the Action and Title Safe Areas. Subtitles should be within the inner box, or Title Safe Area. This assures that the subtitles will be seen clearly in the frame on most every television or monitor.

Now that the workspace is in order, it's time to begin subtitling. Play the video or move the CTI to where the first subtitle will begin.

To insert a subtitle:

Choose the Horizontal Text tool from the Toolbar.

You can use vertical text, but it can surprise the viewers, who don't expect it, and it usually blocks the action in a frame.

Within the Title Safe Area, click on where the text is to be placed.

Type the subtitle.

Press the Return/Enter key to keep text within the Title Safe area. Remember that you can place text anywhere. If a subtitle blocks necessary information at the bottom of the frame, move it to the top or use the Vertical Text tool.

To move subtitles:

Go to the Toolbar and choose any of the Selection tools.

In the Monitor window, click on the subtitle.

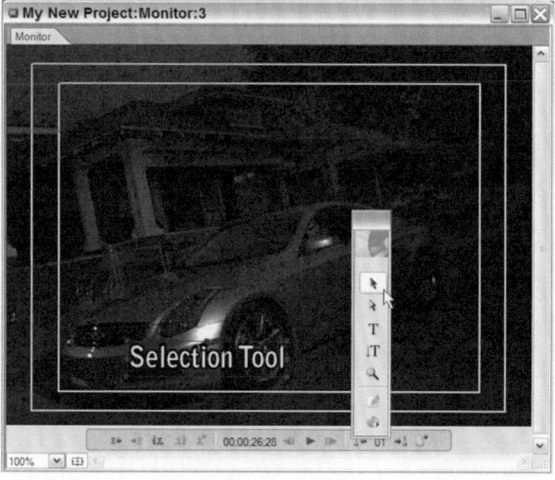

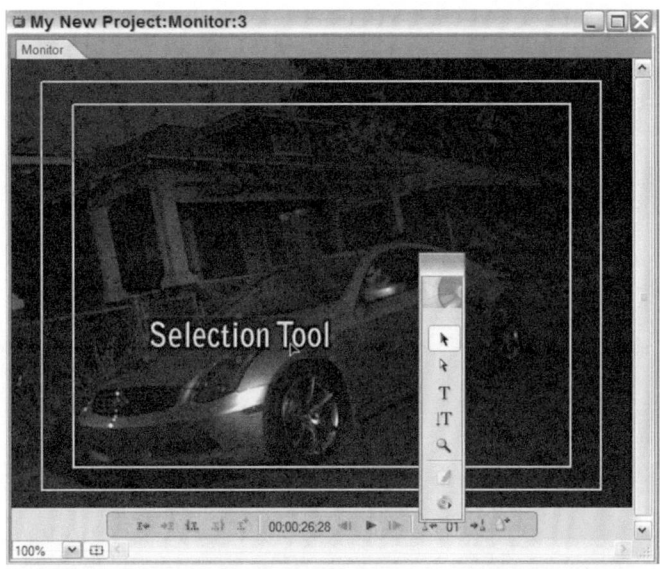

Left-click and hold in the center of the box.

Drag the subtitle to the desired location.

Release the left mouse button.

While it is best to use the Character palette to determine subtitle size, sometimes only a few subtitles need resizing.

To resize a subtitle:

Go to the Toolbar and choose the Selection tool.

Click on the text in the Monitor window.

Hover the cursor over the corner of the box until the diagonal cursor appears.

Click and hold on the corner, and drag the box to the appropriate size.

Release the mouse button.

Choose the Color Group of a Subtitle Clip

A timeline can have up to three different color groups for its subtitles. This allows a color differentiation between speakers during dialog. In each of these groups are three colors. These colors work together to reduce the blockiness of the text.

You can choose the color group for each subtitle from the Properties palette.

To change the color group of a subtitle:

Select the subtitle clip in the Timelines window.

Go to the Properties palette, open the Color Group field.

Choose Color Group 1, Group 2, or Group 3.

At this time you can choose the stroke

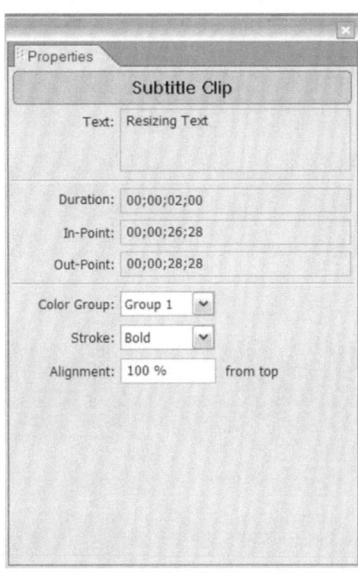

(boldness) of the subtitle. The stroke controls how the colors work together. Chosing None displays just one thin color, while choosing Heavy expands the three colors to an almost ridiculous size. Normal is recommended.

Alignment should remain at 100 percent from the top.

Create a New Timeline Color Set

If you want more control over the color, then you can adjust the color set for the timeline. but when you change the color set for a timeline, all the subtitles will change to match those colors according to their groups. Only three color groups are allowed per timeline, or nine colors total.

Using a new color set for timeline is a two-step process. First you must create a new color set, and then you must apply it to the timeline.

To create a new color set for a timeline:

Go to Timeline>Edit Timeline Color Sets.

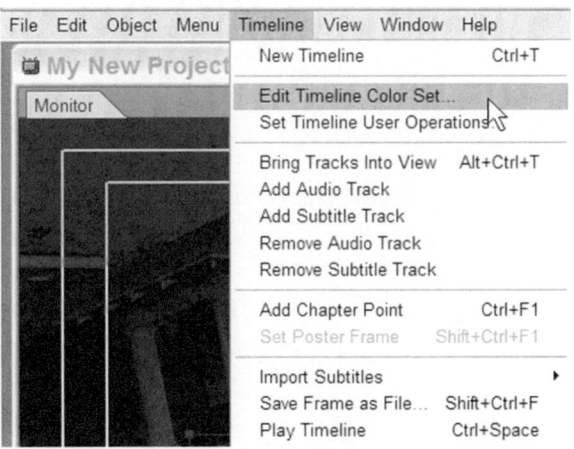

This opens the Edit Timeline Color Set dialog. You can adjust the current or timeline default color set, and the changes will automatically appear in the subtitles.

Click Preview.

If you plan to use only one color set for the project, you'll save a step. But if you want different color sets for different timelines, then you will need to create a new color set. Remember: by changing this default color set, all timelines and their subtitles that use this color set will be affected. Skip the next couple of steps if the default color set is the only one you plan to use.

Click on the Create New Color Set icon.

This prompts for a Color Set name.

Type a name for the color set and click OK.

Now that you've made a new color set, it is time to adjust the colors. Notice that only three colors are in each group. The first color, or the fill color, is really the text itself. The second color, stroke color, provides definition to the inside color. The third color, the

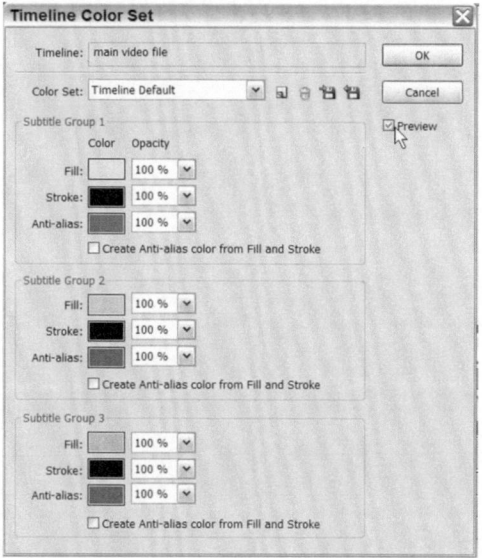

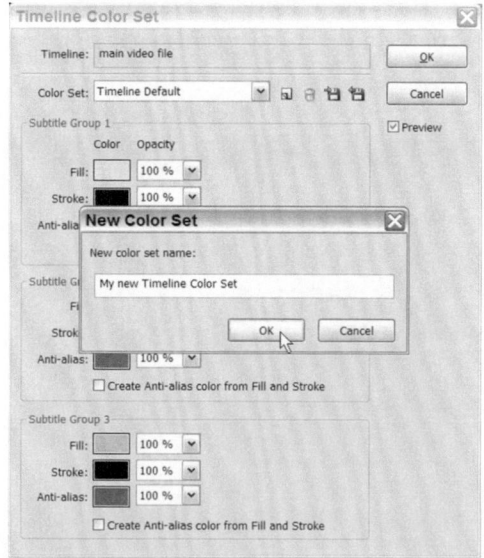

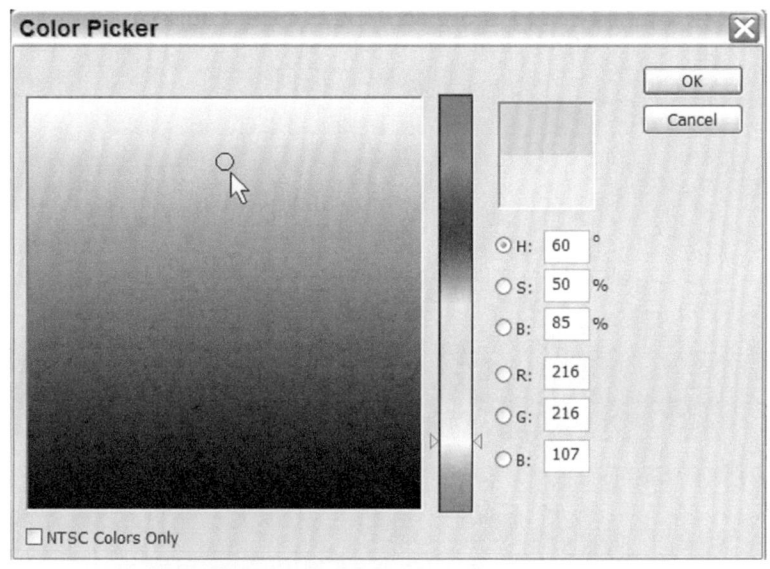

antialias color, counteracts the blockiness of the text.

Click on a block of color to adjust it.

Move the slider up or down to change the hue.

Move the color picker circle in the big box to change the grey density.

Click OK.

You can adjust the opacity, or solidness, of each color. At 100 percent, the color will be completely opaque; 0 percent is completely transparent.

Check the NTSC Colors Only box if this is an NTSC project. This will assure that the best colors will be used on NTSC televisions.

Make all desired adjustments to the color set.

Click OK.

If you created a new timeline color set, then the next step is to apply it to the timeline. If not, then the task is complete.

To apply a new color set to a timeline:

Click inside the Timeline window.

Go to the Properties palette.

Click the arrow next to the Color Set field.

Select the new color set.

The color set has now been applied to this timeline.

Set the Default Length of Subtitles

By default, the length of subtitles is two seconds. However, the length of individual subtitles may be adjusted (see next section). In addition, default length may also be changed.

To change the Default Length of Subtitles:

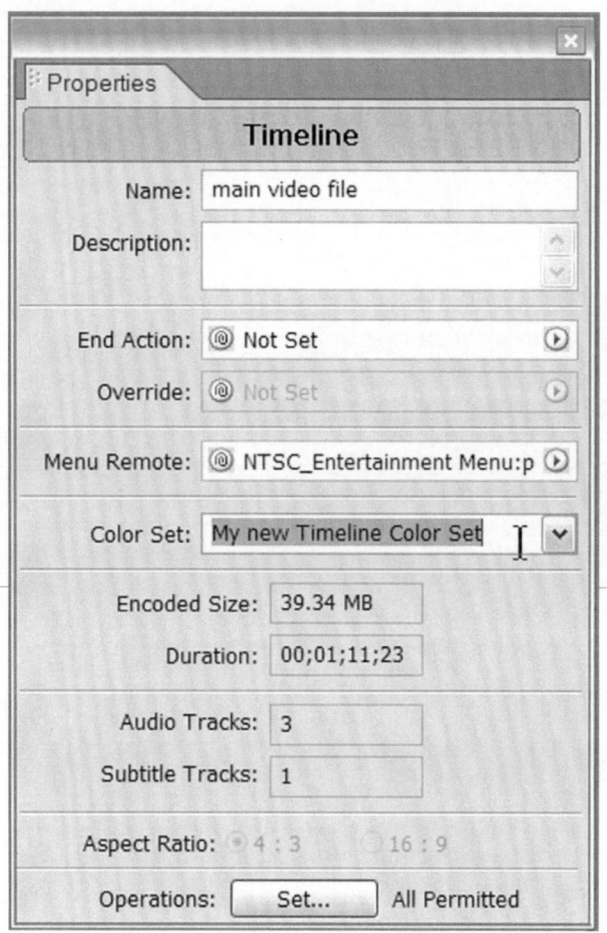

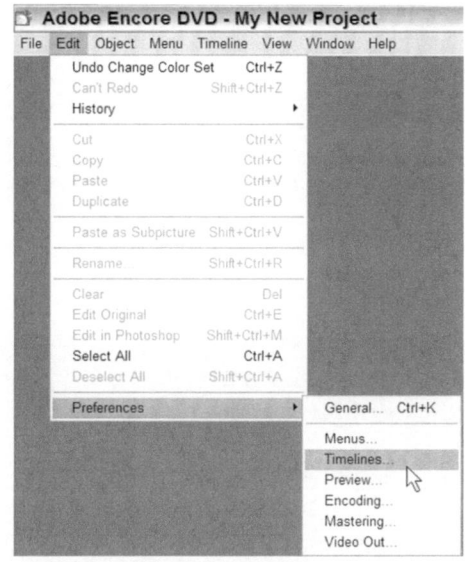

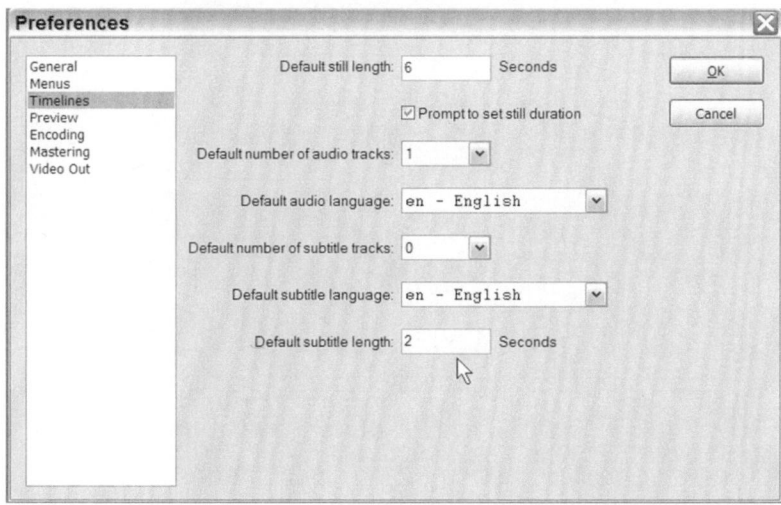

Go to Edit>Preferences>Subtitles.

This opens the Project Settings for Subtitles. The Default Language refers to the language code for which subtitles are automatcally set. (See "Specify Subtitle Language" later in this chapter for more details.) If many of your projects use another language for subtitles, go ahead and specify the language.

When specifying a default length, keep in mind that the average person can read approximately eight (8) words in about two (2) seconds. The default length is appropriate and should not be changed unless the video demands it.

Enter a number in seconds for the Default Subtitle Length.

Click OK.

Now all new subtitles created will automatically be the length specified.

Encore 1.5 Tip: When you create a new timeline, it now adopts the last color set you used. This is useful when you want to create multiple timelines that all use the same color set. Simply create a timeline and choose a color set from the Properties palette or modify the color set of an existing timeline. The next new timeline you create will use the color set you selected.

Remember that color sets are not global settings and must be specified in the properties of a time

Set the In and Out Points of Subtitles

Place the CTI to the frame where you want the subtitle to begin or end, and trim the subtitle clip to that line.

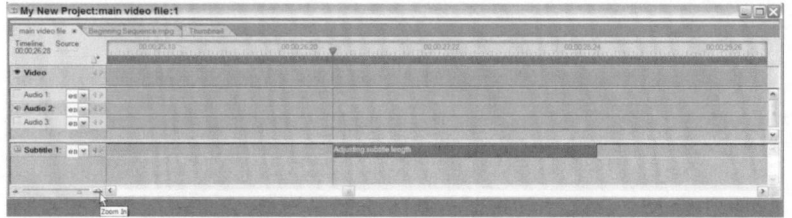

Sometimes subtitles need to be shorter or longer than the default length. Rapid fire dialog and slow, deliberate monologs need special treatment. Encore offers a couple of different ways to adjust the cues and lengths of subtitles.

To set the In and Out points of a subtitle using the Timeline window:

Adjust the Zoom Level of the timeline so that you can adjust subtitles with precision.

Hover over the beginning or end of a subtitle until the red bracket cursor appears.

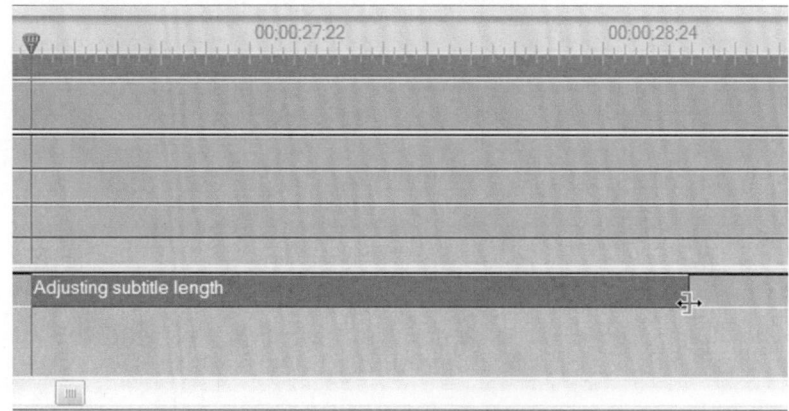

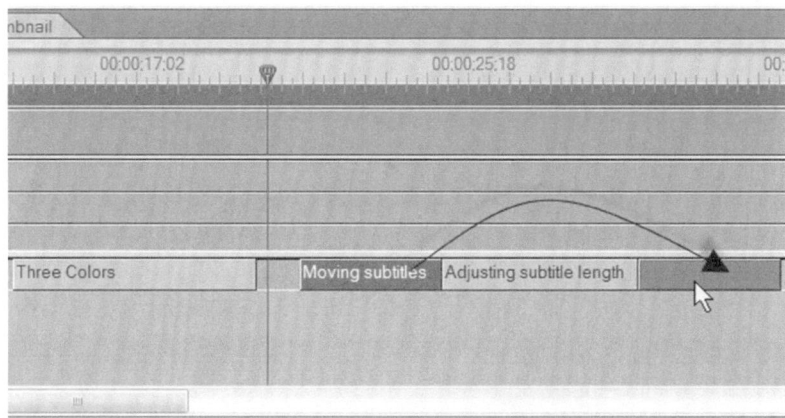

Click and drag the beginning or end of the subtitle to the appropriate size or place.

If the subtitle is the right length but is not in the right place, you can adjust it by moving it.

Click and hold on the subtitle clip and drag it to a better place on the timeline.

Encore offers a better option for trimming the in and out points of subtitles, by using the Monitor window. While a subtitle is displayed, you can set its In point to a later frame or its Out point to an earlier frame.

Trim subtitle clips using the Monitor window:

If a subtitle comes in too early, click the Trim Subtitle In point icon at the frame where it should come in.

If a subtitle lingers too long, click the Trim Subtitle Out point icon at the frame where the subtitle should disappear.

Since only one subtitle clip can be displayed at a time, Encore does not allow subtitles to overlap. If one subtitle is moved into another, it will jump to the other side of the clip it is moving into. In this way, Encore prevents the accidental displacement of other subtitle clips

These Monitor window controls only work if a subtitle is displayed. You must move the subtitle clip's position in the Timeline window if an earlier In point or a later Out point is required.

Import a Text Script as Subtitles

Advanced Tip: Due to the nature of subtitles it is best to start them AFTER chapter points. If a subtitle is started in a previous chapter, and the chapter is directly selected, there is a good chance the first subtitle will not appear when played.

Encore permits the importing of Captions Inc Script, FAB Image Script, and Text Script file formats as subtitles. For plain Text Script, there are few requirements. The text encoding can be ASCII, UTF-8, or UTF-16. Also there is a specified format for using timecode.

1 00;00;01;00 00;00;03;00 This is a subtitle.

The first number, 1, is the subtitle's order. In this case, it is the first subtitle. The next, 00;00;01;00, is the In point of the subtitle. In simpler terms, this subtitle comes in at the first second of the timeline. The other timecode, 00;00;03;00, is the Out point of the subtitle. So the subtitle remains on the screen for two seconds. The final value is the subtitle text itself. "This is a subtitle" will appear on the screen at the first second of the timeline and will disappear two seconds later.

To import a text script as a subtitle:

In the Timeline window, right-click on the subtitle track.

Choose Import Subtitles>Text Script.

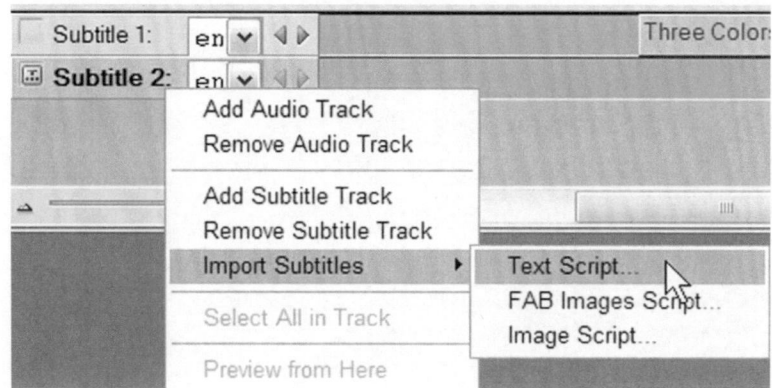

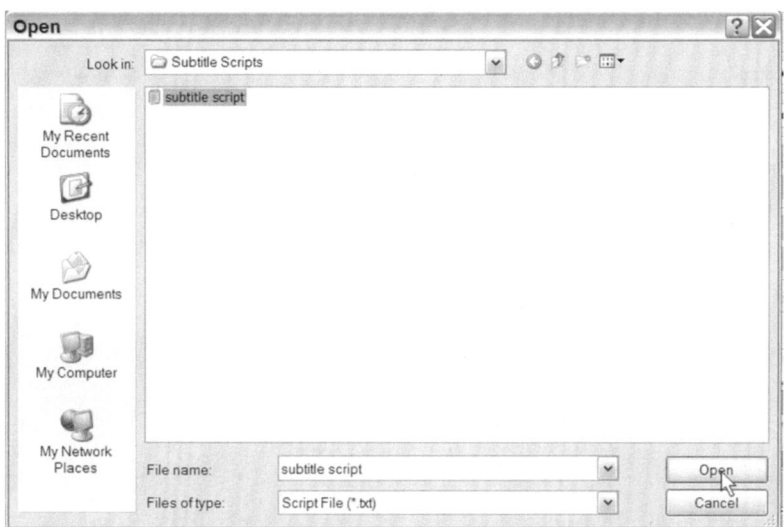

This opens the Open File dialog. Any subtitle clips that exist on this subtitle track will be erased to accommodate the imported file.

Locate and select the text script file

Click Open.

This opens the Import Subtitles (Text Script) dialog. You can be adjust the position and size of the text box on the screen. This offers a few options for the font, font size, and color group options, as well as Asian text options and timecode offset controls.

The Timecode Offset control is a useful feature if the beginning of the video has been trimmed since the subtitle script was created. Choose Relative and insert the proper timecode offset. Leaving it at Absolute maintains the timecodes specified in the original text script.

Make the necessary adjustments, and then click OK.

The text script has now been converted to subtitles. Check the time position of all the subtitles to ensure proper placement.

Making adjustments in this dialog determines how all the subtitles will be placed, not just the first subtitle.

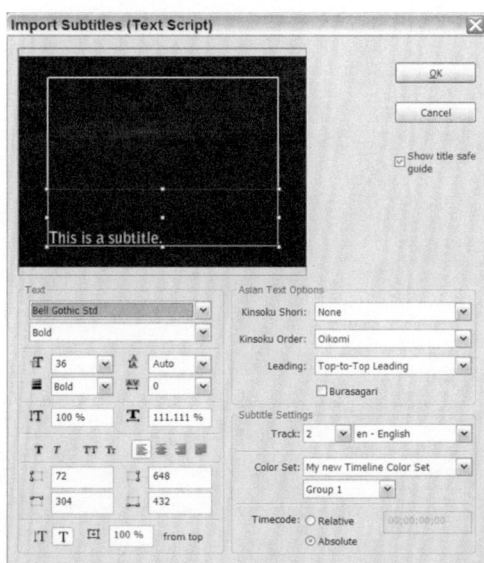

Specify Subtitle Language

Like the audio tracks, subtitle tracks have a specific language code. This code allows DVD players to recognize the language so that direct selection of the subtitle track can be accomplished using the player's hardware.

To specify subtitle language:

In the Timeline window, select the subtitle track.

Open the list of language codes by clicking on the arrow.

Choose the appropriate language code.

Create a Slideshow from Still Images

Encore can create a slideshow from up to 99 graphics. This slideshow can even include audio and subtitles. Graphics must be imported into the

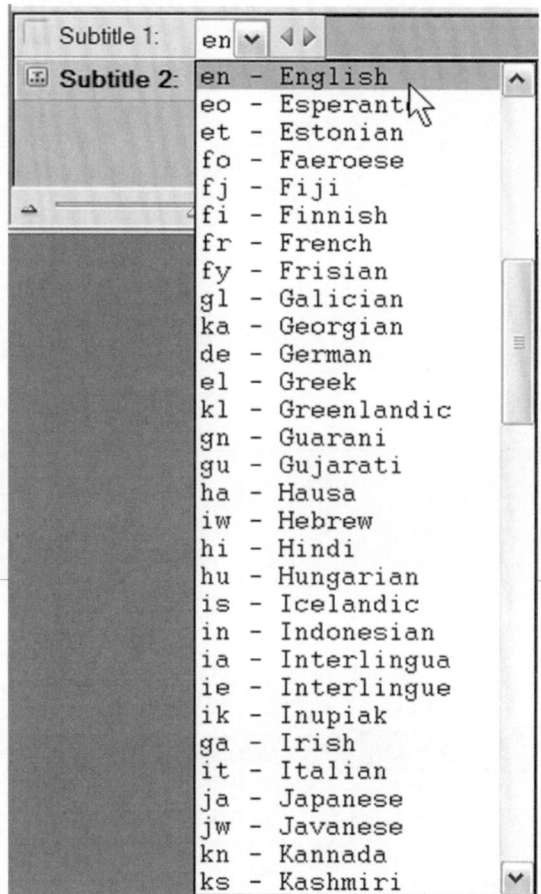

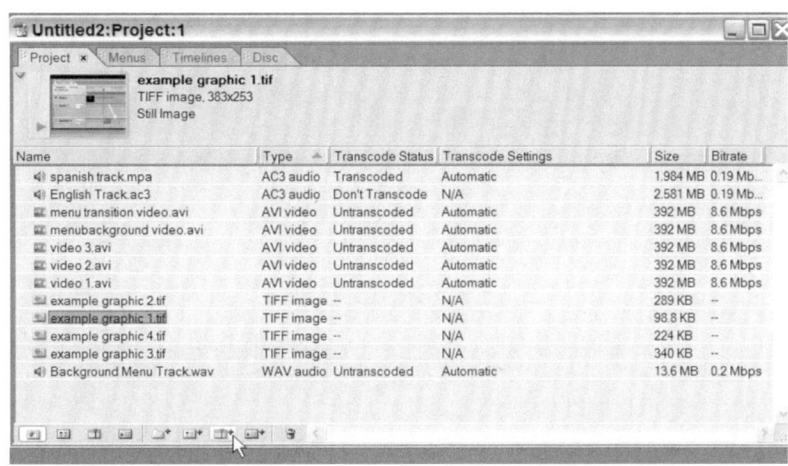

Project tab (see "Import Files as Graphics" in Chapter 1). In order to create a slideshow, you must create a new timeline.

To create a slideshow:

In the Project tab, select the desired first graphic of the slideshow.

Use the keyboard shortcut Ctrl+T or the Create New Timeline icon.

This opens a new timeline with the graphic selected as the first image in the timeline. Now the other graphics must be imported.

In the Project window, select a graphic or a range of graphics to add to the timeline.

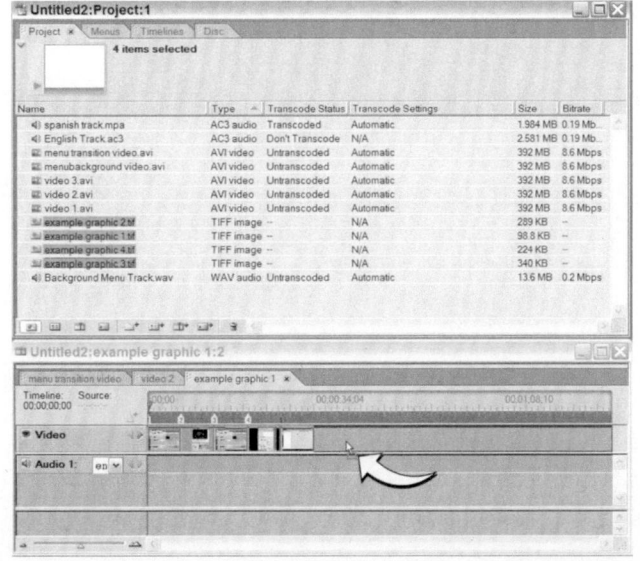

Click and drag the graphics into the Timeline window.

As each graphic is added, it is assigned its own chapter point. If several files were added to the timeline at once, the graphics are ordered alphanumerically. So, for example, pic12 will come before pic2. Changing the order is simple.

To move a graphic to a different place along the timeline:

In the Timeline window, click and hold on the graphic you wish to move.

Drag it to the desired place on the timeline and release the mouse button.

Notice that the chapter points are reordered to maintain the sequence.

Slideshows encode graphics to a single frame and display this frame over time. This process is extremely efficient as it only requires one frame of content to display video over time. For this reason, slideshows can contain a lot of images and are one of the most efficient methods of storing and playing back content on a DVD

Adjust the Duration of Still Images in the Timeline Window

When a still image is added to a timeline, by default it's length is six (6) seconds. You can adjust this length for individual stills.

To adjust the length of still images:

In the Timeline window, select the desired image.

Hover the cursor over the end of the still until the red-bracket cursor appears.

Click and drag the edge of the still to the appropriate length.

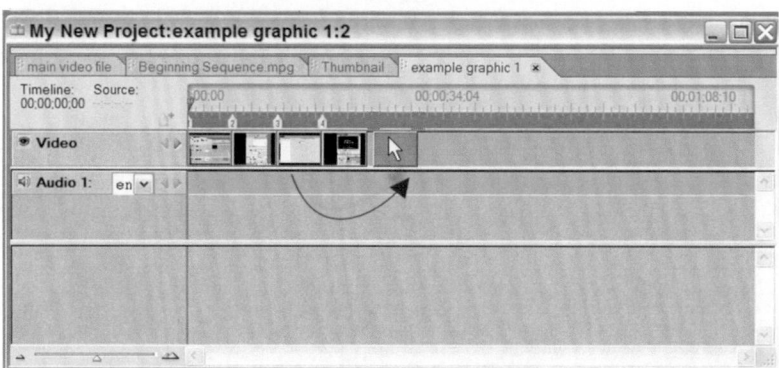

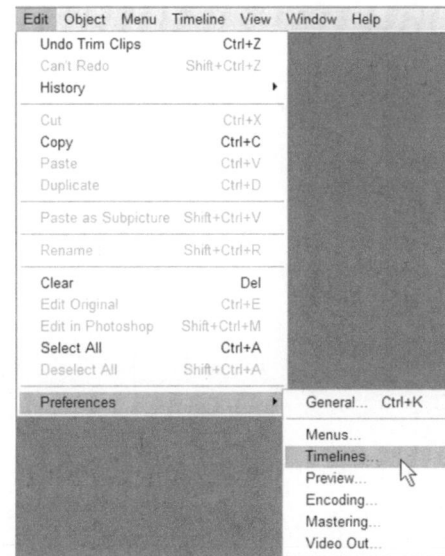

The stills after the clip automatically adjust their positions to fill the gap.

Set the Default Length of Still Images

Encore 1.5: When still images are added to a Slideshow, a dialog appears requesting the length of each image.

Every still image imported into a time-line is automatically assigned a length of six seconds by default. This is controlled by the project preferences. If you want a different default length, you should chang it before creating a slideshow timeline.

To change the default length of still images:

Go to Edit>Preferences>Timelines.

In the Default Length of Still Images, enter a new length in seconds.

Click OK.

Now all stills added to a timeline will be assigned this new default length. However, all stills in existing slideshow timelines will not change their durations.

Chapter 4

Menus, Menus, Art and Function

If Timelines are the highways on a DVD, then Menus are the gateways to those roads. DVD menus offer perhaps the greatest advantages over VHS. With menus, a DVD's features may be seen and accessed instantly. Menu creation has become an art form of its own right with the use of spectacular backgrounds, motion transitions, video backgrounds and motion thumbnails.

Encore is supplied with professionally designed templates that can be put to use in minutes. This speeds the production process and allows a beginning author to quickly create professionally designed menus and buttons.

It is recommended that everyone, not just beginning authors, explore the templates included with Encore. The concepts learned from the templates will pay off dividends when creating menus from scratch.

Open an Existing Template

The first step in using templates is to open one of the menu templates. They are stored in the Library palette.

Templates are a great way to get started in Encore. They can be used to help gather ideas for a project, and can be easily modified to cater to individual projects. A goodies folder, found in Encore's installation CD, provides additional templates and assets.

To open a template:

Open the Library palette.

The Library palette contains three kinds of Photoshop files: graphics, buttons, and menus. The menus in the Library palette contain backgrounds, buttons, text, and graphics. The menu templates all contain the word "menu" in their names. Submenus are generally used for chapter selection menus.

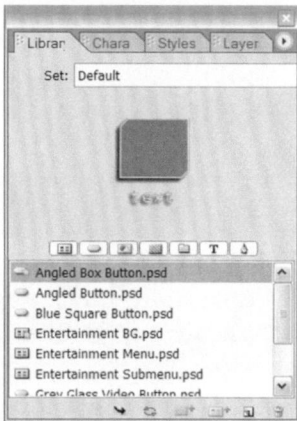

You can preview the look of a menu by selecting from the list. A thumbnail view of the menu or graphic appears.

Select the desired menu from the list.

Right-click on the selected menu and select Create New Menu.

This loads the template into the Menu Editor window. For this example, the Entertainment menu is used.

At this time it's a good idea to reorganize the workspace. Minimize the Project window, Monitor window, or

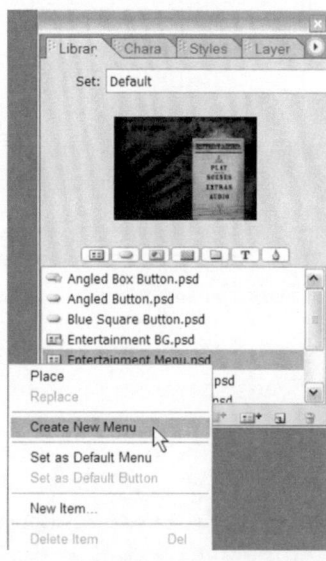

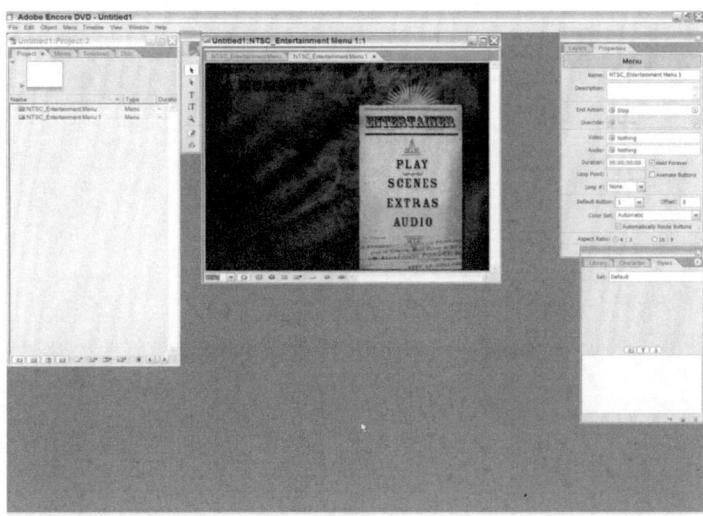

Timeline window. The Menu Editor, palettes, and Toolbar should be easily accessible. Drag the Properties palette out of the Palette window.

Understanding Basic Layers and Layer Prefixes

Encore inherits one of the best innovations of its sister program Adobe Photoshop—Layers. All Encore menus, buttons, and graphics exist on layers separated with sensible naming conventions.

Encore uses layers and layer sets to organize various aspects of a menu. A layer can be a specific graphical aspect of a file. For example, there is a specific layer for text, a specific layer for a graphic and a specific layer for the background. These layers are organized into layer sets. For example, a button of a DVD is a group of layers organized into a layer set.

A button is a functional aspect of DVD. The viewer can press it to perform an action. Encore must make a distinction between an ordinary graphic and a button. Encore does this by assigning a (+) prefix to a button's layer set.

It's a very good idea to own and comprehend Photoshop if a lot of work is anticipated for Encore. However, the many applications of Photoshop to the Encore/visual workflow are another book by itself. I recommend Richard Harrington's Photoshop CS for Non-Linear Editors.

Another important aspect of a DVD menu is the Subpicture Highlight. This is an interactive graphic generated by the DVD player. It aids navigation by highlighting the buttons, and confirming selection. In many ways, the subpicture is really the menu itself. You can create a menu using just the subpicture. But because the subpicture is a crude two-bit image that can use a maximum of three colors at once, it is best used as a highlight for a more elaborate background menu.

Use an existing template to reverse engineer the menu structure. This is the easiest way to understand how all of the different elements are combined to create a menu.

The subpicture highlight layers are identified by the (=1),(=2), and (=3) prefixes. The subpicture highlights just one layer inside a button's layer set.

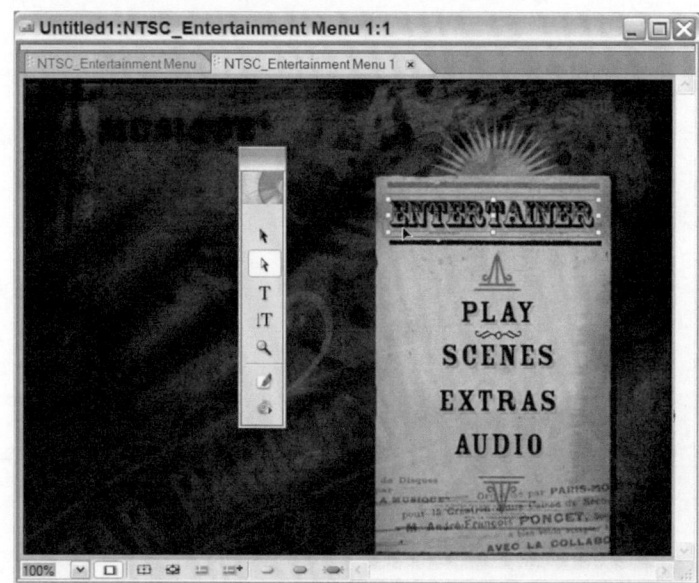

Modify the Text in an Existing Template

You can change a template to suit individual needs with the Menu Editor. You can add or delete text and buttons. Making changes to a template does not affect the original template. See "Saving a Modified Template" in this chapter.

Don't let the text of a menu limit your perception of what it should or can

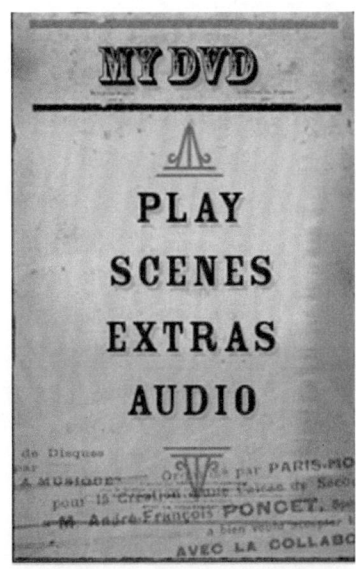

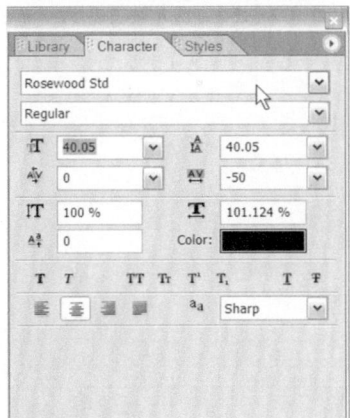

possibly do. You may set buttons in a menu to link anywhere, and you may modify the text to indicate the changed link.

To change the title text of a menu:

Select the Direct Select tool (the white arrow) from the Toolbar.

In the Menu Editor, double-click on the title text.

While you can use the Text tools to perform this function, it is best to use the Direct Select tool to modify existing text. This prevents the accidental creation of blank text layers.

When the Insert Text cursor appears, delete the existing text

Type in the new title.

The title text has now been changed.

The font and font size can also be changed for the text using the Character palette and Direct Select tool.

To change the font or size of text in a menu:

Use the Direct Select tool and single-click on the text .

A blue bounding box will appear around the text. At this time you can move the text or resize it using the corners of the box. But for consistency, use the Character palette.

Open the Character palette.

Select the font and/or font size for the text.

Although you can adjust the color in the Character palette, the existing colors match the scheme of the menu and have a very professional look.

To modify the text of a button:

Open the Layers palette.

Click on the arrow to twirl down the button's layer set and reveal its individual layers.

Select the Text layer of the button (the layer with the T).

A blue bounding box now appears around the text. There is a second bounding box around a larger area; this represents the entire area of the button.

You may now modify the text in the same way as the title text.

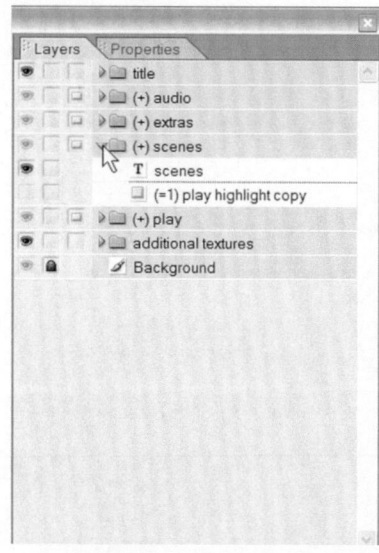

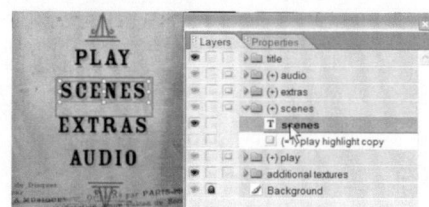

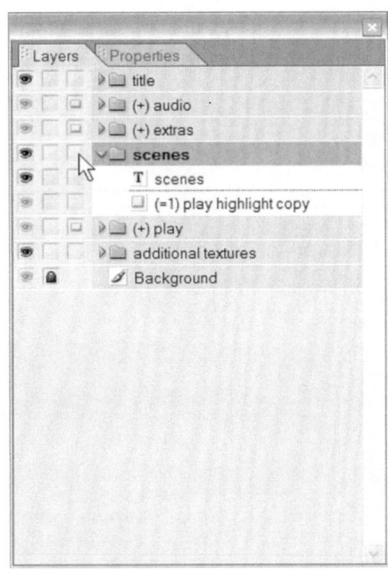

Deactivate or Remove Extra Buttons from a Template

Most of the templates have four buttons for the usual options in a DVD's main menu. If you need fewer buttons, then you can the delete or deactivate the buttons. Simply deleting the text does not remove a button. The best way to hide a button is to deactivate it in the Layers palette.

The text for the buttons is changed in much the same way the title text is changed. Since the text is a layer of the button, however, it is easy to select the wrong layer of a button. The easiest way to modify the text of a button is to use the Layer's Palette to directly select the text layer first.

To deactivate a button:

Open the layer's palette.

Select the layer set of the button.

Click on the Button icon in the Button/ Object column.

Notice when clicking on the Button/ Object column (the third column from the left side of the palette) that the (+) prefix in the layer set is removed. Encore no longer treats this as a button and considers it an object. The next step is to hide the object.

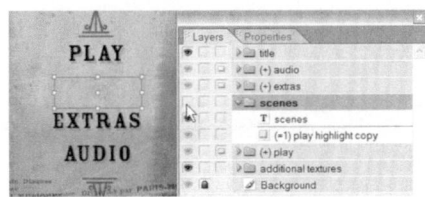

Click on the Eyeball icon in the first column's box to deselect it.

Now that the Eyeball icon is deselected, the object and its text no longer appear in the Menu Editor.

Of course, you can delete the entire button from the menu.

To delete a button from a template:

Buttons can be deleted in Photoshop by simply deleting layers that contain button layer sets.

In the layer's palette, select the button's layer set.

Press the Delete key.

The button and text have now been completely removed from the menu.

Edit in Photoshop Feature

Experienced Photoshop users will appreciate the ability to use Photoshop to edit their DVD menus. Photoshop offers several options for creating graphics and editing colors.

To edit in Photoshop:

With the Menu Editor open on the menu, go to Menu>Edit in Photoshop.

This opens Photoshop (if installed) and imports the current menu.

After you've made all the adjustments to the menu in Photoshop, go to File>Save in Photoshop.

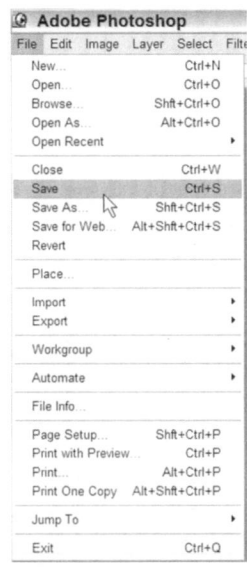

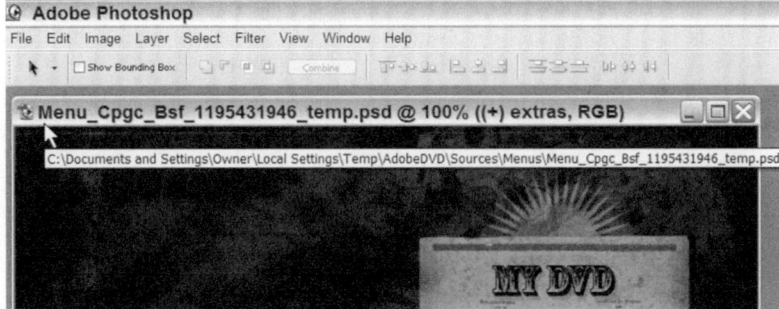

The menu in Encore has now been updated with the changes to the file.

Save a Modified Template

When a template is used, a copy of that template is created. This way the original template is not changed by the user and safeguards against accidentally corrupting a useable menu. While this is a nice feature, it can be frustrating if one template is changed the same way every time it is used.

To save a modified template:

With the desired final template in the Menu Editor, go to Menu>Edit in Photoshop.

This opens and loads the template into Photoshop. Notice that the file name of the menu in Photoshop is completely different than the original name of the template.

Tip for Encore 1.5: You can access the Edit in Photoshop feature using a convenient toolbar button. To edit a menu in Adobe Photoshop, open it in the Menu Editor and then click the Edit in Photoshop button.

After a file has been saved in Photoshop, the live link with Encore is severed. The Edit in Photoshop command must be used again to make additional changes to the menu using Photoshop.

In Photoshop, go to File>Save As.

In the Save As dialog, give the template a new file name that is different from the original template name.

Choose the desktop as the saved file destination.

Click Save.

Now you need to import the menu into Encore's Library palette.

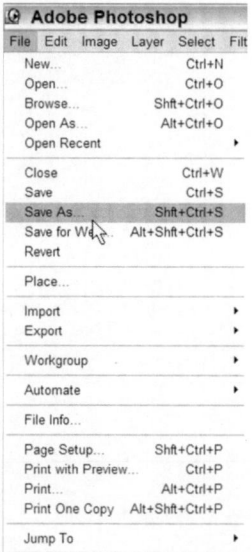

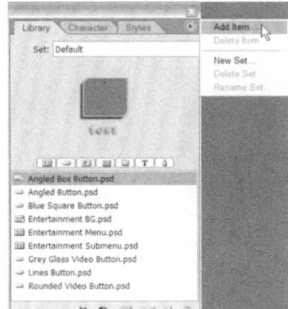

In Encore, open the Library palette.

Right-click inside the library, and select Add Item.

This opens the New Library Item dialog.

Locate and select the new template from the desktop.

Click Open.

The new template has been added to the Library palette.

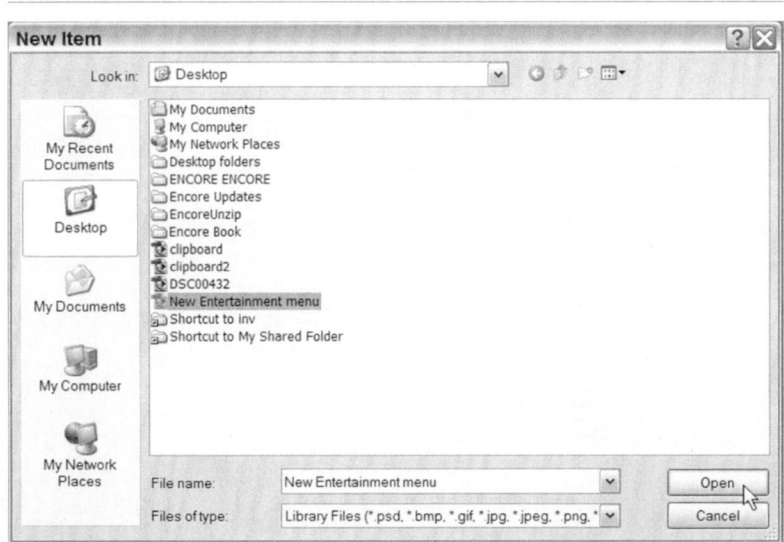

Use the Library Palette to Organize Graphics, Menus, and Buttons

Items can also be dragged and dropped directly into the Library Palette.

You can set Encore's Library palette to view only certain types of PSD files. This is rather helpful if you have multiple files in the Library palette. By default, all the file types are shown.

To hide a file type in the Library palette:

At the bottom of the window there are three icons.

Click on the icon of the file type you wish to hide.

To show just one type of file, click on the other file types to hide them.

Encore 1.5 allows even greater organization. You can create library sets to file the different items away under categories you define.

To create a new library set:

From the Library palette flyout menu, select New Library Set.

Enter a name for your library set and click OK.

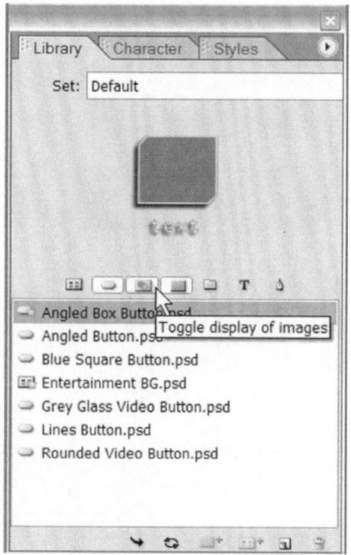

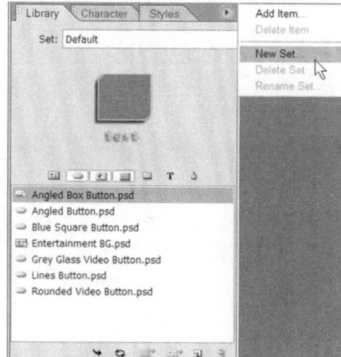

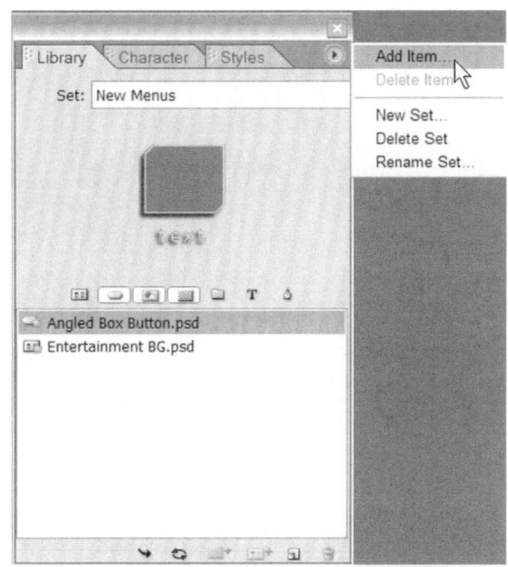

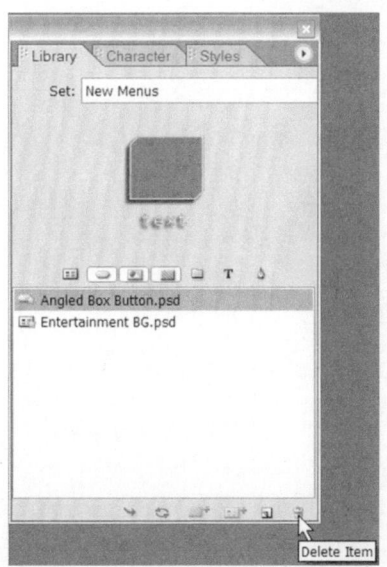

To add items to a library set:

In the Library palette, display the library set to which you want to add items by selecting it from the set drop-down box.

Click the Add Item button or select Add Item from the Library palette fly-out menu.

In the file browser, locate the item you want to add and then click OK.

Library Palette Maintenance

After several projects have been created, the Library palette might appear cluttered and disorganized. It's a good practice to perform a little spring cleaning from time to time to keep the file list short. Encore will not allow the built-in templates, buttons, and graphics to be deleted.

To delete an item from the Library palette:

Select the item to be deleted.

In the lower-right corner of the palette, click the Trash icon.

One of the most significant changes between 1.0 and 1.5 is the Library Palette. In version 1.5, the show and hide file type icons are above the list of items and includes backgrounds, text, and shapes. Hold shift and click on the file types you wish to display. To display one file type just click its icon.

Encore will warn that this deletion cannot be undone.

Confirm the deletion by clicking OK.

Another recommendation is to prioritize your menus and buttons according to use. By default, Encore uses the blank menu as the default menu, but you may set any menu as the default menu. The same is true for a button. The default menu and button have asterisks next to their names.

To set the default menu/button:

Select the desired menu/button and right-click.

Select Set as Default Menu or Default button.

Each time a new menu is created from the Menu pulldown dialog, this will become the new default menu.

Using Photoshop to Create a Menu

Not only can you modify Encore's menus in Photoshop, but you can create them within Photoshop without ever using Encore's Menu Editor. Because Photoshop and Encore share

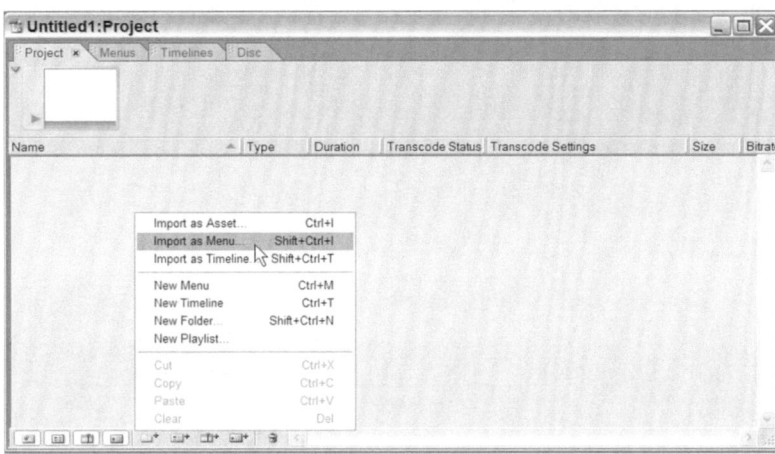

the same layer conventions, importing a Photoshop menu is a breeze.

Keep in mind that Encore's menus are Photoshop (PSD) files. There are several ways to import a PSD file as a menu. However, a PSD file should never be imported as an asset. When a PSD file is imported as an asset, it flattens the layers, making the menu unusable for anything other than a background.

To import a PSD file to use in only one project:

In the Project tab, right-click in a blank area of the pane.

Select Import as Menu.

In the Import as Menu dialog, locate and select the desired psd menu(s).

Click Open.

Of course, if a PSD file is slated for multiple use, the best way to import the menu is through the Library palette.

To import a menu for future use in projects:

Go to the Library palette, right-click in the list.

Encore 1.5 tip: Create Library Sets of your frequently used menus and buttons. You can access them instantly by changing the library set displayed in the palette.

Select Add Item.

In the Add Item dialog, locate and select the menu(s).

Click Open.

Once a menu is added to the Library Palette, consider it a master template. When opened in subsequent projects, Encore creates a duplicate copy, leaving the original menu completely intact.

Now the menu is a part of the Library palette and is available for use in any project. Keep in mind that a menu uses multiple layer sets. If the PSD file has just one layer set and a background, Encore will treat the PSD file as a button. Also, the layer sets must have the appropriate prefixes. See the sidebar "Understanding Basic Layers and Layer Prefixes Using the Library Palette" earlier in this chapter.

Create a New Menu Inside Encore

Creating a menu from scratch inside Encore is easy, but requires a greater understanding of the menu architecture. While Encore can certainly be used to create menus, it's safe to say that Adobe intended Encore to be used in cooperation with Photoshop.

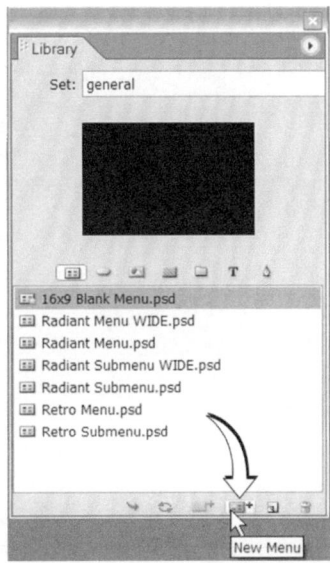

Open a Blank Menu

All menus start with a background. Encore's default menu is a blank background. Buttons, text, and other graphics are added later.

To create a blank menu:

Open the Library palette, and choose the blank menu.

Note: Encore offers a 4x3 and a 16x9 blank menu.

Right-click on the menu, and select Create New Menu.

The Menu Editor opens and displays the blank menu background.

Encore 1.5 now supports Photoshop CS layer comps. This allows layer sets to be placed inside other layer sets.

Use Non-Photoshop Files as Menus

Photoshop has been used by DVD authors for a very long time, and it is the graphics editor of choice. However, if the graphics/photo editor you use is not Photoshop, yet does support Photoshop layer conventions and prefixes, it is still possible to create and import a menu to Encore. To accomplish this task, you must first convert the file to PSD format before importing the file.

If your graphics editor doesn't support PSD layers or cannot export to the PSD format, the recommended workflow is to use the non-Photoshop application to create the various components of a menu separately. Save them in a bitmap (BMP), JPG, or GIF format, and then import them into Encore as individual files.

Any supported graphic may be imported into the Library palette; Encore will treat them as flat graphics. Import the background and buttons individually into the Library palette, and then use Encore's Menu Editor to apply the attributes to the buttons. (See "Convert a Graphic to a Button" in Chapter 5.)

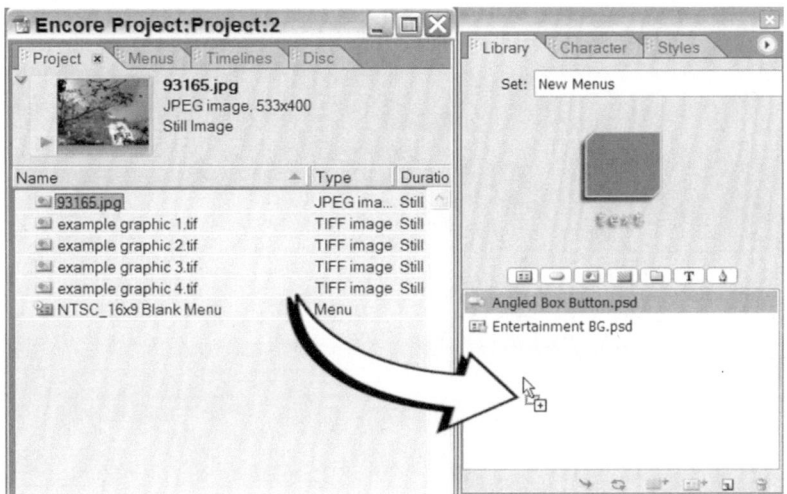

Gimme Some Background

A graphic that is imported from the Project tab into Encore's Library palette can be used as a background for a menu. If the image is not the correct size for the project, it will be rescaled to fit within the dimensions of the normal blank background.

To import a graphic as a menu background:

Open the Library palette and the Project tab.

Select the graphic file in the Project tab.

Click and hold on the file, and then drag it into the Library palette.

Notice that the file becomes a PSD file after it is imported into the Library palette.

Click the Place icon in the Library palette.

When the Menu Editor is opened, the graphic is displayed as a part of the background. However, it is not locked to the background yet. This is especially apparent if the image was rescaled in any way.

Click on the graphic in the Menu Editor to display the blue bounding box.

Resize the image with the corner bounding boxes or click and hold on the image to reposition.

When the image is the desired size and is in the right position, it is best to lock the image to the background layer. This way it cannot be accidentally repositioned or resized.

Go to the Layers palette.

Click on the box in the second column of the layer.

The Lock icon will appear in the box. This indicates that the layer cannot be adjusted, unless it is unlocked. Now the background graphic will stay in place. If desired the black background layer can be deleted, but it is not necessary.

Encore 1.5 users will enjoy the more intuitive approach to adding a background to a menu.

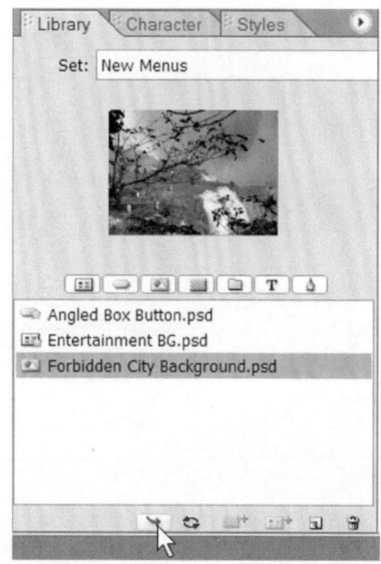

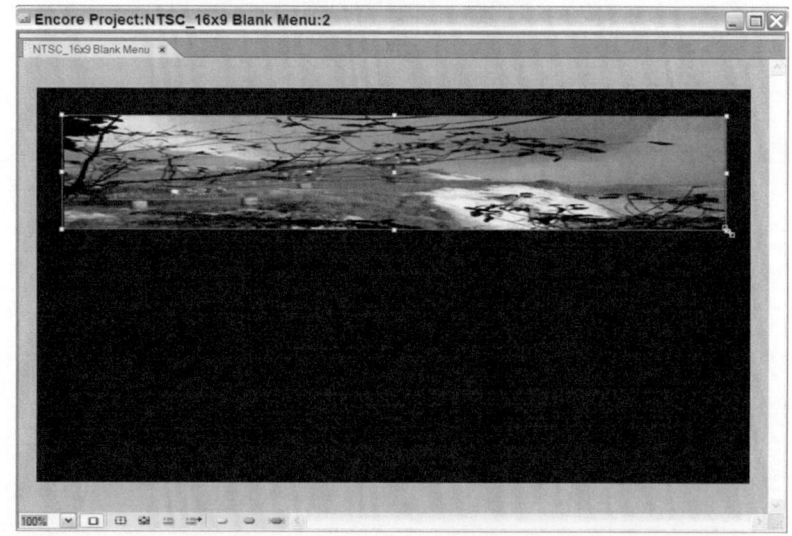

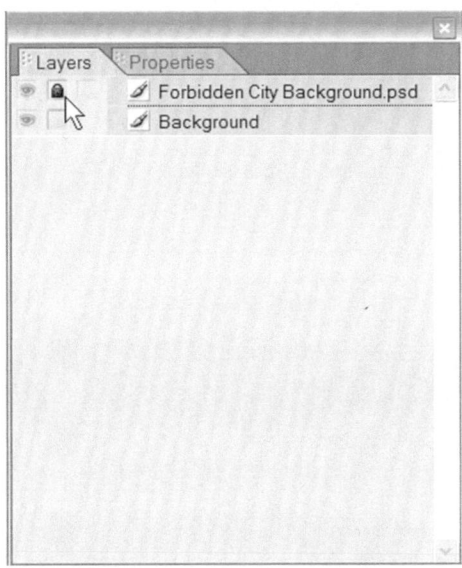

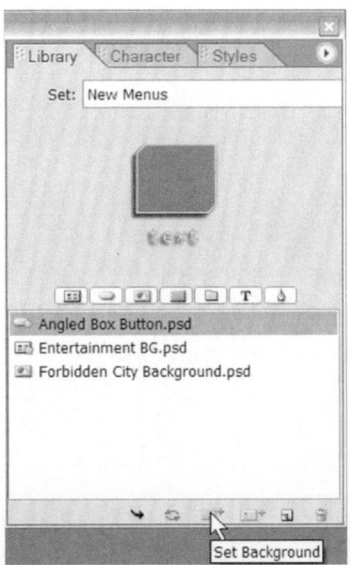

To set a background in Encore 1.5:

With the Menu Editor open, go to the Library palette and select the desired background.

Click the Set as Background icon.

Encore 1.5 tip: It is not necessary to resize or lock your menus when opening a new menu with the 1.5 Library palette.

What's My Name?

It's best to properly label your menus as soon as you create them to minimize confusion. You can rename menus in the Menu tab, the Project tab, or the Properties palette. Renaming in the Menu or Project tab is accomplished by right-clicking on the file name and choosing Rename. But it is better to get into the habit of using the Properties palette instead.

To rename a menu:

Click on the background of a menu in the Menu Editor, or have the menu selected in the Menu tab or Project tab.

Go to the Properties palette.

In the Name field, change the name of the menu.

What Do I Say?

When text is added to a menu, a text layer is created in the Layers palette. Exercise care when using the Text tools, because clicking multiple times on the menu with the Text tools could inadvertently create blank text layers.

You can add text horizontally or vertically.

To add horizontal text to a menu:

With the Menu Editor open, select the Horizontal Text tool.

Click the tool on the menu to set the inserted text position.

A blinking vertical line will appear; text will be entered from left to right.

Type in the text and hit return to add a line break.

Vertical Text places letters from top to bottom in a column.

To Insert Vertical Text:

Select the Vertical Text tool.

Click on the menu where you want the top most (first) letter to go.

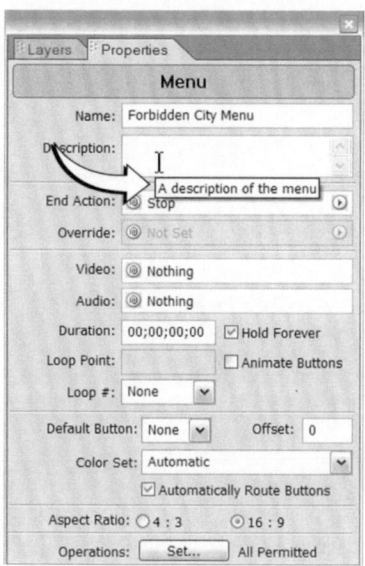

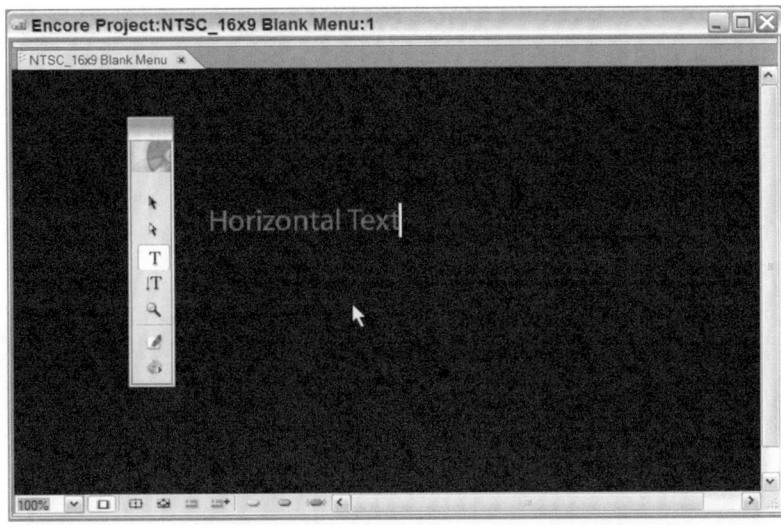

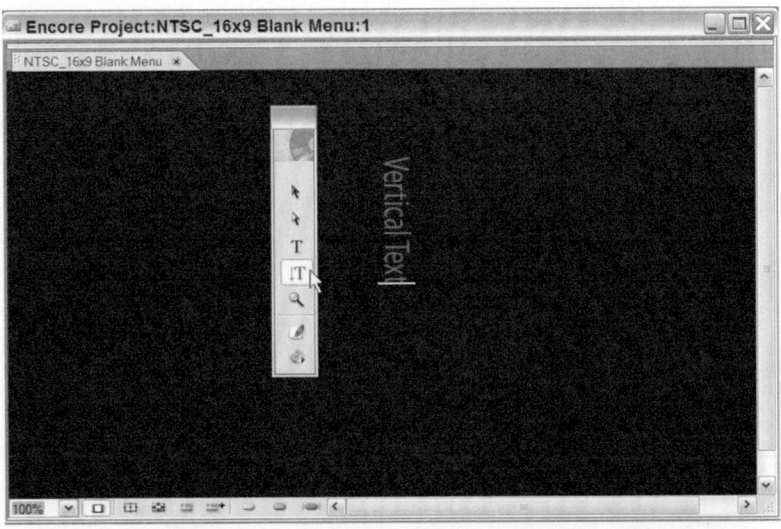

Type in the text, and press Return to put in a column break.

The Character palette offers a wide array of fonts and tools to adjust the look of the text.

To change the font or attributes of text:

Open the Character palette.

Adjust the Font, Font Size, Letter Spacing, Text Style, or Color.

After you've made the adjustments, begin typing in the menu using the Text tools.

Changing the look of existing text is fairly simple and there are a few ways to do it, but the best way is to use the Layers palette and Character palette together.

To change the Font/Attributes of Existing Text:

In the Layer's palette select the text layer or hold Ctrl while clicking to select multiple layers.

Go to the Character palette and make the desired adjustments.

Now the all the text in the layers will be adjusted simultaneously.

How Does it Look?

Text should be placed in an area that can be readily seen on all televisions and monitors. If text is placed too close to the edges, some televisions might cut off that text. Encore's Menu Editor includes guides known as the Action and Title Safe areas.

To turn on the Action and Title Safe Areas:

In the Menu Editor, click on the Action/Title Safe icon.

This will display two white boxes on the menu. Always place text within the inner box. Text is not locked in place until the project is built, and it should be adjusted to respect these Safe Areas if you want to assure that text will not be clippedby various television bezels.

To reposition text:

Using the Direct Select tool, click and

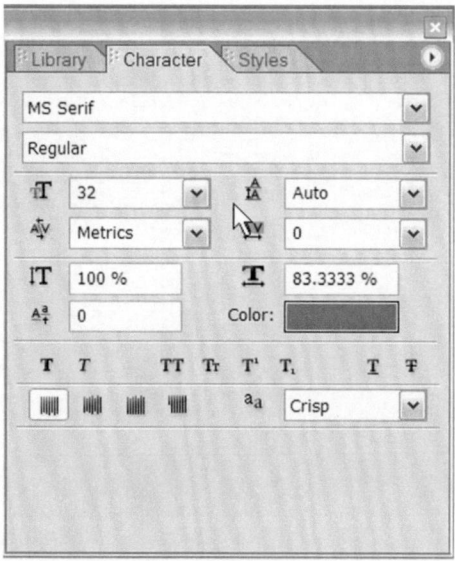

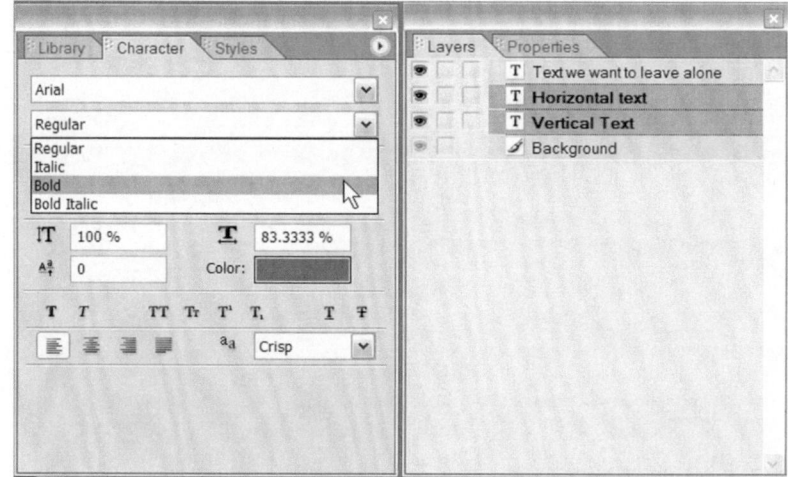

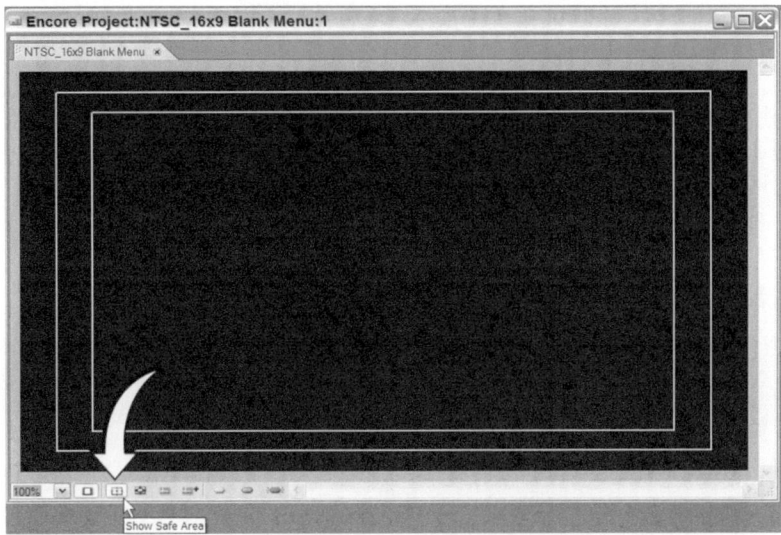

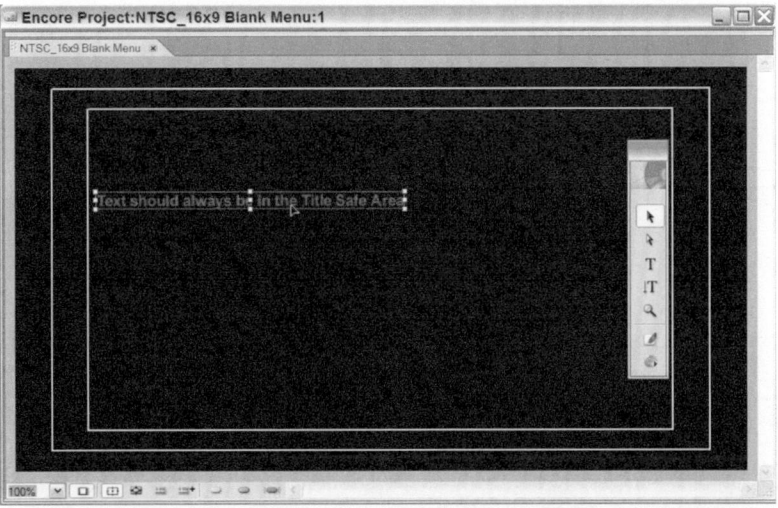

hold on the center of the text in the Menu Editor.

Drag the text to the proper position within the Title Safe Area.

Release the left mouse button when done.

While the blue bounding box is in view, you can resize the text using the corners or sides of the box. It is always better to use the Character palette to adjust text. Avoid distortion of the text by holding the Shift key while resizing the text. The Shift key constrains the proportions, making the height and the width scale together.

To resize the text:

Using the Direct Select tool, click on the text.

Hold down the Shift key.

Click and hold on the corner of the blue bounding box with the mouse.

Drag the corner of the box to resize the text.

When the text is the desired size, release the mouse button.

Only the Shadow Knows...

A three-dimensional look can be given to text by adding a drop shadow. A drop shadow is an illusion that gives the appearance of light shining down on the text and casting a shadow on the background, as though the text were elevated.

While not recommended, it is acceptable to resize the text without the Shift Key. The text can be made longer or wider by just dragging the corner. Also by using the Ctrl Key while selecting the text boxes, multiple text layers can be selected and resized or repositioned simultaneously. This can insure the same "look" to the text is preserved in all text layers.

To add a drop shadow to text:

Select the text layer(s).

Go to Object>Drop Shadow.

This opens up the Drop Shadow dialog, which offers several options for the shadow's appearance.

Color: Black is the Default, but any color can be selected. It is best to use shades of grey. On a dark background, use a lighter shade, on a bright background go darker.

Opacity: Determines the transparency of the shadow. At 100 percent, the underlying background is blocked out, while 0 percent won't appear at all. It is best to find a medium between the extremes, because a shadow doesn't always block out what it is cast upon.

Angle: Sets the angle of the imaginary

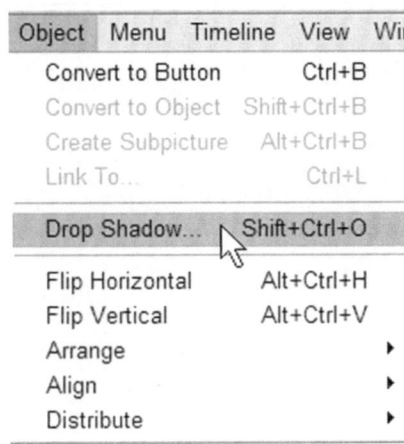

light source. Can be between 0 and 360 degrees.

Distance: Sets the length of the text from the background. A higher number increases the perceived distance between the text and the background.

Size: Determines the size of the shadow. The default size is best. But the size should increase with the distance from the light source.

Spread: Set to Zero. This determines the diffusion or spread of the shadow.

Make all desired changes to the settings.

Click OK.

Now the text appears to hover over the background.

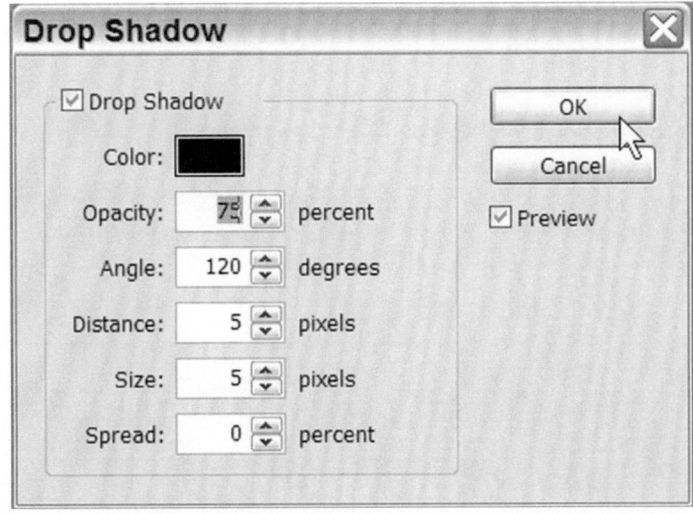

Encore 1.5 Authoring with Style!

Another significant improvement in the 1.5 release is the ability to use preset styles. Styles let you quickly change the appearance of an element in a menu. Styles are Photoshop layer effects, such as shadows, glows, bevels, overlays, and strokes. When you move or edit the element, the effects are modified correspondingly.

Styles are located in the Styles palette. Styles come in three categories: text, shape, and image. You may sort styles by category by clicking on the Style Types icon. Styles behave differently, depending on whether they are applied to an individual layer or to a layer set, such as a button. You can apply text, shape, or image style to any individual layer. A text style could be applied to a shape, for example.

To apply a style to an individual layer or layer set:

Select the layer in the Layers palette, or click on the element in the Menu Editor.

Go to the Styles palette and double-

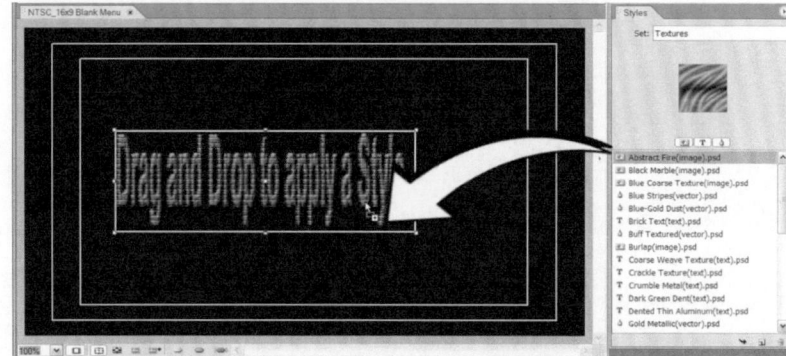

click on the style you wish to apply—

Or simply click and drag the style from the palette and drop it onto that element in the Menu Editor.

You can undo styles by applying the Plain Shape, Plain Text, No Image Edge Effects, and No Image Fill Effects styles, just as you did in the previous examples. This function removes any styles applied to the element.

Photoshop Tip: Custom Styles may also be imported from Photoshop. A style is a Photoshop file containing one or more layer effects. The Photoshop file must contain a single layer but no background layer. Create a Photoshop file with a text layer for a text style and a shape layer for a shape style. For image styles, create a layer that is not a text or a shape layer. Apply layer effects and configure them to obtain the style you want. You can then save the Photoshop file and import it into Adobe Encore DVD as a style.

Chapter 5

Push My Buttons

Buttons are an integral part of the DVD experience. Aside from providing navigation information, buttons also create an ambience that compliments the DVD presentation. Buttons consist of 2 primary elements; the background button graphic and the Subpicture Highlight.

The subpicture highlight is the inter-active part of a button. It allows the viewer to see which button is selected and if it has been "pressed." A sub-picture highlight is typically used to accent an underlying graphic.

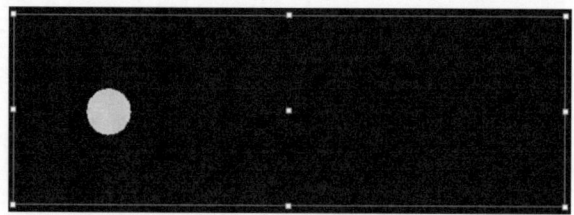

With this in mind, it is possible and recommended that the design of the background button graphics be in-depth, colorful, and creative. Using the subpicture highlight to complement that design scheme is also recom-mended.

If you are using templates with pre-ex-isting buttons, feel free to skip directly to the Linking Buttons section of the next chapter.

Buttons often consist of graphics that are part of a background video stream. In this case, graphics are used as window dressing for the subpicture highlight, the overlay that provides selection information. Because of the limited graphics potential of the sub-picture, the background button

graphic often exists in the MPEG-2 video stream. Because it exists as part of a background video stream, it offers far better color depth, quality and detail. In addition, background video provides almost limitless animation options, in stark contrast with static overlays.

Use Buttons from the Library Palette

Creating a button from scratch can be a trying experience for a novice DVD Author wanting to create a DVD quickly. Fortunately, Encore supplies pre-made buttons in the Library Palette.

To start, a Menu must be opened in the Menu Editor, even if it is a simple black background.

To Add a button from the Library Palette into the Menu Editor:

With the Menu Editor open, go to the Library Palette

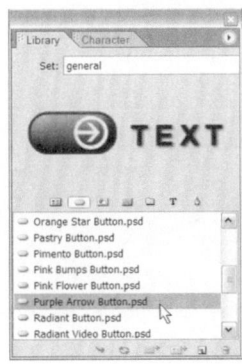

Select a button from the Library.

Buttons are designated by small plain square icons beneath the preview thumbnail in the Library Palette. In this example the Angled Button is used.

Buttons known as thumbnails are available. To learn more about using thumbnails, see Chapter 6.

With the button selected Click and Drag the button into the Menu Editor.

The button now appears in the Menu Editor with a bounding box around it.

If you are using Encore 1.5 then all of the above behaviors will work, but it has more advanced features, such as the place command.

PSDs Can Be Buttons Too!

All buttons used in Encore exist inside Photoshop (.psd) files. They use special Layer prefixes that designate the layer set as a button. When a single layer set with a (+) prefix is imported into Encore, it treats the file as a button.

When creating a button in Photoshop, remember that all the layers of the button are contained within a layer set

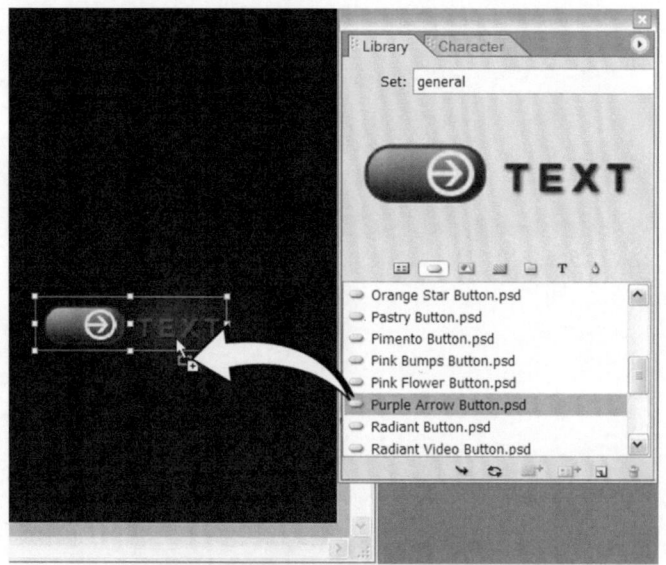

marked with the (+) prefix. Individual layers inside the layer set indicate things such as text, graphics, subpictures and thumbnails.

Several different prefixes are used to assign the different layers. First, the (+) prefix in the Layer Set. Without this prefix, Encore treats the graphic as an object. Secondly, the (=1) (=2) (=3) layers identify the subpicture highlights. Each represents a different color that can be used for the subpicture. One layer can be used for one color, or all 3 can be used to create subpicture containing 3 individual colors. The final prefix is the (%) prefix, which represents the thumbnail layer. This layer is a placeholder for the video information that will be displayed in a thumbnail.

To Import a Photoshop file as a button:

Open the Library Palette in Encore

Right click on the list of items and choose Add New Item.

In the Add Item Dialog, select the psd button file

Click OK

Now the button can be dragged into the Menu Editor using the steps specified in the previous section.

A button should ALWAYS be imported into the Library Palette NOT the Project Tab. If imported into the Project Tab as an Asset, Encore will discard the layers and flatten the image. If it is imported as a Menu, any background information will be preserved.

Use Non-Photoshop Files as Buttons

As mentioned before, Encore is designed with Photoshop integration in mind. The Photoshop layer conventions are the key to Encore's Menu and Button functions. However if your Graphics Editor of choice supports PS Layer conventions and can save the file in the .psd format, then successful button creation can be achieved.

If your Image/Graphics Editor does not support PS layers or the .psd format, graphics can be imported into Encore directly. Once the file is imported, use Encore's layer capability to assign the button attributes to the graphic. See the Convert a Graphic to a Button section of this chapter for details.

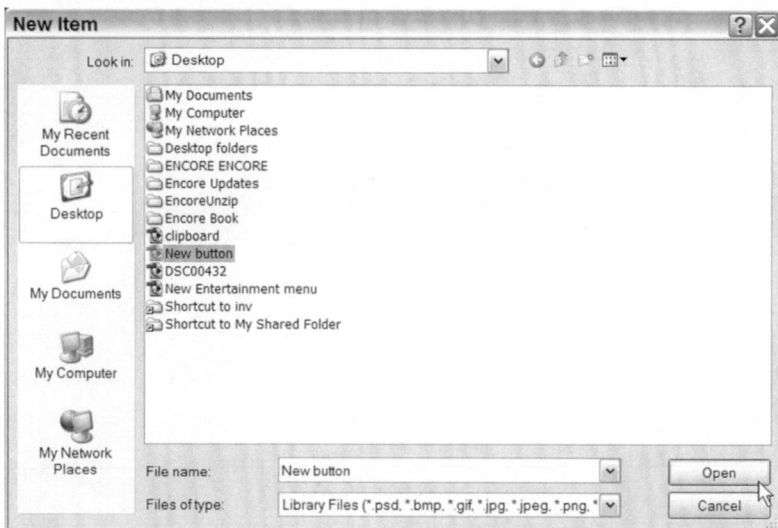

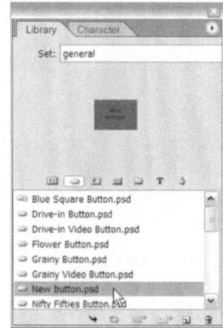

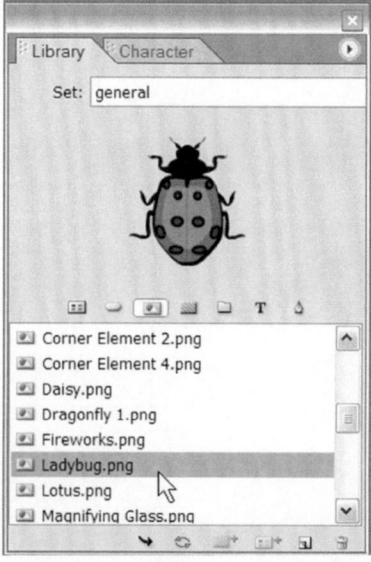

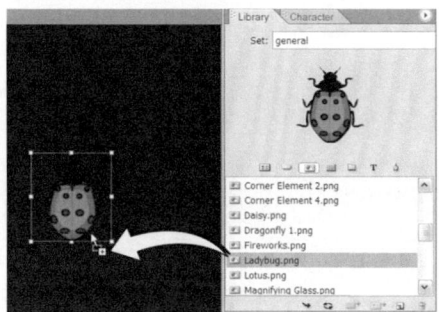

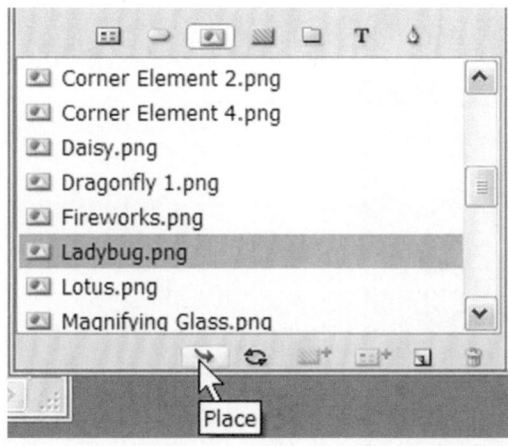

Place

Use Shapes and Images from the Library Palette

Encore has a set of ready to use graphics/objects in the Library Palette. Shapes can be used to create background graphics, button graphics and even subpicture highlights. The shapes are extremely intuitive and easy to use. At the same time, they provide a huge variety of creative options. (See next section).

To Add a graphic from the Library Palette into the Menu Editor:

With the Menu Editor open, go to the Library Palette

Select a graphic from the Library

With the graphic selected Click and Drag the button into the Menu Editor.

The graphic now appears in the Menu Editor with a bounding box around it.If you are using Encore 1.5 then all of the above behaviors are supported. It also offers additional features, such as the place command and new replacement behaviors.

Using the place command sets the object in the center of the menu. If you want to replace an object/graphic in the Menu Editor with an object from the Library, use the Replace command.

Use the shift key to constrain proportions while creating a shape.

To replace an object:

In the menu, select the object you want to replace.

In the Library Palette, select the desired object.

Click the Replace Icon

The object in the Menu Editor will be replaced with the one selected in the Library Palette.

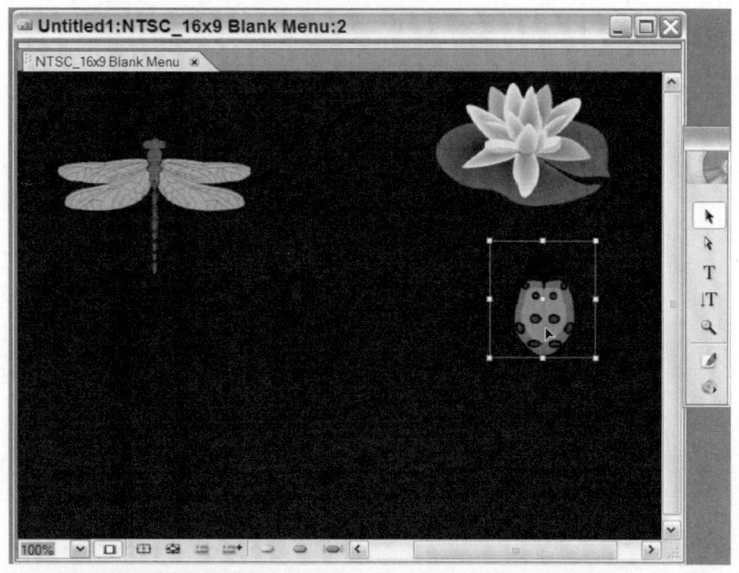

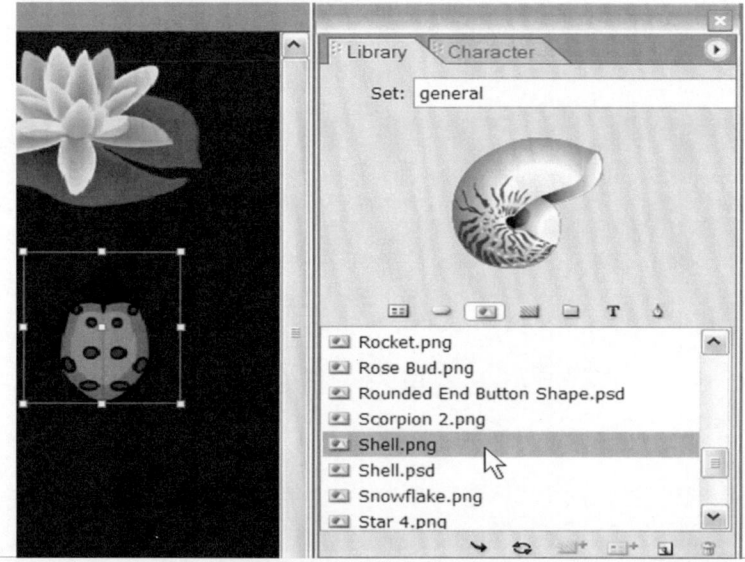

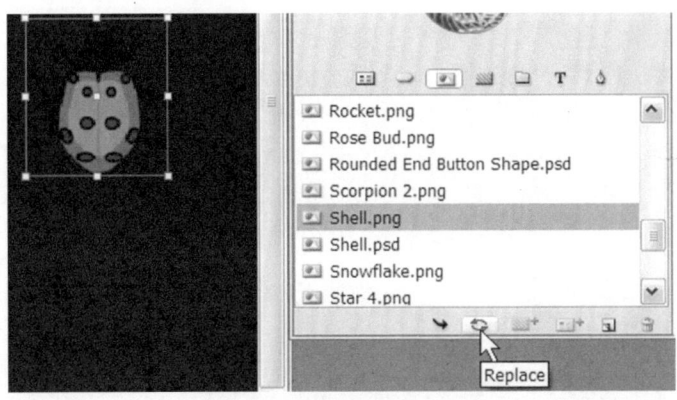

Convert a Graphic to a Button

Encore has the power to convert a simple graphic into a fully functional button. This can be a photograph or an elaborate design, only imagination limits what can be used. Any graphic imported into Encore's Project Tab or Library Palette can be utilized.

To use a graphic from the Project Tab:

With the Project Tab and the Menu Editor open, select the desired graphic.

Click and hold on the graphic, then drag it into the Menu Editor

Imported graphics should either be flat (non- .psd files) or in a one layer set. (.psd files) Multiple layer sets are preserved in the Library Palette, but Encore will treat the graphic as a collection of Objects or a buttonless menu.

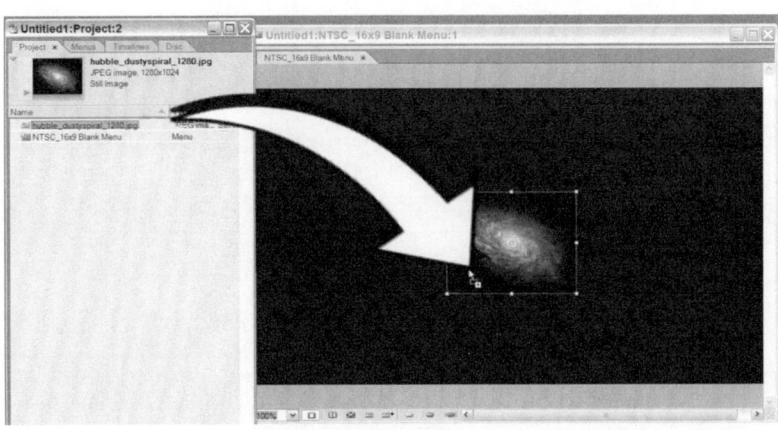

If you plan to use the same graphic in several projects, import it into Encore's Library Palette. Any graphic is instantly converted into a .psd file. You may add a graphic as an Item, as described in the "Import Photoshop File as a Button" section, earlier in this chapter. Once the graphic is in the Library Palette, simply drag it into the Menu Editor.

Speed Tip: Select the graphic and use Ctrl-B to instantly convert it to a button.

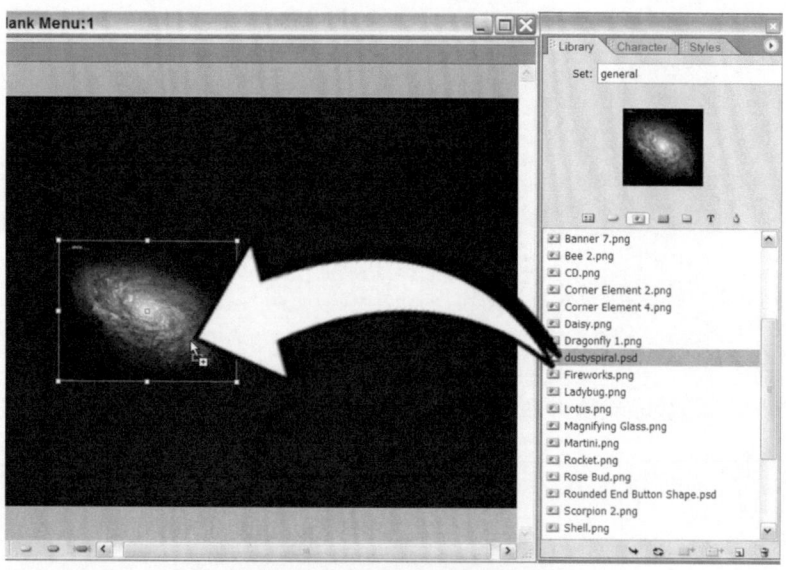

Once a graphic is dragged into the Menu Editor it's time to convert it from an object to a functional button.

To convert a Graphic (Object) to a Button:

Select the object in the Menu Editor

In the top bar go to Object>Convert to Button

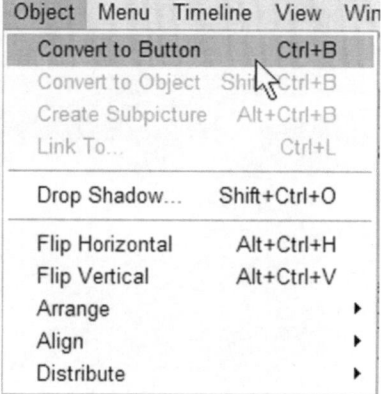

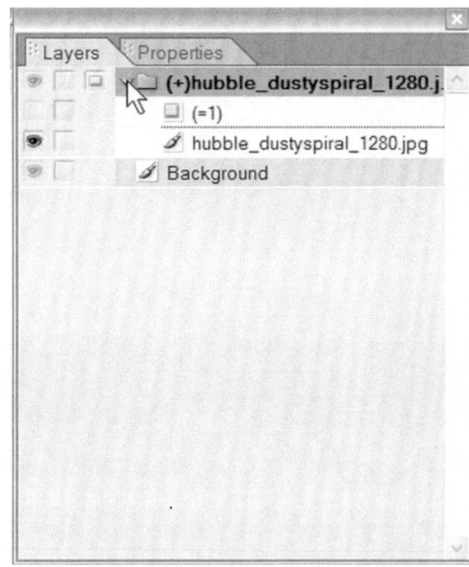

If you open the Layers Palette you will see that the Graphic is now within a Layer Set with a (+) Prefix.

Whenever a button is created in the menu editor it's a good idea to rename the button so it is instantly recognizable from one of the other windows.

To Rename a Button:

With the button selected open the Properties Palette

In the Name Field type in an appropriate name (i.e. play all or special features)

Also, by renaming buttons, the layer set name itself will change, making it easy to select the proper buttons with the Layers Palette.

Subpicture highlight creation is covered later on in this chapter. In Encore 1.5 subpictures are created automatically when a button is created.

Copy and Paste Buttons in the Menu Editor

If the imported button is obviously too big or small for the menu, having to resize and rescale buttons could be a challenge. But it doesn't have to be. Before replicating a button, resize it (see next section.) Every button thereafter will match the resized button's dimensions.

Encore allows several methods for duplicating buttons in the Menu Editor. Of course, one could pull a button out of the Library Palette several times, but mouse and keyboard shortcuts are much faster.

Encore DVD, like most modern applications, supports the standard Windows copy and paste shortcuts.

To Copy and Paste a button using Windows shortcuts:

With the Selection Tool, click on the button.

Use Ctrl-C to copy the button into the Window's Clipboard

Move the cursor to the desired location of the next button

Use Ctrl-V to Paste the copied button into the Menu Editor

While this is a convenient approach for users familiar with standard shortcuts,

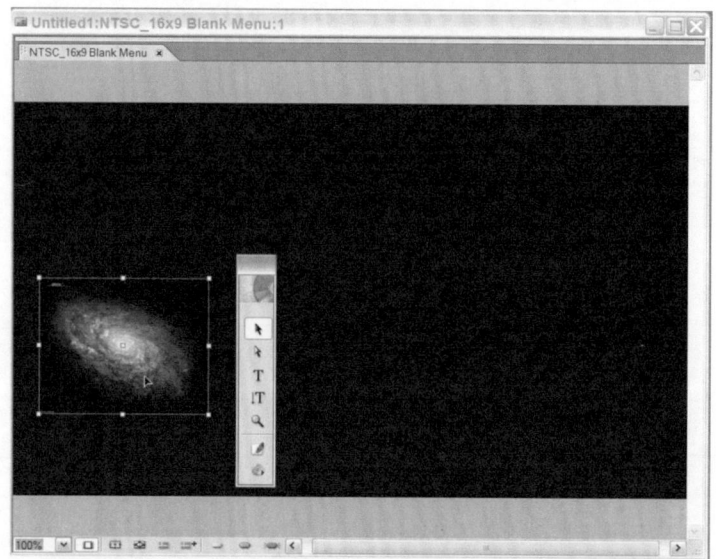

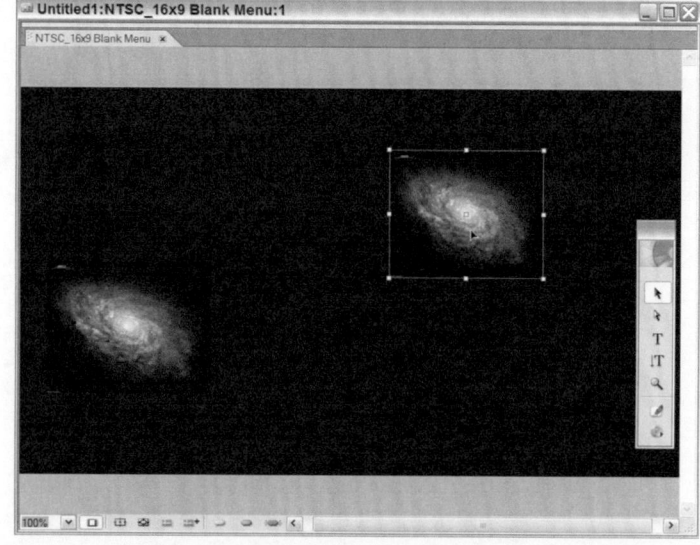

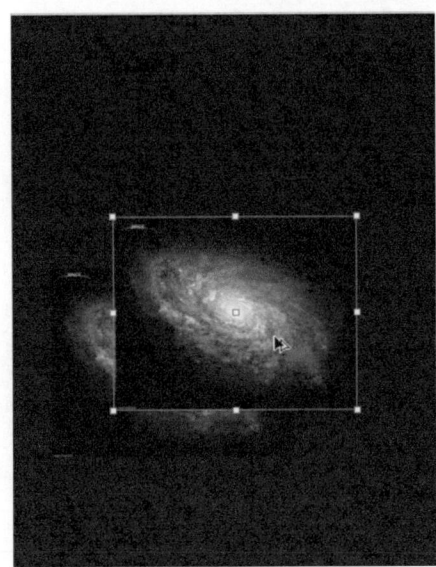

there is one duplicate command that makes it even easier. Using the Alt key.

To Duplicate a Button using Encore's mouse-keyboard shortcuts:

With the Selection Tool, click on the button you wish to duplicate

Hold the Alt Key, left click and drag the new button out to an appropriate spot.

After all your buttons are present, it's a good idea to rename the buttons.

Multiple buttons can be selected by clicking and dragging a box around the buttons. Or specific buttons can be selected or deselected by using the Ctrl key while clicking.

Resize Buttons in the Menu Editor

Not all buttons fit all menus. More often than not a button will need to be resized or rescaled in order to fit the scheme of a menu. Encore DVD allows several buttons to be resized at once.

Another important consideration is scaling. Most buttons look best when they are resized with respect to their proportions, also known as constraining.

To resize a button while constraining proportions:

In the Menu Editor using either Selection Tool, select the button(s) to be resized.

A blue bounding box appears around the button(s). On each corner of the box is a solid blue square.

While holding the Shift key, click and hold on the bounding box's corner

Drag the box until it is the correct size, then release the mouse button.

Notice that the buttons maintain their proportions, and the height and width grow and shrink at the same rate. Using the Shift key assures that there isn't unusual scaling of the buttons. This is ideal for buttons with text, because it won't skew the look of the characters.

There will be times when rescaling the buttons is necessary to make the button longer or shorter. On the four sides of the bounding box are blue squares. By clicking on those squares, the box

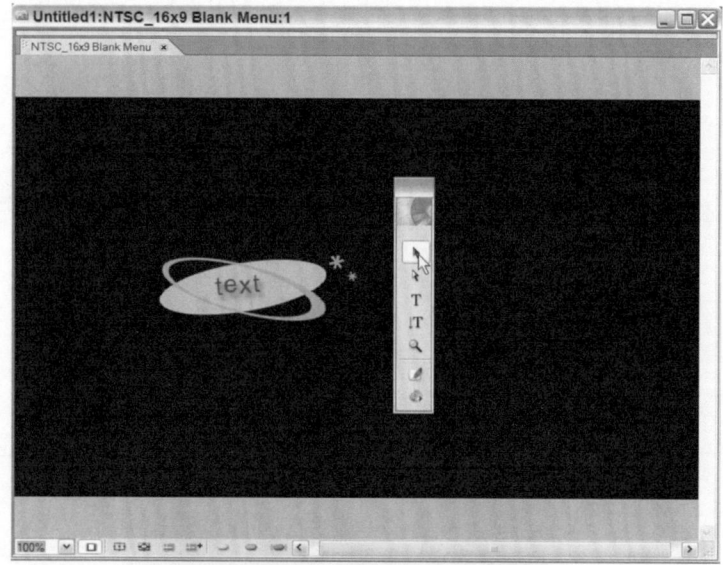

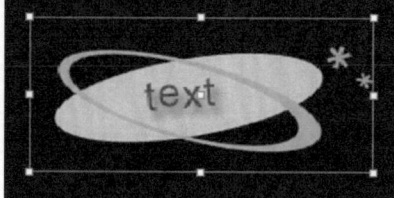

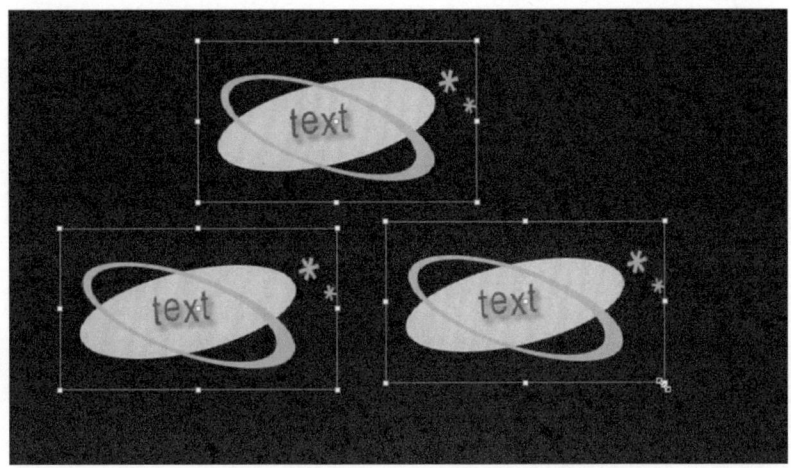

will grow or shrink on the adjacent sides (i.e. clicking and dragging the top, will adjust the length of the left and right sides.)

Using the Shift Key while adjusting the top, bottom or sides of the bounding box has no effect.

To rescale a button using the corners, follow the above steps, without pressing Shift.

Use the Selection Tool, instead of the Direct Selection Tool, to move entire buttons.

Arrange Buttons in the Menu Editor

Now is a good time to point out the major difference between the Selection Tool and the Direct Selection Tool. The Selection tool selects an entire group or layer set. The Direct Selection Tool selects whatever layer the cursor is on top of when clicked. Many complicated buttons have multiple layers. If the Direct Select Tool is used to move an item, sometimes only one layer in that set is moved, which may interfere with the look of the button.

Trying to arrange buttons by sight can be a tedious task. Consider that buttons, like any text on a screen, should be arranged according to the Title and Action Safe areas. If a button extends into a non-Title Safe area, it might not be seen by the viewer on some televisions. Fortunately Encore includes alignment, arrangement and distribution tools.

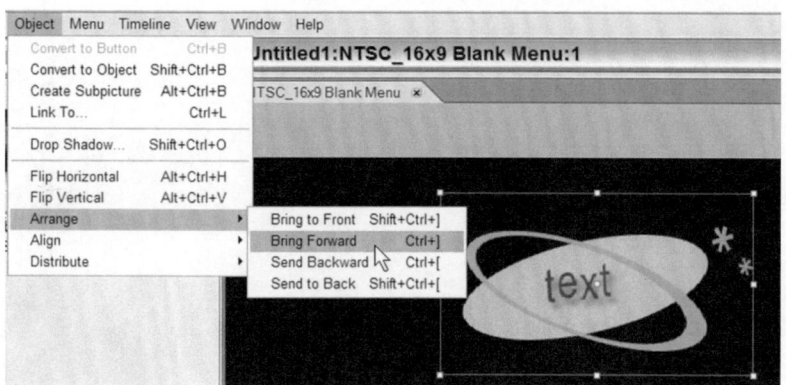

Arrangement moves a button or objects back or forward throughout the layers of a button. This is helpful when a button or a part of text was inadvertently put behind the background, or should be set farther back.

Most DVD Authors will be using the Align and Distribute Functions to give the buttons an even spacing and a nice, flush look.

To Distribute Buttons Evenly:

In the Menu Editor, select the buttons to distribute

In the Object Menu go to Distribute>Relative to Safe Areas

By selecting this, when Encore distributes the buttons, it will not allow the buttons to extend past the safe areas.

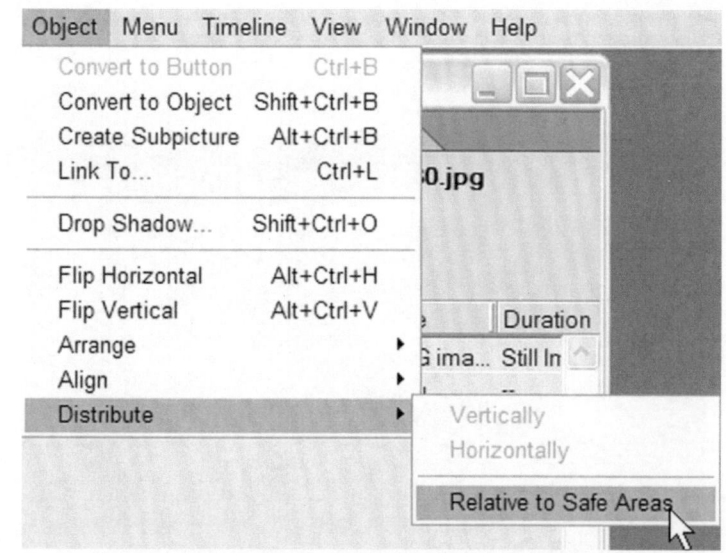

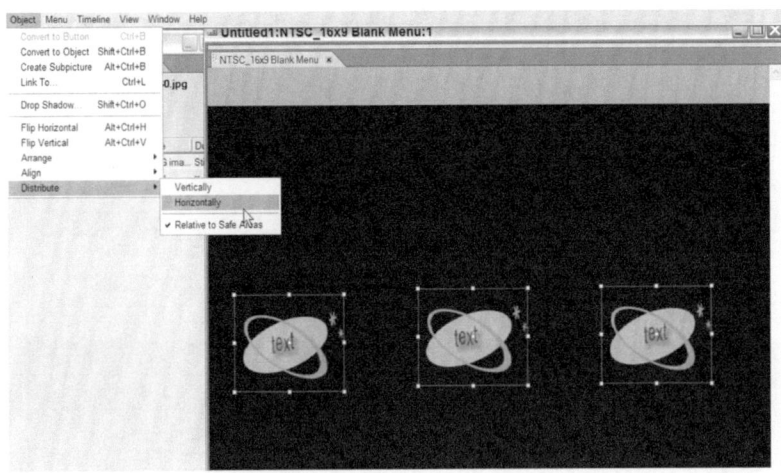

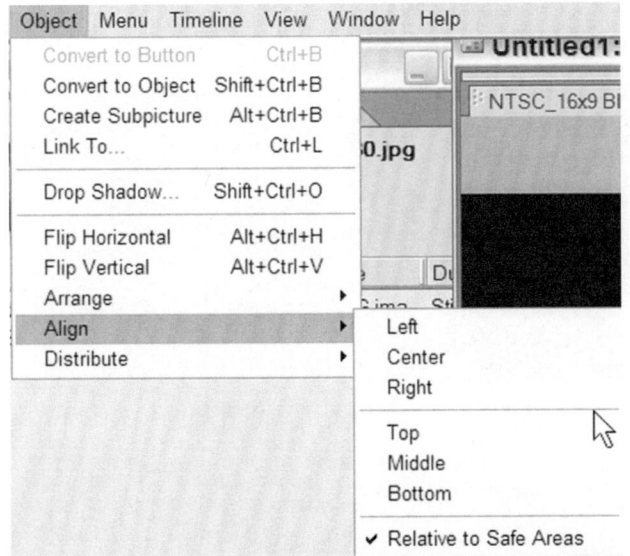

Go to Objects>Distribute>Vertically

This will line the buttons up and down. If there are several large buttons they will crowd together.

Or Go to Objects>Distribute>Horizontally

As the name implies, the buttons are spaced evenly across the width of the menu and take advantage of more screen area than vertically placed buttons. Notice also that the Relative to Safe Areas is still checked.

The Align command repositions the buttons according to the sides or centers of the bounding boxes, depending on the alignment chosen.

To Align Buttons:

Select the buttons you wish to align

Go to Objects>Align>Relative to Safe Areas

Again this command is essential to assuring the buttons will be visible on most televisions. This command also sets the Title Safe Area as the box to which every button selected aligns.

Go to Objects>Align

Don't let Buttons overlap under any circumstances. It interferes with mouse selection of buttons when viewing the DVD with a computer.

The alignment options are divided into a top and bottom panel. The top panel is best for use with buttons that are vertically distributed. Left and Right will bring the boxes flush with the Safe Area border on their respective sides. Center will bring the boxes into the horizontal center of the screen.

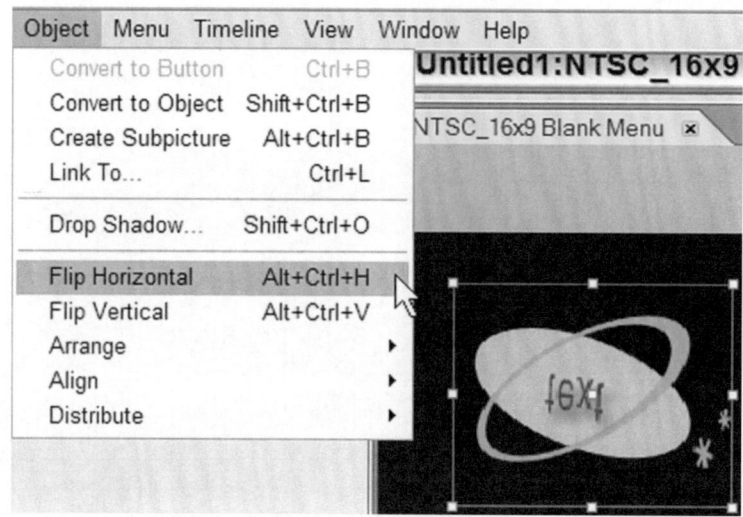

The bottom panel is great for boxes that are horizontally distributed, divided into Top, Middle and Bottom. As the names suggest, these commands will bring the boxes into those respective positions.

Using Gridlines in Encore 1.5

One of the nicer additions to 1.5 is the ability to use gridlines to orient your buttons or objects on the menu. You can add buttons, and move buttons, so their top, bottom or specific side is aligned with a gridline that you specify.

To show or hide guides:

Make sure the Menu Editor window is active and choose View > Show Guides.

To place a guide:

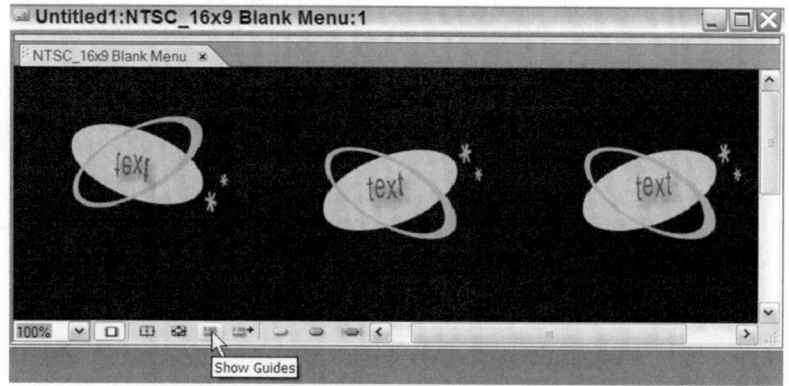

Experiment with these Alignment options. If you make a mistake use Ctrl-Z (Undo) to bring the boxes back to their original positions.

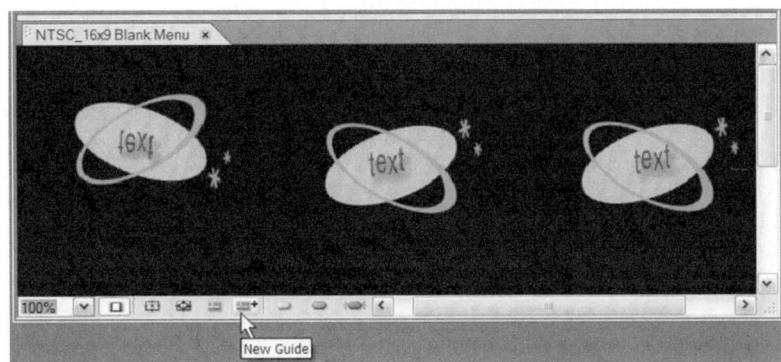

With the Menu Editor window active, choose View > New Guide.

In the dialog box, select Horizontal or Vertical orientation, enter a position, and click OK.

If you are unsure of which pixel from the left or top you want the guide to rest on, you can always move it later in the Menu Editor.

To move a guide:

Select the selection tool.

Position the pointer over the guide.

Drag the guide to move it.

Lock the guides to prevent accidental movement of the guides once they have been set.

Encore 1.5 Tip: You can now flip buttons or graphics using the flip Horizontal or Flip Vertical commands in the Object Menu

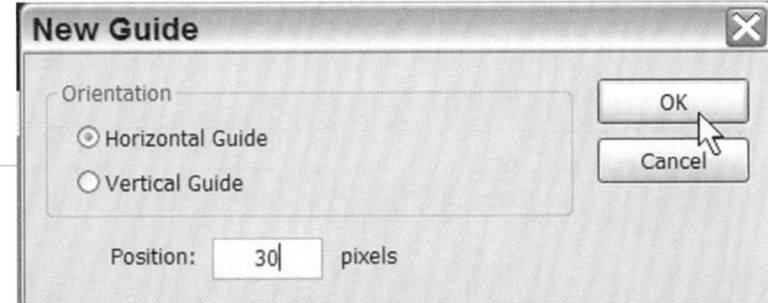

To lock all guides:

With the Menu Editor window active, choose View > Lock Guides.

Once the guides are set, click on the button and move it to the line. Encore will snap the button's edge to the line.

You may also align a button's midpoint to the gridline, centering the button or object on the gridline.

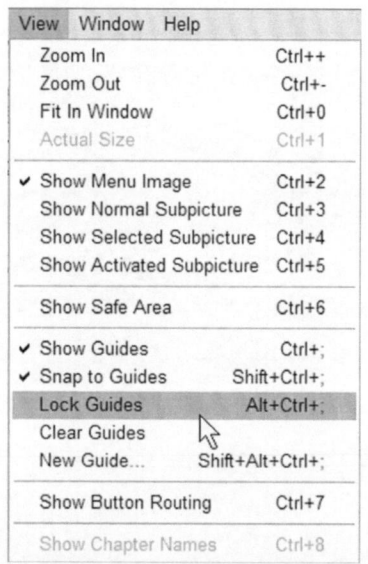

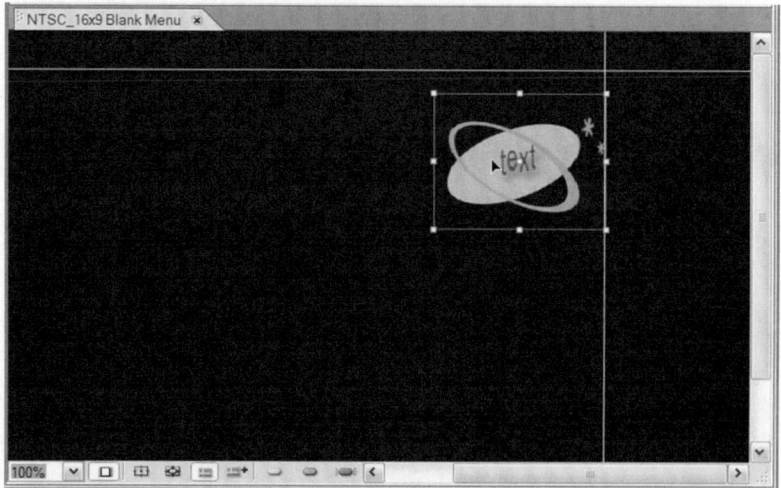

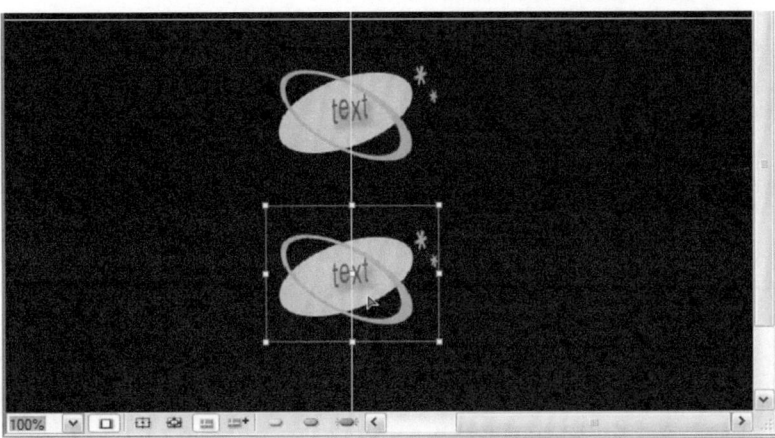

Getting Stylized: Applying Styles to Buttons in Encore 1.5

Encore 1.5 is now equipped with a Styles Palette that can apply Photoshop styles to elements in an Encore menu. Anyone who has used styles in Photoshop will appreciate the ability to use and create styles in Encore. Styles create many different looks including bevels, textures and strokes. These styles can be applied to instantly stylize objects, shapes or text.

Encore uses three categories for styles: Image, Text, and Shapes. Experiment with styles to create unique looks for your project. If you don't like the style applied simply hit Undo (Ctrl-Z) and try another one.

To apply a style to a button:

Select the button's layer set in the Layers Palette or click on the element in the Menu Editor

Go to the Styles Palette and double click on the style you wish to apply.

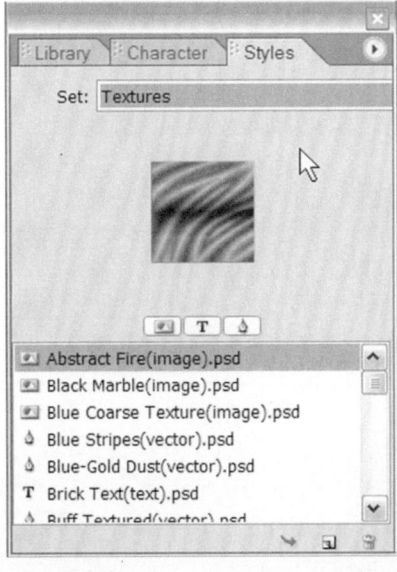

Or simply click and drag the style from the palette and drop it onto that button in the Menu Editor.

If you applied a style and cannot Undo it, you may be able to workaround the problem by applying the Plain Shape, Plain Text, No Image Edge Effects, and No Image Fill Effects styles.

Create a Subpicture Highlight for a Button

The Subpicture highlight is probably the most important aspect of a button. Without it, the button will not function. The subpicture highlight is a simple, crude picture displaying up to 3 individual colors. It is generated by the DVD Player as an overlay. Therefore, it does not exist as part of the MPEG-2 video. It is best reserved as a subtle highlight to compliment this background video.

When creating a Subpicture Highlight inside Encore, Encore maps out the shape of the button and "cuts" a highlight to match the visible dimensions of the button including the text.

To Create a Subpicture Highlight for an entire button:

Select the button(s) in the Menu Editor

Go to Object>Create Subpicture

Or use the quick shortcut Alt-Ctrl-B.

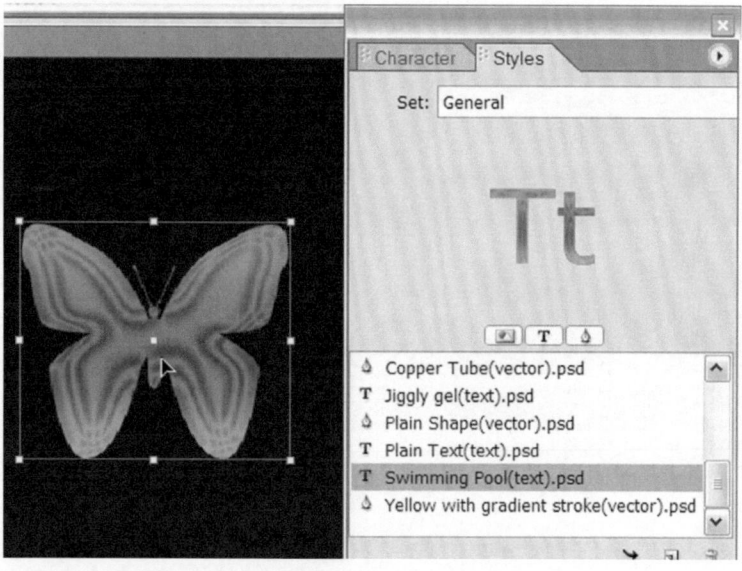

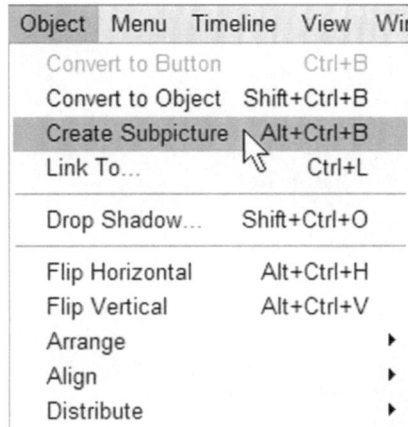

Now Encore has created a subpicture for the button.

Create a Text Subpicture Highlight

Creating a Subpicture Highlight over an entire button is a simple task, but it covers the entire shape and could possibly block the design. Fortunately, Encore comes equipped with the ability to create a text subpicture highlight. This way, only one part of the button is highlighted and brings attention to the title of the button without blocking the entire design.

When multiple buttons are selected, the Properties Palette can change them simultaneously.

Note: If you used Encore's supplied buttons, you cannot apply a subpicture highlight to the text, since most of the buttons have a (=1) shape already.

To create a Text Subpicture Highlight:

Select the button(s) in the Menu Editor

Go to the Properties Palette, check the Create Text Subpicture box

If you are using the pre-made buttons in Encore, you do not need to create a subpicture highlight for it. It has already been provided.

Encore 1.5 Tip: You no longer have to create a subpicture highlight as a separate step. Once a button is created, the subpicture highlight is automatically created for you.

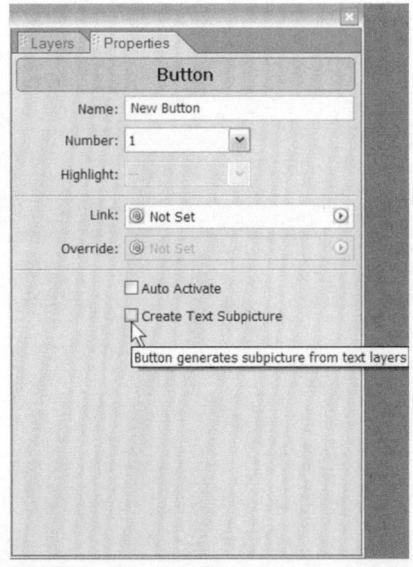

View the Selection States of the Subpicture Highlights

For more control over the shape of the subpicture highlight, use Photoshop to create accent layers to the main button. Prefix those layers with (=1) or (=2) or (=3). See Edit In Photoshop feature in Chapter 2.

Subpicture highlights typically have three states: Normal(unselected), selected, and activated. On most DVD's, the Normal subpicture highlight state is transparent. By default Encore's Menu Editor shows no subpicture highlights.

At the bottom of the Menu Editor screen there are three buttons that control the display of those different states. When none of the icons are selected, no subpicture highlight is displayed.

To view the Selected Subpicture Highlight State:

Click the middle icon.

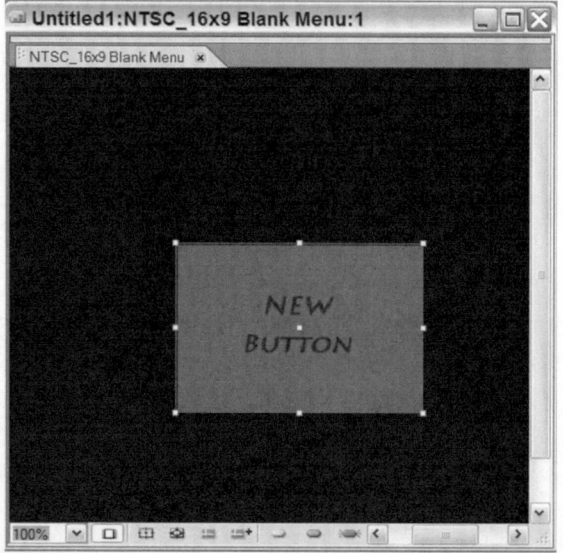

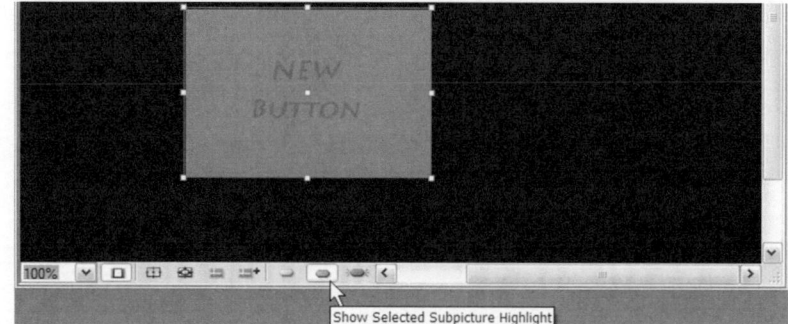

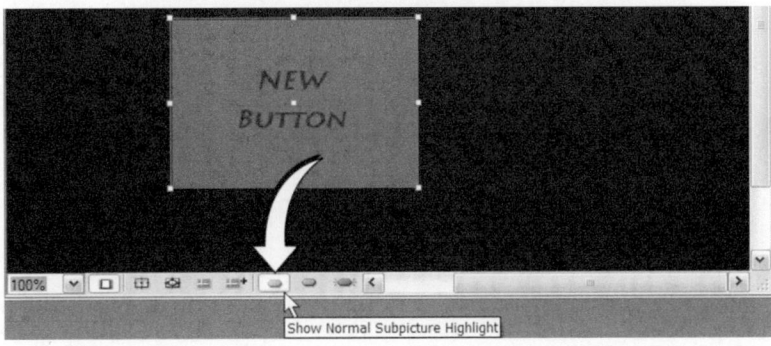

To view the Activated State:

Click the last icon

To view the Normal State:

Click the first icon.

The keyboard shortcuts CTRL + 3, CTRL + 4 and CTRL + 5 may also be used to toggle between the different states.

Chapter 6

Navigation

Intuitive navigation is the goal of every DVD author. Every button should link to an asset on the DVD. This link may be to another menu, such as an Audio/Subtitle selection menu, or to a chapter point along the major timeline of the DVD.

How the viewer of the finished DVD navigates from button to button is addressed, managed, and changed by the DVD author. Even the Title, Menu and number buttons on the viewer's remote control can be assigned functions.

Link Buttons to Chapter Points

Use Still or Motion Thumbnails to spice up these chapter selection menus. See related sections in the next chapter for more detail.

Many DVD's have submenus that allow the viewer to directly access chapters in a timeline. This way the viewer doesn't have to skip through the chapters while viewing the timeline.

While this may not be a feature in some DVD's, the Play or Play All button nearly always exists. This is linked to the first chapter point of a timeline. Also any buttons for slideshow presentations are linked to the first chapter point.

Encore offers many ways to link buttons to chapter points.

To link a button in the Menu Editor:

Right click on the button

Select Link To...

This will open the Link To dialog

From the list of selections, open the Timeline this button will link to.

All the chapter points on that particular timeline are now displayed.

Select the desired chapter point.

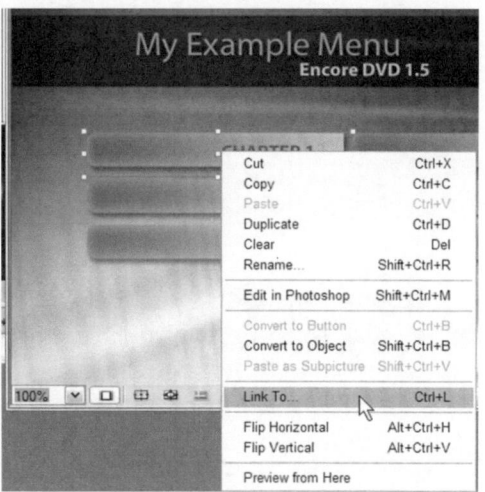

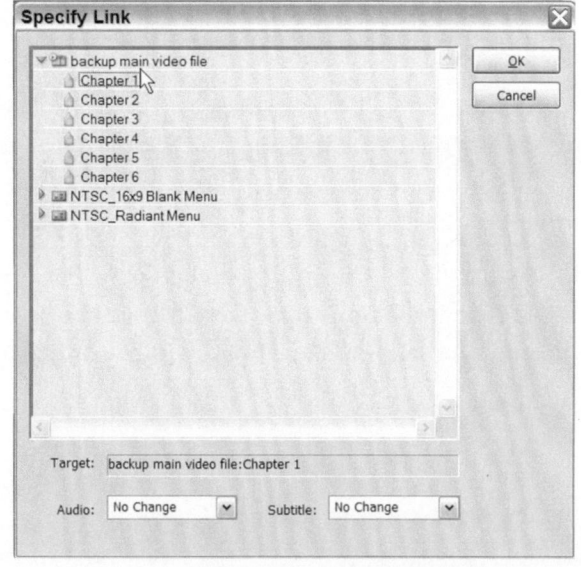

Click OK.

The button, when pressed, will link to this chapter point.

If the Timelines Window and Menu Editor are open, chapter points can be dragged and dropped onto the desired buttons.

To Drag and Drop Chapter Points onto Buttons:

In the Timelines Window, select the chapter point.

Left click and hold on the chapter point.

Drag the cursor up to the button.

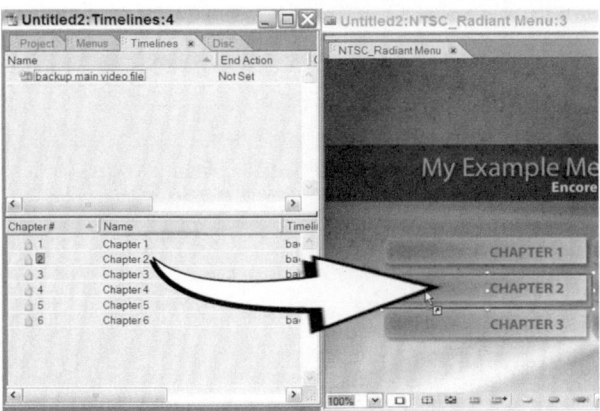

Release the mouse button once the lighter box appears around the button.

And of course the Properties Palette offers another way to link buttons creatively.

Chapter points can also be selected in the Timelines Tab and dragged onto buttons the same way.

To link buttons using the Properties Palette:

With the button selected, go to the Properties Palette

Click on the arrow in the Link To field.

Go to the desired Timeline and click on the appropriate chapter point.

Menus to menus; who's got the hook-up?

When multiple menus are used in a project, then buttons must be used to link the various menus together. All the methods specified in the previous section will work when linking menus (except of course, the use of the Timelines Window), but there is one difference that could be potentially confusing. When linking a button to another menu, Encore asks for a button on that destination menu.

Encore allows the author to specify which button is highlighted when navi-

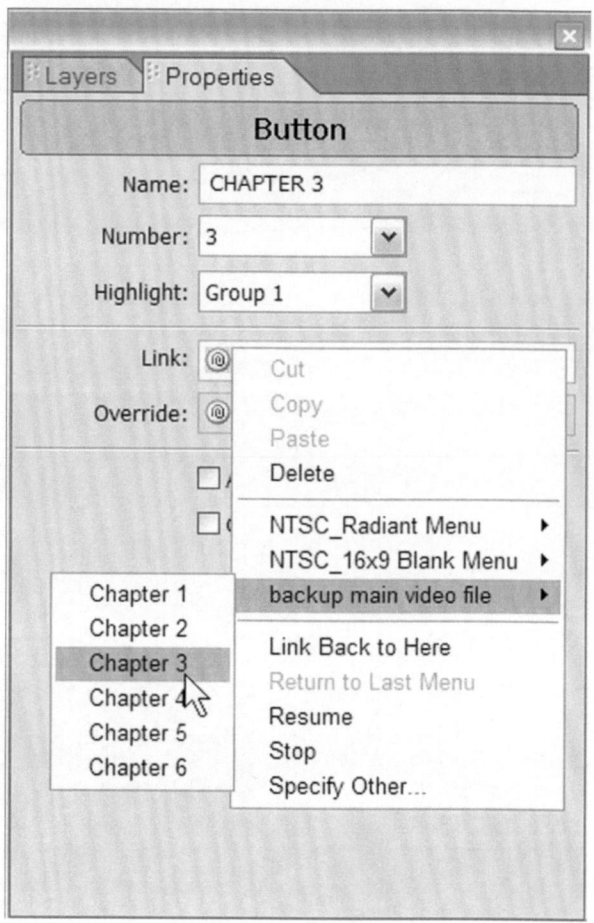

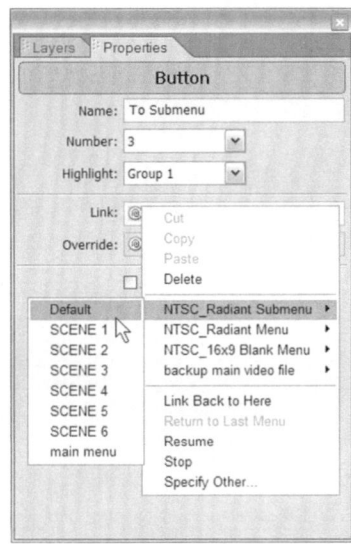

gating to that menu, potentially making it faster for the viewer to locate the appropriate button. In most cases the default button is the better choice, but having this level of flexibility remains useful.

Buttons from other menus can be dragged and dropped from the Menu Tab into the buttons of a menu in the the Menu Editor.

To link a button to another menu using the Properties Palette:

With the button selected in the Menu Editor, go to the Properties Palette

In the Link To field, click on the arrow to display the choices.

Choose the menu you wish to link to.

Choose the button that should be highlighted first when the viewer navigates to that menu.

A new addition to Encore 1.5 is the Resume Link. Now you can set a "Back" button that will link the viewer back to the menu from which they accessed the current menu. So if one menu can be accessed from several other menus, this link will take them back to the previous menu.

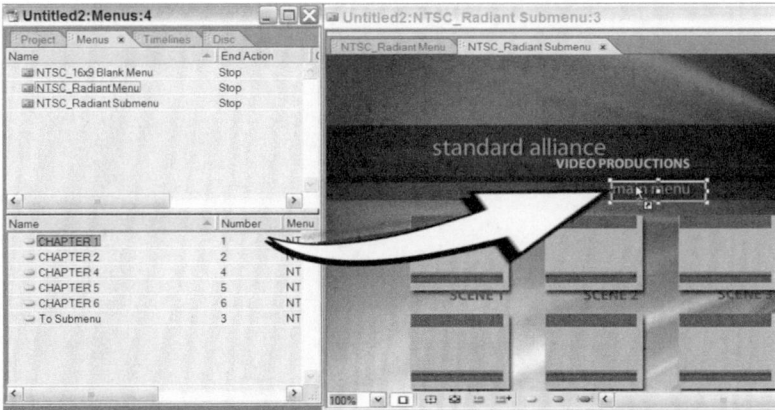

Use Pickwhips for Button Linking

Pickwhips offer yet another great way to link buttons. If you have never used a pickwhip before, now is a good time to start. A pickwhip allows you to create a link by simply dragging it to what you want it to link to, instead of dealing with pull down menus or dialogs.

The pickwhip icon appears on the left hand side of the Link To field in a button's Properties Palette. (It looks like a coiled up whip or a snail.) If you can see the item you wish to link to, you can use the pickwhip. This is why good workspace organization is essential; making another great argument for a dual monitor setup.

To use the Pickwhip to link to a chapter point:

With the button's Properties Palette open and the Timeline Window open, click and hold on the pickwhip icon in the Link to field

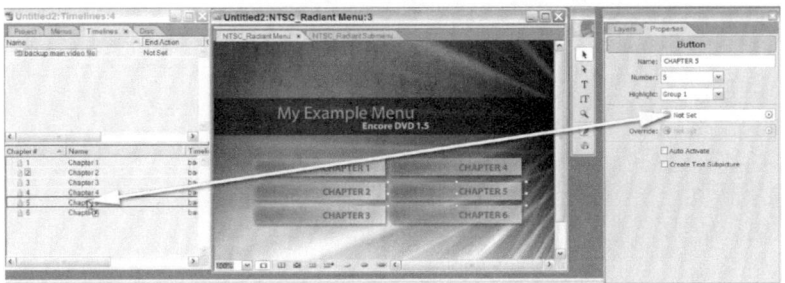

Drag the cursor to the appropriate chapter point in the Timeline.

Once the item is selected, let go of the left mouse button.

And just like that, the button's link is set to that chapter point. This method of linking chapter points works in the Timelines Tab as well.

This works for menu in the same way. Just drag the pickwhip to the appropriate menu in the Menus Tab and it's automatically set to the default button in that menu.

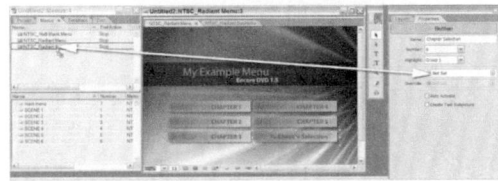

Encore will not allow you to link to something that cannot be linked. If what you're trying to link to is not allowed, the pickwhip simply withdraws and the Link field remains unchanged.

Set an Override Action of a Button

Override is a tricky and potentially confusing aspect of DVD creation, therefore this is an advanced feature and should be used by experienced authors. Put simply, Button Override allows you to change the end action of whatever that button links to. For example, a timeline is set to return to the main menu after it is done playing, but you want the viewer to return to the chapter selection menu, if they accessed the timeline through the buttons on that menu. By using button override this is not only possible but easy to do.

To set the Override Action of a button:

In the button's Properties Palette, click the arrow next to the Override Action Field

Select the timeline or menu you want the LINKED item to return to when it is done playing.

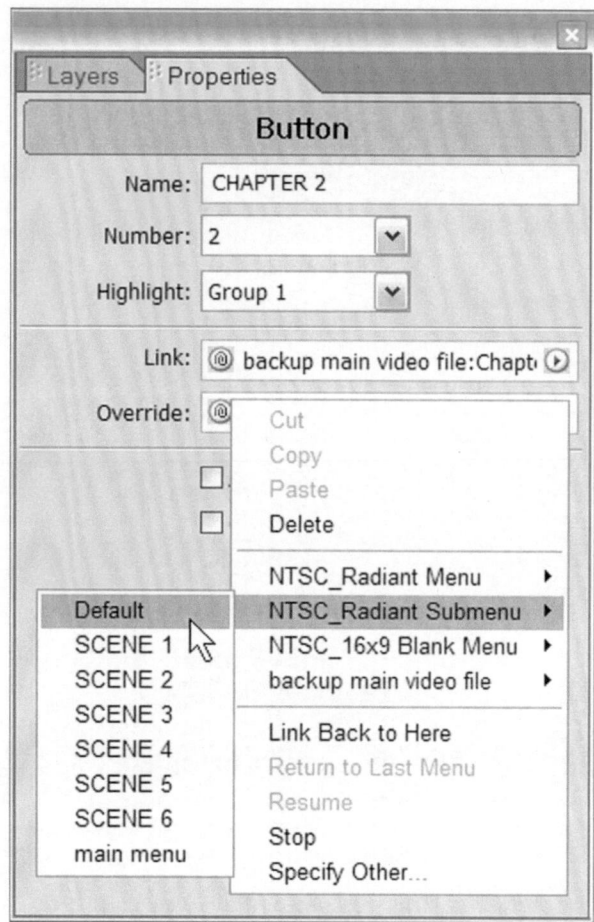

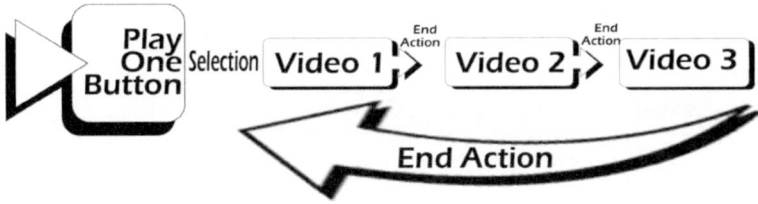

Play One, Play All and Play One

If your project uses multiple timelines, you might want the user to have more control over the way the timelines are played. For example, if you have a DVD with three music videos. You may want the viewer to be able to watch the videos in sequence, but if they desire they can select one video and return to the menu after it is done playing.

The solution is to create individual timelines for each clip, simply using Button Override and Timeline End Actions to create multiple navigation paths.   .

First, you'll want to set up the timelines for Play All. This means that when the Play All button is set, it plays all three timelines then returns to the main menu once the third timeline is finished.

Link the Play all button to the first timeline. Link the first timeline's End action to the second timeline. Link the second timeline's End action to the last timeline. And then link the last timeline's End action to the menu.

Now set up the Play One, Play Two and Play Three buttons. With these items

When doing chapter selection menus, multiple buttons can have their overrides set at the same time. Just select all the buttons, and set the Override in the Properties Palette.

Encore 1.5: It is no longer necessary to set an override end action to return to a previous menu. Simply select Return to Last Menu as the end action of the timeline, and the DVD will return to the menu it was accessed from.

selected, the DVD player will show only one timeline, then return to the menu.

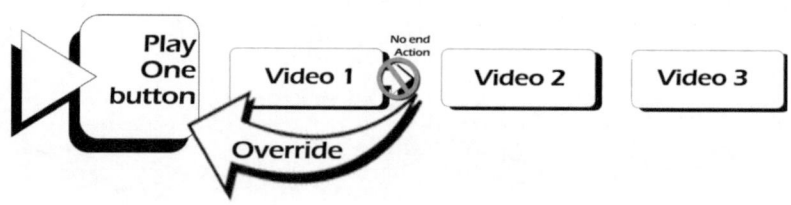

Now all that's needed is to link the Play One button to the first chapter point of the first timeline.

Then set the Play One button to override the End Action of the first timeline.

You would repeat this process with all the buttons, except the button linking to the last timeline. Its timeline is already heading back to the main menu when it is done. So all you have to do is link the button to the timeline. No override needed.

It is not currently possible to instruct an override at the end of a chapter (i.e. When chapter one is finished, don't play chapter 2, return to the main menu.) DO NOT ATTEMPT TO WORK AROUND THIS BY CREATING TIMELINES FOR EVERY CHAPTER! You will end up encoding the asset multiple times for every timeline. (99 chapters, will turn into 99 timelines, and 99 full assets must be encoded to the disc.) Plus there is a DVD track access snag between timelines, which would put a glitchy pause between chapters.

Use Playlists in Encore 1.5

One of Encore's most awaited features, Playlists, allows you to skip the complicated routing outlined in the previous section. Think of playlists as Override on steroids. With Playlists, you can program a button to play a series of timelines in any order you choose. Plus you can start those timelines at any chapter point. For example, you can program a playlist to play the second chapter of one timeline, the first chapter of the second timeline, and

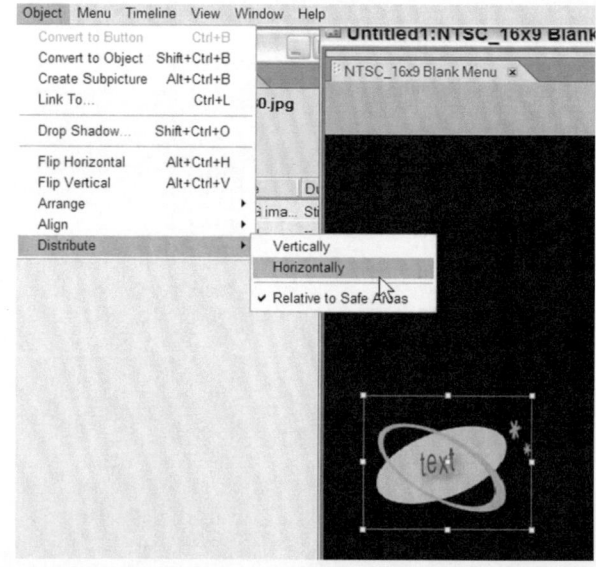

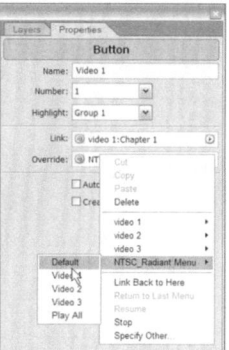

the last chapter of the last timeline. You can even have the playlist play the last timeline, then the first, then the second and go back to the menu at the end of the second timeline.

To create a playlist:

In the Project tab, choose File > New Playlist.

Note: The timelines must still play to the end before continuing to the next timeline on the playlist.

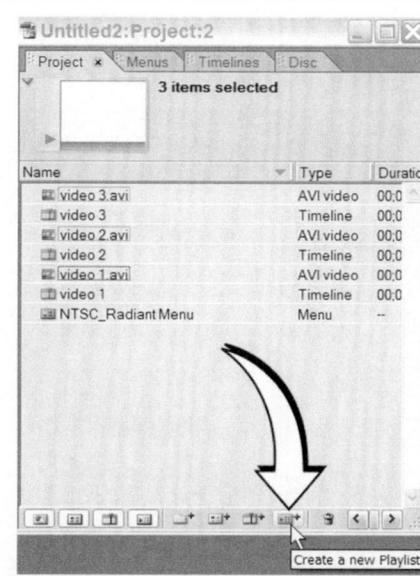

Enter a name for the Playlist and click OK.

Select the playlist in the Project tab and open the Properties palette.

Drag the pick whip from the Timeline section of the Playlist Inspector to a timeline in the Project tab.

Encore adds the specified timeline to the playlist.

If desired, set an end action to link to a timeline or a menu using the pick whip.

Now all you must do is link a button to that playlist.

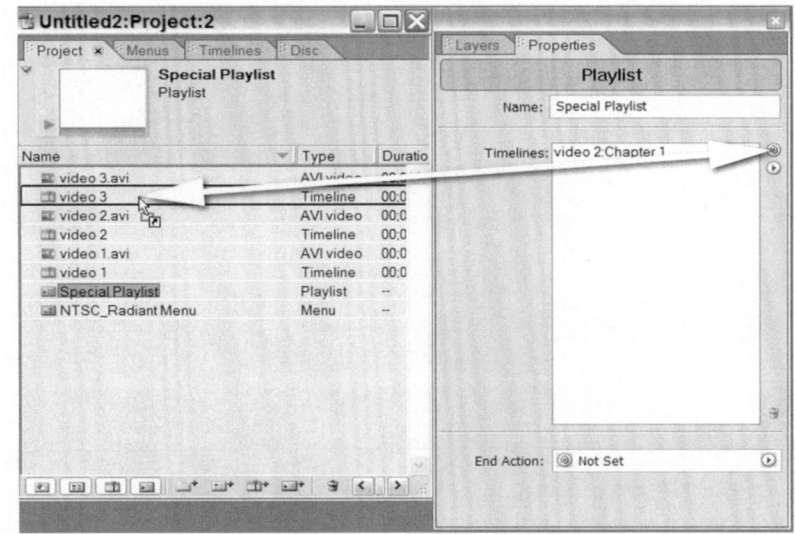

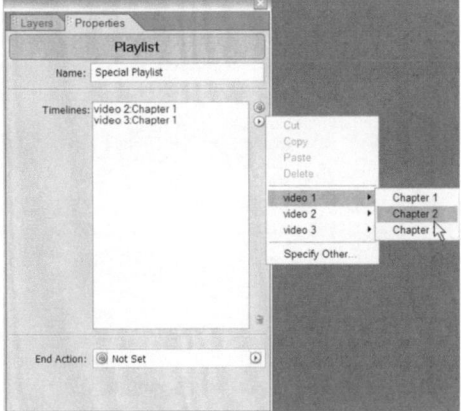

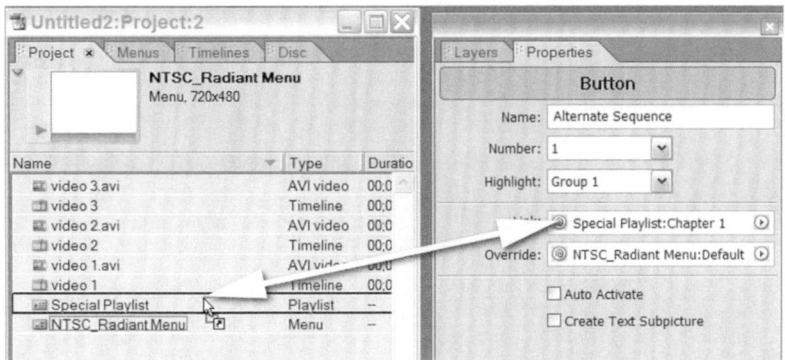

Change the Automatic Routing of Buttons

Authors new to DVD creation don't always realize that they control the viewer's navigational experience Encore takes most of the guesswork out of button routing by handling it automatically. Yet the method in which Encore automatically routes those buttons can be adjusted.

To change the Automatic Routing of Buttons in Encore:

Go to Edit>Preferences>Menu

Note: it is recommended that new DVD Authors leave these settings alone until a good familiarity with Encore techniques is established. Adjusting these settings may limit or completely disable the ability to navigate menus.

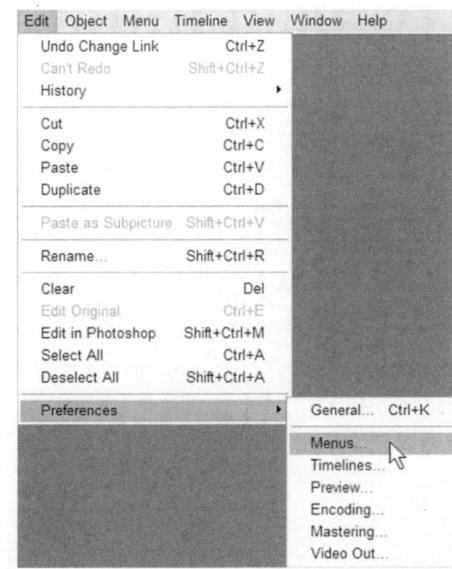

This opens the preferences dialog for menu button routing.

Route Buttons up/down: Unchecking this box disables the feature's ability to route buttons for the up and down arrows on a DVD remote control, limiting routing to the left and right.

Wrap Around Up/Down: Unchecking this box disables the automatic wrap from the bottom or top button to another button. In other words pressing down on the bottom button in a column does nothing. When checked it offers the option of wrapping to the same column or an adjacent column.

Route Buttons Left/Right: Unchecking this box disables the use of the left or right keys to move the selection left or right.

Wrap Around Left/Right: Unchecking this box disables the automatic wrap from the leftmost or rightmost button to another button. If the box is checked it offers the option of wrapping to the same row, or wrapping to an adjacent row.

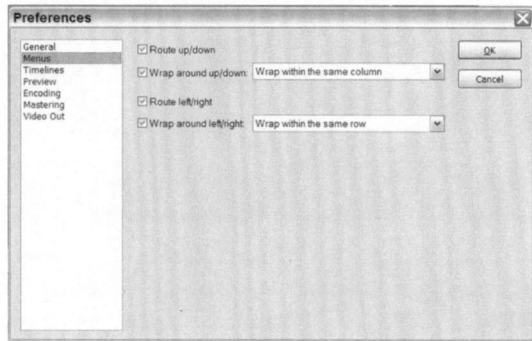

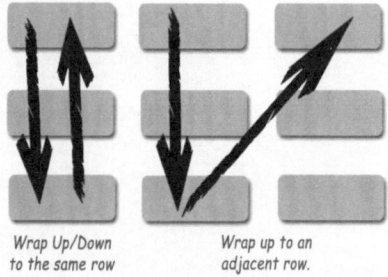

Wrap Up/Down
to the same row

Wrap up to an
adjacent row.

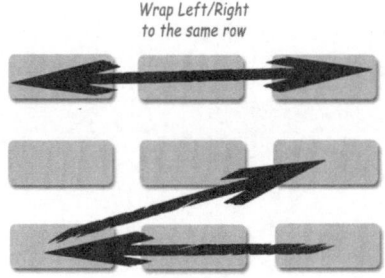

*Wrap Left/Right
to the same row*

*Wrap Left/Right to an
adjacent row.*

Let Me Do It: Change the Routing of Buttons

While Encore's Automatic Button Routing feature is reliable there are times a unique button routing is required. When your buttons are in a novel layout, sometimes Encore doesn't route them in an intuitive manner.

First, Automatic Routing must be disabled, then the buttons can be assigned new routes.

To manually change the routing of buttons:

Go to the Properties Palette of the menu.

Uncheck the Automatically Route Buttons box.

**Warning:
Unchecking all
boxes disables
Encore's Automatic
Button Routing
feature. Unless
you plan to route
the buttons
yourself, it is best
to leave some
of the routing
functional and test
the navigation
yourself.**

Now the Menu Editor will allow you to change the routing of buttons.

Go to the Menu Editor and click on the Show Button Routing Icon at the bottom of the window.

Now the buttons have numbered crosses in their centers. These represent the directional buttons on a DVD player's remote control. In the center of each cross is the button's number. The numbers in each direction indicate exactly to which button, pressing in this direction, will move the selection. If you want the directional key to take the selection to another button instead of the one indicated, you must drag it to select the different button.

Click and hold on the direction and drag the line to the desired button.

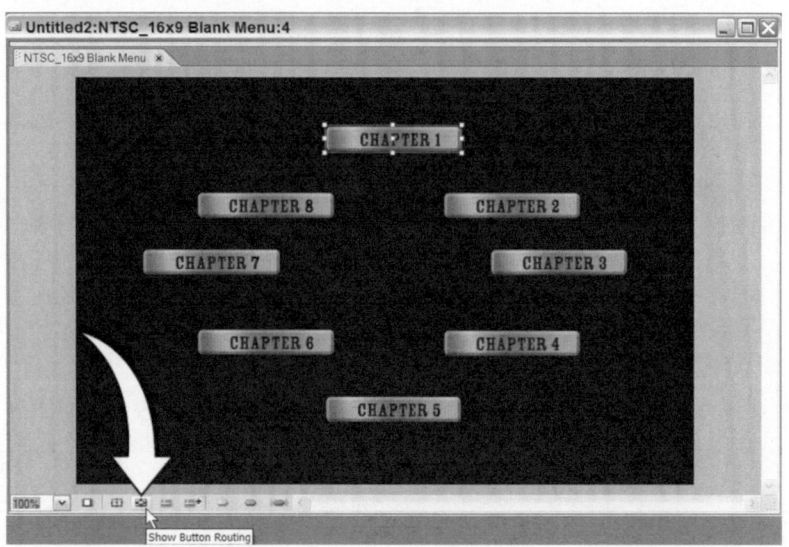

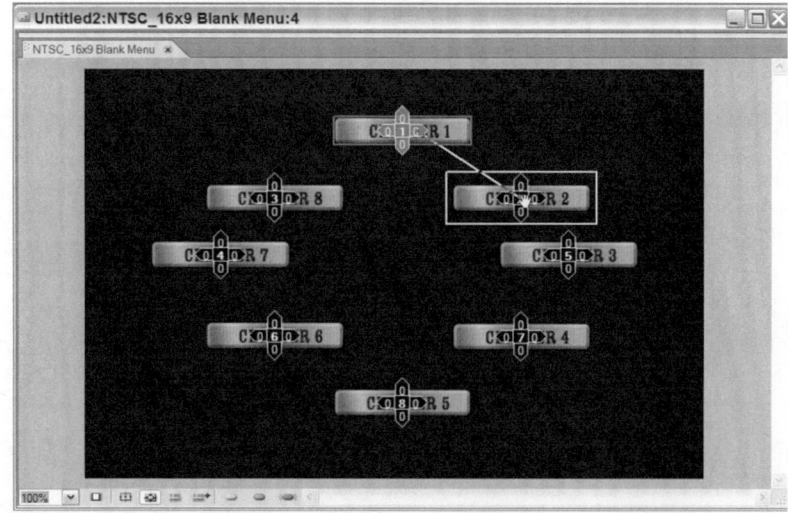

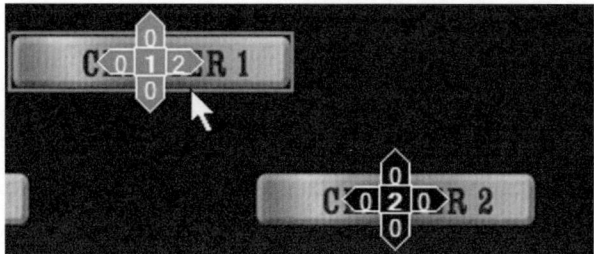

You'll notice as you drag the line away from the button a pickwhip-like line draws out. If you drag this line to another button it will change the routing of this direction to that button, BUT if you drag the line to the center of the button itself, it will disable the routing of that direction altogether.

Once the desired button is selected, release the mouse button.

If the pickwhip was dragged to its own button, a zero will appear in that arrow, meaning routing in this direction has been disabled.

Note: Make sure all buttons are routed and can be accessed from at least one other button. If not, some buttons cannot be accessed using traditional DVD player remote controls.

Proper Mouse Selection Area

Encore 1.5: The selection area error has been corrected, text layers no longer affect the size of the selection area.

Many viewers like to watch DVD's on their computers. For this reason, buttons have mouse selection areas so when the mouse is in this area clicking will activate the button. To prevent glitches when a viewer uses a mouse, the selection area of the buttons must be checked.

By using the Show Routing of Buttons feature in the Menu Editor, the selection area can be viewed. The borders of the area are shown as a solid box. These boxes should never overlap, or problems will occur when viewing the DVD on a computer. Also this is a good time to check the size of these selection areas. If one button's selection area is bigger than every other button, it is probably because there is a blank text layer in the button's layer set. Deleting these blank text layers will usually reduce the size.

Set the Default Button

The default button is the first button highlighted when a menu is displayed. Usually this button is button number one, but the default button can be any

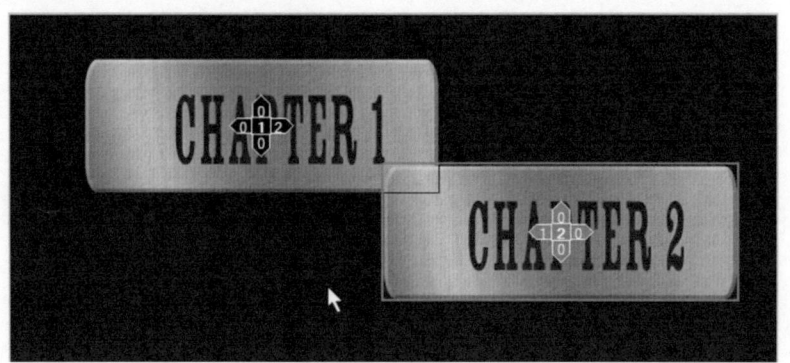

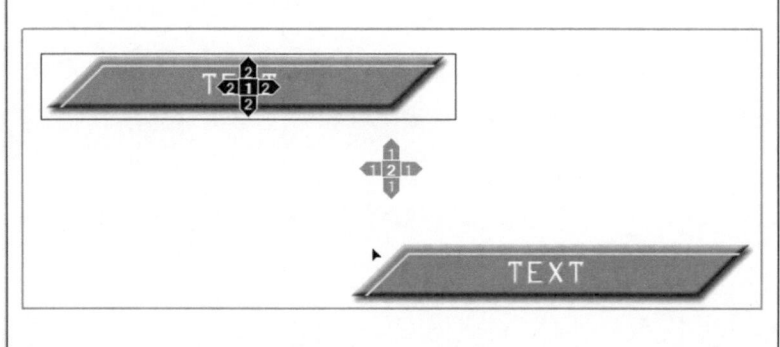

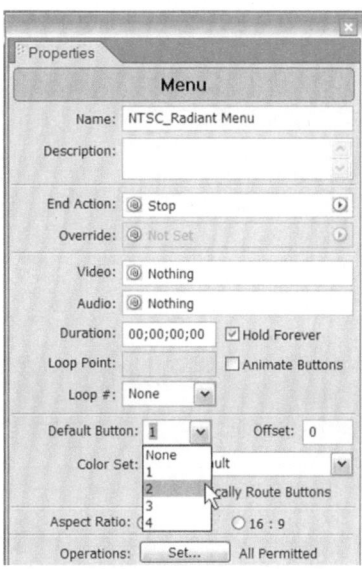

button on the menu.

To Change the Default Button of a Menu:

Select the menu and open its Properties Palette

Click the arrow on the Default button field and select the desired button number.

Now when this menu opens, this button will be highlighted.

It is never a good idea to change a button's number to make it the default button.

Offset the Button Numbers

Many DVD viewers use the number keys on their remotes to select and activate buttons. For the sake of consistency it is sometimes best to offset the button numbers to account for navigating between menus. For example, a menu has three chapter selection buttons and the next menu has three buttons also. You would want to offset the second menu's button numbers by three to account for the change. So, instead of the buttons being numbered 1, 2, and 3 an offset of 3 would change the values to 4, 5 and 6.

To offset the button numbers:

Select the Menu and open the Properties Palette

Click inside the Offset field and enter the offset number.

Set the Remote Control Title Button of a Disc

On most DVD remote controls, there is a Title button. This button allows the viewer to go to a default menu or timeline on the disc, from any location on the disc. Normally, this is set to the main menu. But it may be set to any menu or timeline on the disc.

To set the Remote Control Title button:

Go to the Disc Tab in the Project Window.

Open the Properties Palette for the Disc

In the Title Button Field click on the arrow to open the drop down menu

Select the menu or timeline you want this button to link to.

Title Button vs Menu Button

Most DVD player remote controls offer the Title button and Menu button. And the vast majority of people cannot tell

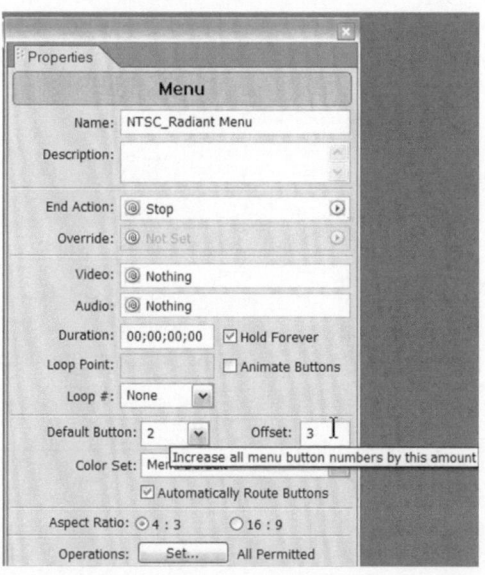

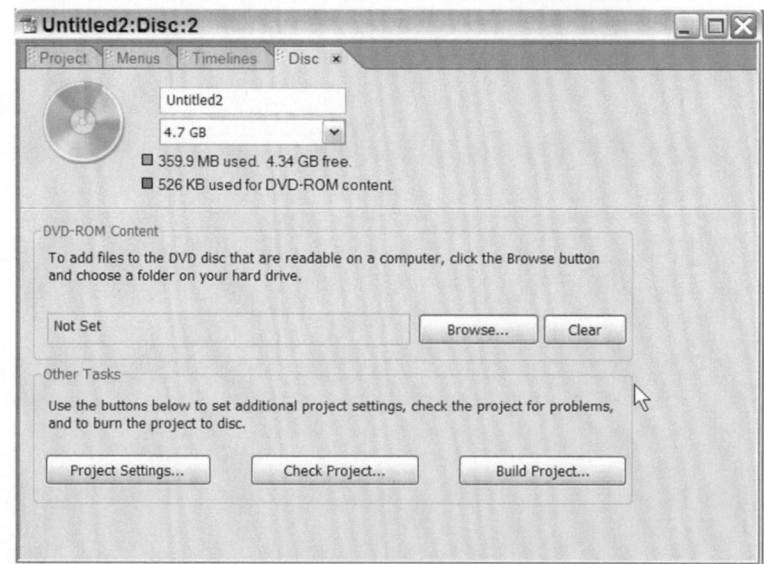

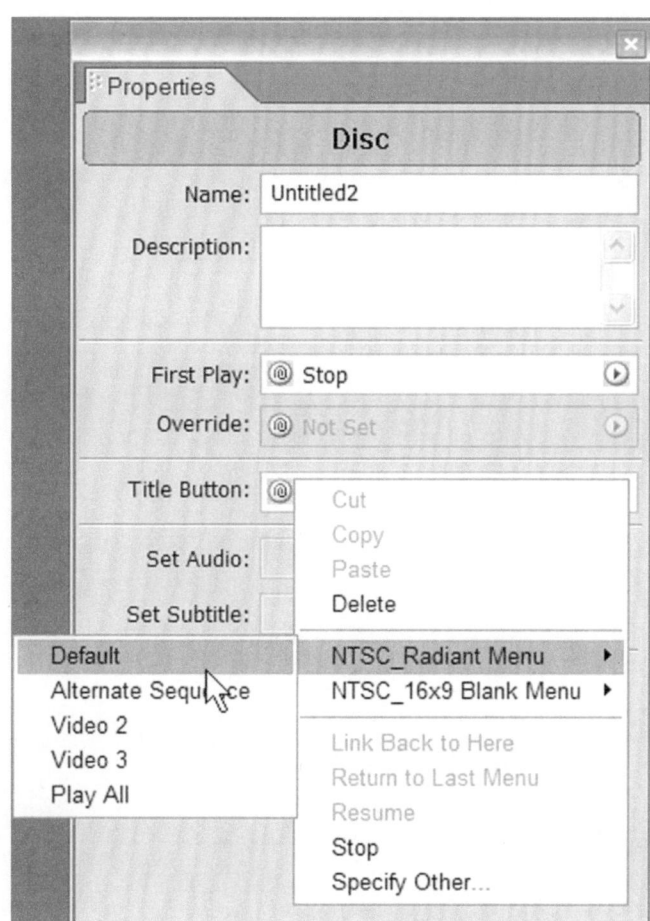

the difference between the functions of the two. Unfortunately many DVD authors have not taken creative advantage of their respective functions.

Regarding functionality, the Menu and Title buttons do the same thing. Whenever the button is pressed, the DVD player pauses whatever it is doing and goes to the menu. If it is pressed again, it returns the viewer to their previous place. This allows the viewer to stop the feature, return to a menu and adjust something (such as subtitles or languages) then return right back to when they first pushed the button.

As far as scope and adjustability, the Title and Menu buttons are very different. The Title button is a constant; it doesn't matter where the button is pressed it returns to the same menu every time. The Menu button, however, can be set specifically to suit the needs of every timeline. So in essence, you can give your viewers two menu options while watching a DVD. They can watch a Timeline from the Chapter Selection Menu, and return to the Chapter Selection menu by pressing the Menu button. Or they can hit the Title button and return to the main menu.

Chapter 7

Takin' on Hollywood:
Advanced Menu Authoring

Once you've become familiar with creating simple menus and buttons in Encore, you quickly branch off into some of the more complicated and creative facets of DVD authoring. None of these features are required for a basic DVD, but the creative author will enjoy taking their DVD's to the next level.

Create Audio/Language and Subtitle Submenus

If you imported several audio tracks or created subtitle tracks for one feature, it makes sense to create a DVD menu that allows the viewer to access those additional tracks.

Basically a button on an audio/language/subtitle submenu instructs the DVD player to play another audio or subtitle track while playing the timeline. Start by creating a menu that identifies the available tracks. Then when linking buttons, a special command must be included with the button's linking instructions.

To set a button to play an audio or subtitle track:

Select the button and open its Properties Palette.

In the Link To Field click the arrow and select Specify Other

This opens the Link To Dialog with options for linking and track selection. The simplest way to switch audio tracks is to link this button to the first chapter point of the timeline.

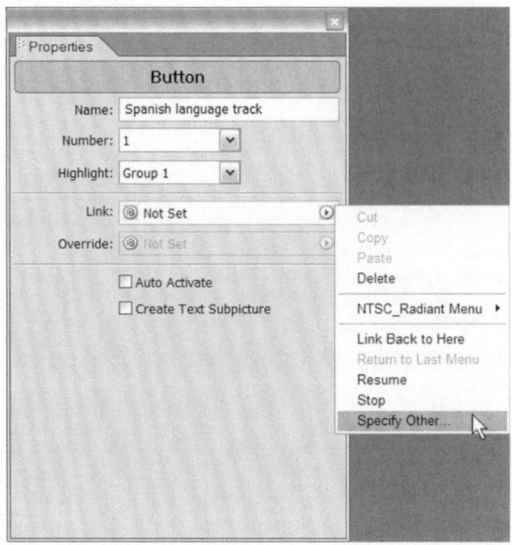

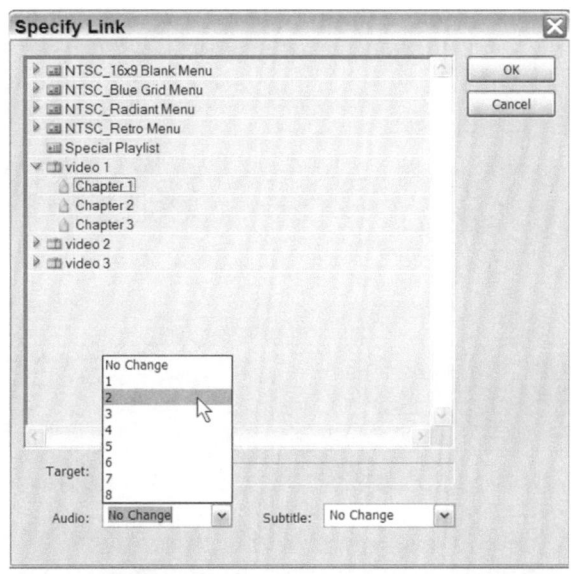

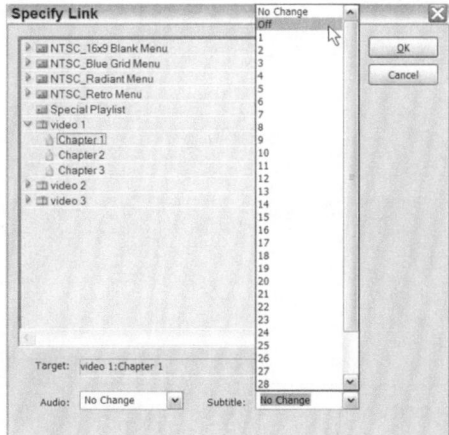

Link the button to the first chapter point of the timeline.

Then in the Audio Field, select the desired audio track number

Or

Select the Subtitle track number.

Click OK

Now when the button is activated it will go directly to the first chapter of the timeline and play the audio or subtitle track specified. You can also link the button to another menu such as the main menu.

Create Still and Video Thumbnail Menus

One of the valuable features of many DVD's is the ability to display a single frame, or a short sequence from a chapter in the button that links to the chapter. This way the viewer can get an idea of the contents of the chapter without having to go to the timeline.

Encore provides a set of Chapter Selection submenus, complete with thumbnails.

Whether you are creating Still (single frame) or Video Thumbnails, the first step is to link the thumbnail button to the chapter point.

To link a thumbnail to a chapter point:

Click on the button and go to its Properties Palette

In the Link To field, click the arrow.

Select the Timeline and the desired chapter point.

Immediately, the first frame of the chapter point is displayed in the thumbnail frame. If you selected a poster frame then the poster frame will be displayed in the thumbnail. (See Set Poster Frames in Chapter 2.)

Now at this point if all you wanted to create was still-graphic thumbnails you're done. However, if you want to generate motion video thumbnails, you must animate the menu's buttons.

To Animate Video Thumbnails:

Select the Menu and open its Properties Palette

Check the Animate Buttons box

When creating multiple timelines, I recommend you be certain to have the same number of audio and subtitle tracks in each timeline. If one timeline doesn't have the audio or subtitle track specified, the DVD player will default to track one and will NOT return to the track specified when playing another timeline.

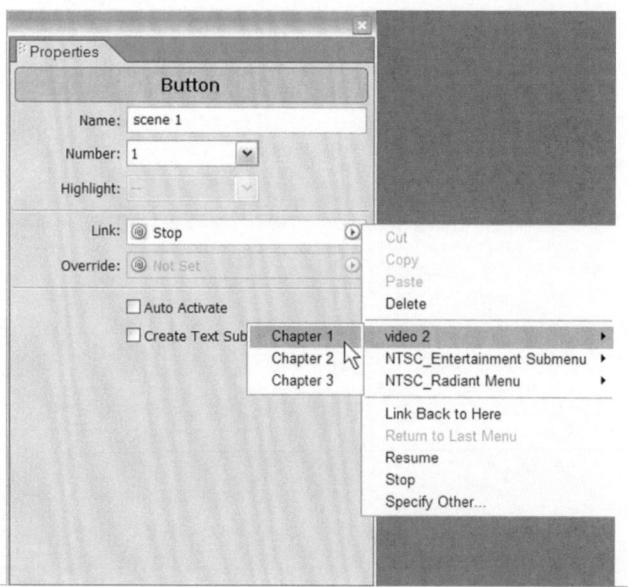

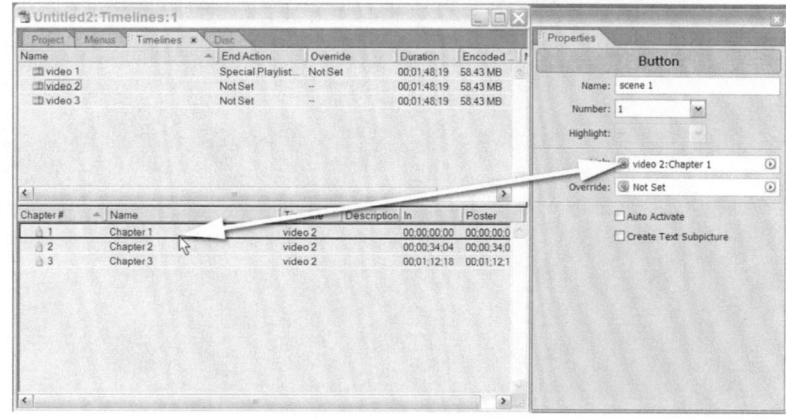

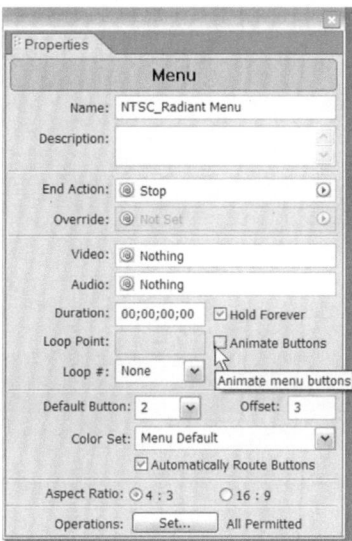

Now Hear This: Menu Audio

Adding audio to a menu can serve as the perfect complement to the DVD experience. By the same token, however, choosing the wrong audio can make a menu annoying. Choose a subtle background audio track preferably without lyrics or dialogue. In other words, find something that will loop cleanly; otherwise after a few minutes the menu will begin to wear on the viewer. Using loops found in Adobe's Audition library serves as a good starting point, or find a library of Acid loops that fit the musical style. These loop seamlessly, and are generally generic and rarely contain any 'surprises' that viewers might find irritating.

Choosing the right audio is the hard part, but putting it in is a breeze.

To add background audio to a menu:

Select the menu you wish to add audio to.

Work with a sound editing program and find a good loop point on the audio track. Write down the time code of the loop point.

Open the Properties Palette and go to the Audio Field

With the Project Tab in view, Drag the pickwhip to the desired audio track in the Project Tab.

Have a second or two of silence just after the loop point and just before the end of the clip. This will reduce pops and/or stutters when the clip snaps back to the loop point. This can also be dealt with by using Audition loops or ACID loops, as they are pre-faded at the beginnings and ends of each loop file.

Release the mouse button.

The pickwhip will retract and the name of the audio file will appear in the audio field. Also notice that the duration of that audio file becomes the duration of the menu itself. If you change nothing, the menu will stop being displayed when the track is over. To change this, see the section Loop Menu/Subpicture Highlight Delay in this chapter.

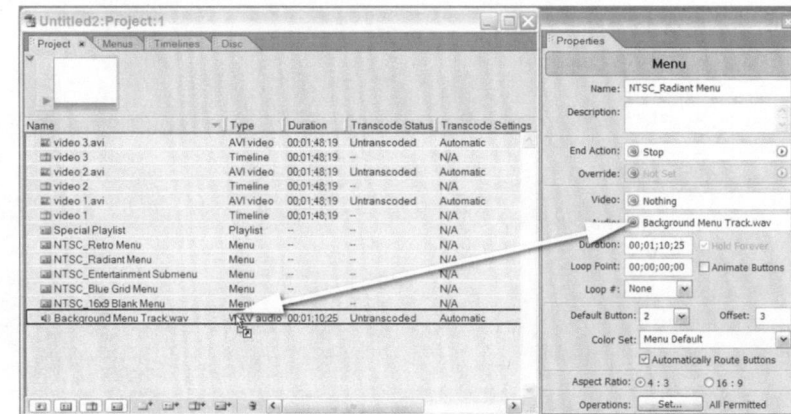

Add Background Video to a Menu

Many beginning DVD authors see video backgrounds in professional DVD's, and wonder how they were made. The truth is, every menu has a video background. The basic menus become

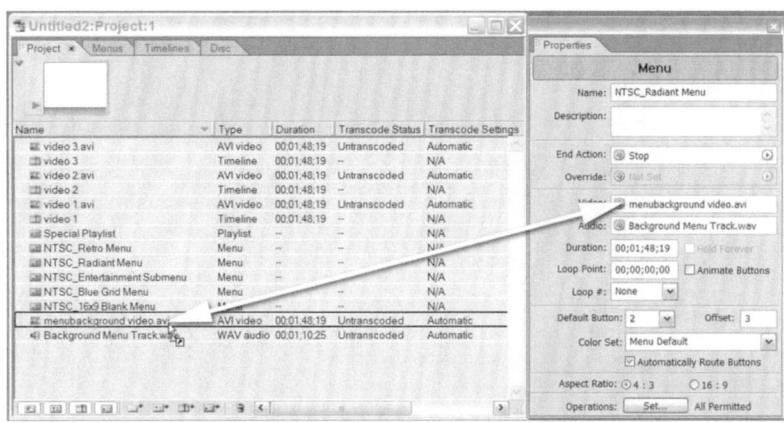

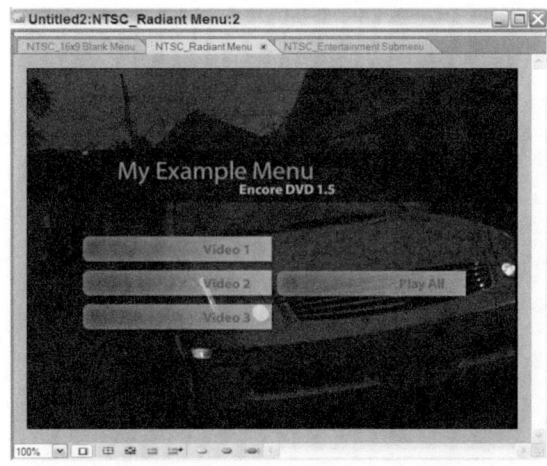

video streams and the same rules apply to motion menus as they do to basic "still" menus. If you want a video clip to play in the background it is a very simple process.

To add background video to a menu:

Select the menu and open the Properties Palette.

With the Project Tab in view, go to the Video field.

Click on the pickwhip icon and drag the whip to the desired video file in the Project Tab.

Release the mouse button and the whip will retract.

Notice the menu's duration is now the duration of the clip. When the clip ends, the menu will stop being displayed if left alone. (See next section.)

Note: If a background video and audio clip are used, but they are of different lengths, Encore will set the duration to match the longest clip.

Notice that if you have any buttons they will be displayed on top of the background video.

Creating Motion with After Effects

The more ambitious author thinks of those sleek motion menus where the buttons fly onto the screen, or lightning jumps from one button to the next, illuminating the buttons in series. Encore is not capable of creating those kind of effects, but its sister program, After Effects, is perfect for unleashing that creative potential.

After Effects is not a simple program by any means, and a lot of time and patience must go into creating high voltage menus. If you are comfortable with After Effects then importing AE MPEG-2 or AVI compositions into Encore is easy. For those just getting into After Effects, check out books by Chris and Trish Meyer for solid information on how to use AE to create great motion menus.

Also Encore 1.5 has added interactivity with After Effects.

To save a menu for use in Adobe After Effects:

Select the menu in the Project window or in the Menu Editor

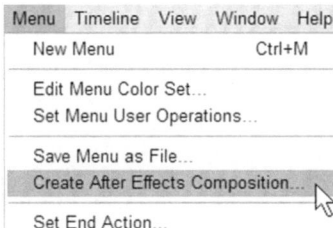

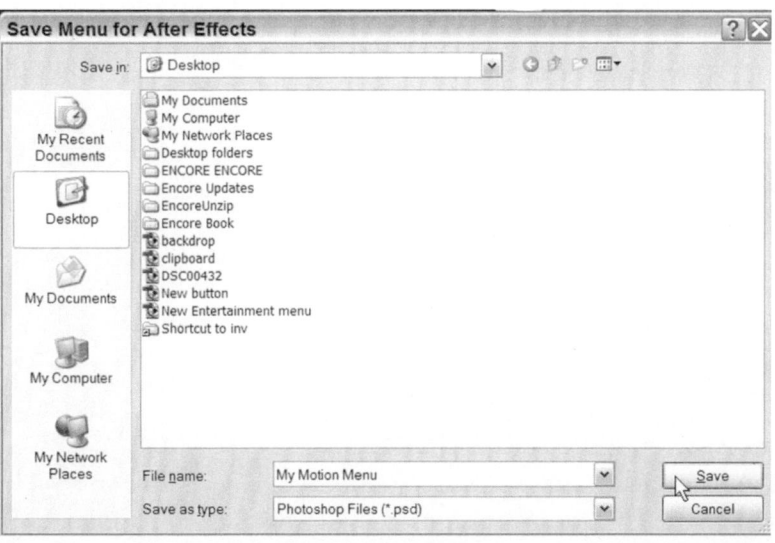

Choose Menu > Create After Effects Composition.

Choose a file name and destination and click OK.

Keep a few simple tips in mind when creating menus with AE.

At some point the buttons should stop moving! The subpicture highlights cannot move with the buttons, they will appear in the same place regardless of where the background button may be. However, WHEN the subpicture highlights appear is covered in the next section.

It helps to work backwards from the "resting position" of the menu. Create a Photoshop file that will act as a placeholder for creating the subpicture highlights in Encore. Use that same Photoshop file as the base composition in After Effects.

Hide all but the subpicture highlights in the .psd file once you've set the final placement of the buttons. If you leave the graphic layers visible they will remain in the menu the entire time.

If the motion menu is designed to loop, leave a few seconds of inactivity just after the loop point and before the end of the clip. This will help smooth out the stutter when the video snaps back to the loop point.

Once you have finished creating the AE composition, you will need to save the file as either MPEG-2 or AVI. Then Import that file into Encore's Project window as an asset. Use that asset as your background video for the menu.

Loop d' Loop; Looping a Menu.

Once background audio or video is added to a menu, it can no longer be Held Forever like a still menu. Once the clip is finished, the menu will carry out its end action. (See Set an End Action for a Menu later in this chapter.)

However, the menu can be set to loop several times or forever if need be. If it is set to Loop Forever, the menu's End Action is irrelevant since it will never end.

To Loop a Menu:

Open the Menu's Properties Palette

Click the arrow in the Loop Field

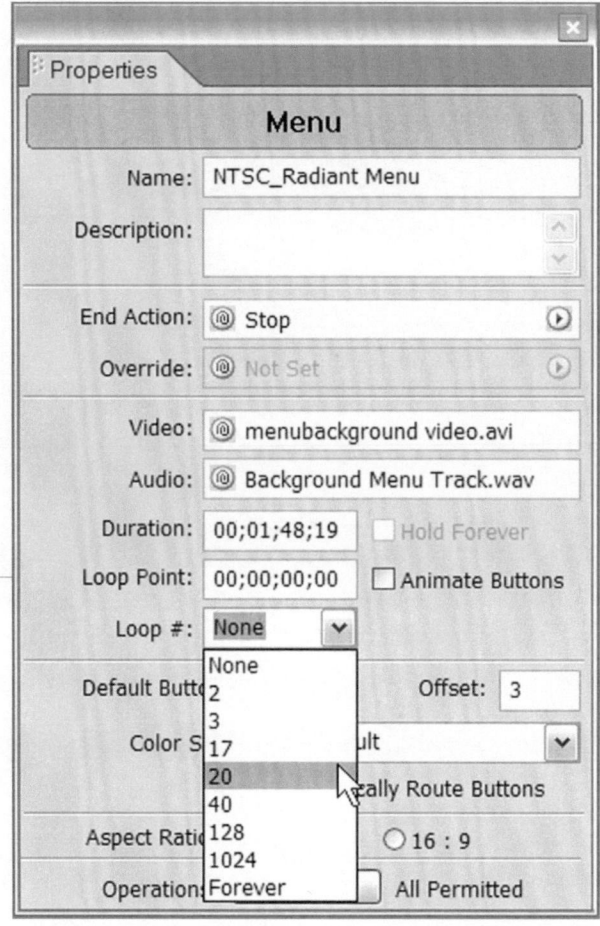

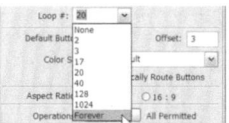

Select the desired number of loops from the list

Or type in the number of loops

If you have set up a complex motion menu where, for example, the buttons slide in or fade in, having this repeat itself could get annoying. Plus the subpicture highlights appear when the menu first opens, not when the buttons are in the "correct" positions.

Fortunately, loop point accomplishes several tasks in an intuitive manner. Not only does it allow you to set a point in a clip to loop back to, it delays the subpicture highlight, keeping highlights out of view until the loop point is reached.

To set the loop point of a menu:

In the menu's Properties Palette, click in the Loop Point Field.

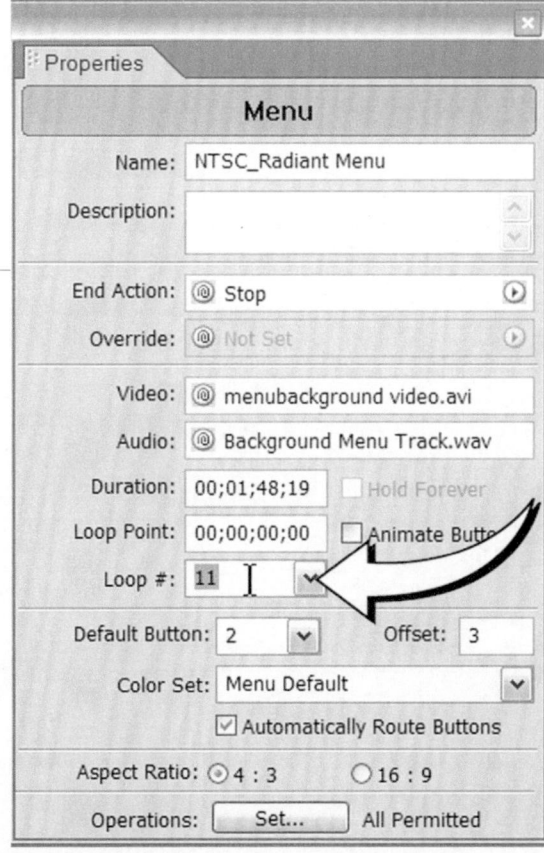

Type in the precise time code for the loop point.

Unless a number of loops are selected, the loop point does not matter. Make sure both loop features are set.

Exit Stage Left; Transition Videos for Menus

For the After Effects savvy, exit transitions are a must. If your opening sequence had buttons flying in, why not have them flying out? Depending on the DVD and menu scheme the exit could be the same no matter which button was pushed (i.e. all buttons zoom out to a blur), or each button could have its own exit motion (i.e. the play button spins and flies out when pressed, while the chapter selection button expands and morphs into the chapter selection submenu.) In any case, the buttons aren't linked to their destinations; rather they are linked to a transition timeline. That timeline's end action serves as the real link to the desired material.

If you have one button that links to one special transition timeline, setting the transition difficulties easy.

To set the transition timeline for one button:

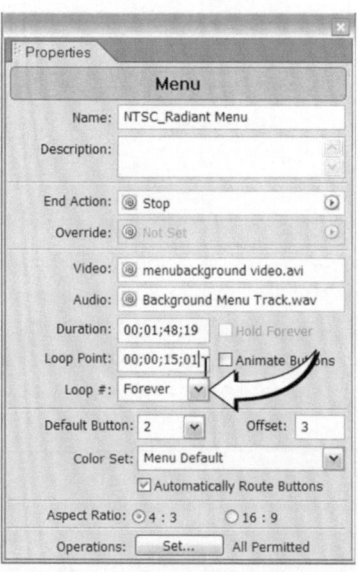

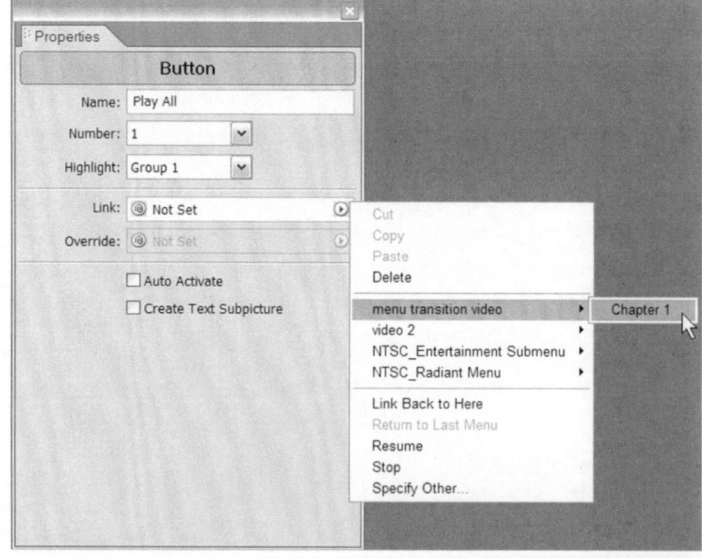

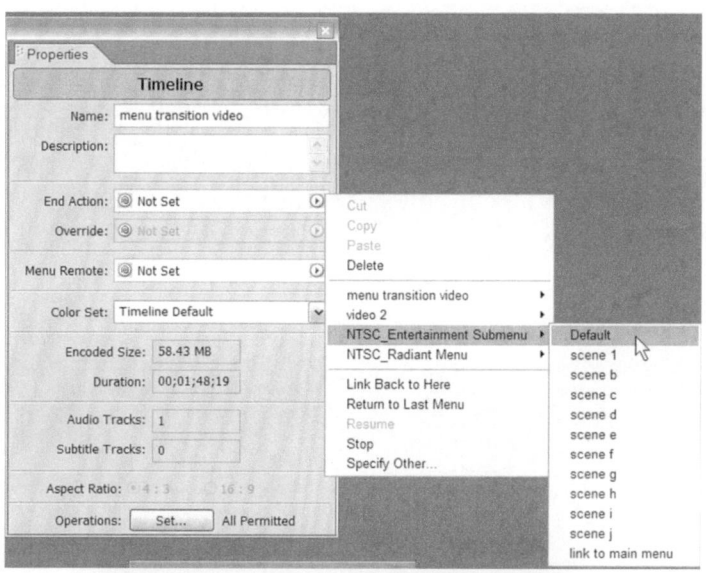

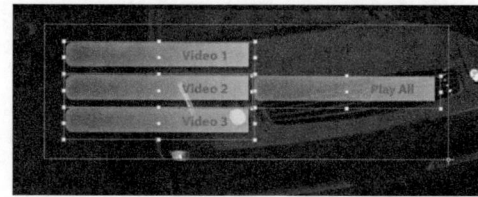

Select the button

Open its Properties Palette and click the arrow in the Link To field

Select the transition clip's timeline from the list and click on chapter one.

The next step is to set the end action of that transition timeline to link to the right destination.

In the Timelines Tab, select the transition clip's timeline.

Go to the Timelines Properties Palette and click on the arrow in the End Action field

Select the desired menu or timeline from the choices.

As a time saver, many DVD authors have one general exit transition for all of their buttons. Some blur the menu so that it is indistinguishable from the next menu or timeline. One transition can serve many functions. The only problem is, a timeline can only be set for one end action. Each button must override that end action to get where the viewer wants to go.

To link multiple buttons to the same transition timeline:

A timeline should be created for any video clip that acts as a transition FROM a menu. Use background video for transitions TO a menu.

Draw a box or hold the Ctrl key to select multiple buttons in the Menu Editor or the Menus Tab.

Once the buttons are selected go to the Properties Palette.

Notice that the specific characteristics of each button are not shown, but the buttons can be linked to the same item, or for this purpose, exit transition timeline.

In the Link To field, click on the arrow

Select the transition timeline from the list

Now all buttons will link to the same exit clip timeline. Each button must be set to override the timeline in a different way.

Select the button and go to the Properties Palette.

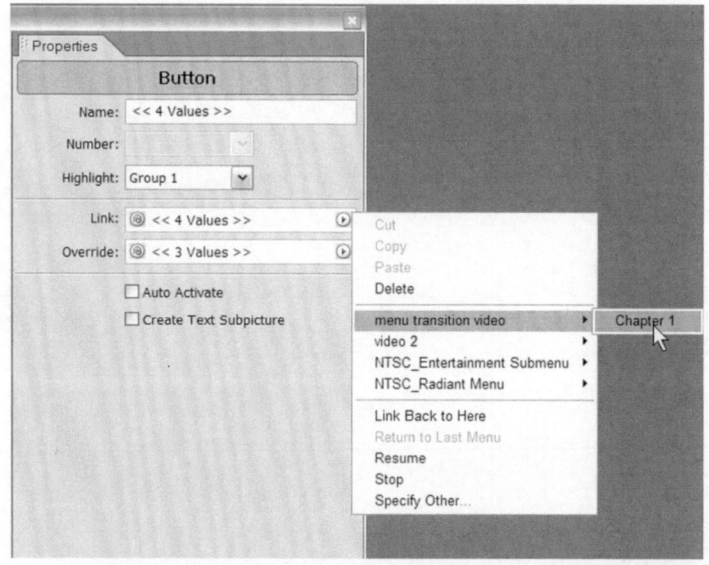

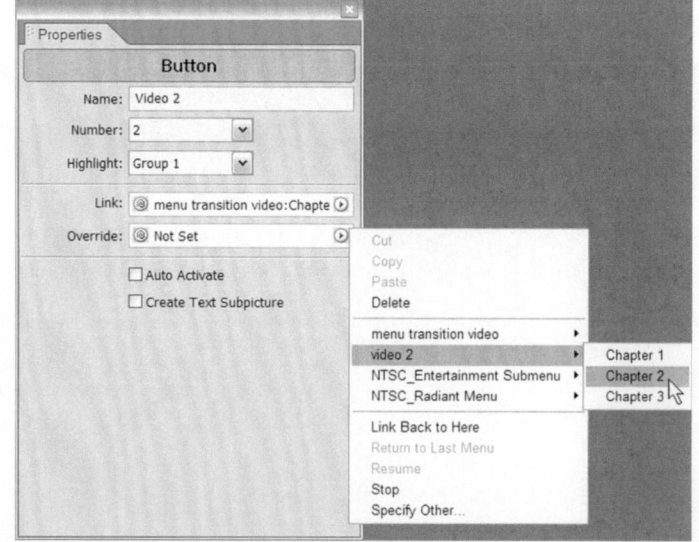

Go to the override field and select the appropriate destination

Repeat for all buttons that require a different destination.

Now when the transition is accessed from this button, the transition clip's timeline End Action will proceed to where the button override directs it.

The override function of a button only overrides the end action of the menu or timeline it links to.

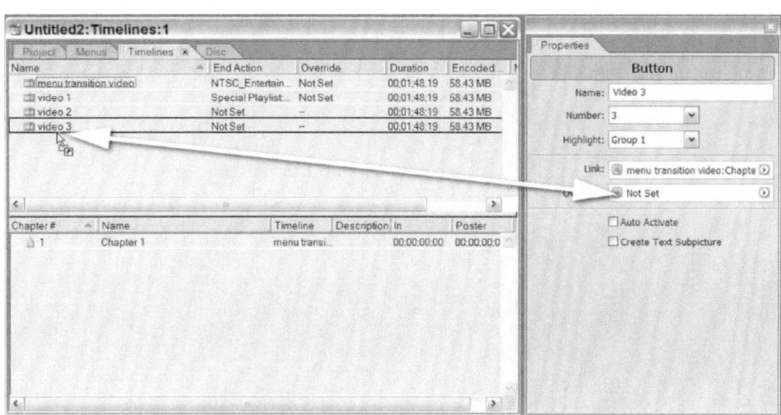

Create a Menu Color Set

Every menu can have one color set. Usually the color set is handled automatically, based on colors used in the Photoshop file when Photoshop is used to create a menu. However, entire color sets can be created to suit your needs. Before a new color set can be applied to a menu, the color set must be created.

To create a new color set:

Go to Menu > Edit Menu Color Set

This opens the Menu Color Set Dialog. If you have never used this dialog before there should only be one Color Set in the list, the Menu Default. If you don't want to deal with creating a new color set you can always adjust the menu default. Until you are comfortable with changing the color sets, it's probably best to have a fail safe color set, so create a new color set.

If this is an NTSC project, check NTSC Colors Only. This will assure that the colors will be safely shown on most NTSC Color TV's.

Click the New Color Set Icon.

Name the new color set and click OK

Now it's time to adjust the subpicture colors and opacity to suit your needs. The first set of three colors represents the normal or unselected state. Usually these three colors are set to 0% Opacity (Transparent). The next group down has six available colors, this represents the selected and activated states for the first color group. The next group of six colors represents the second color group selected and activated states.

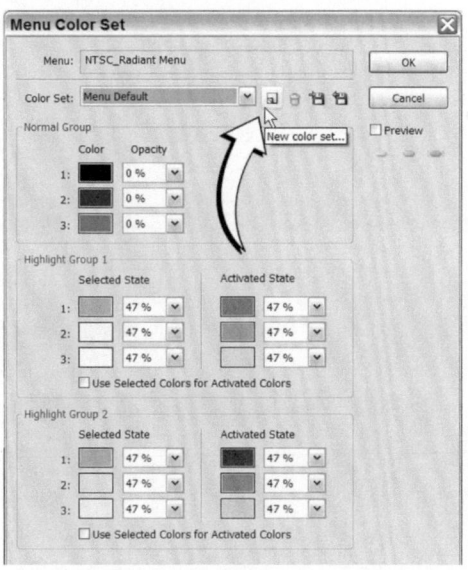

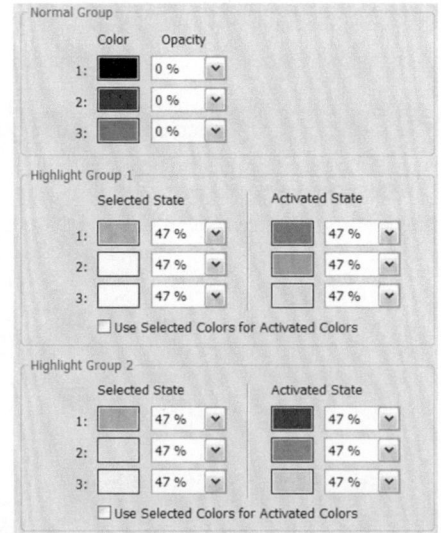

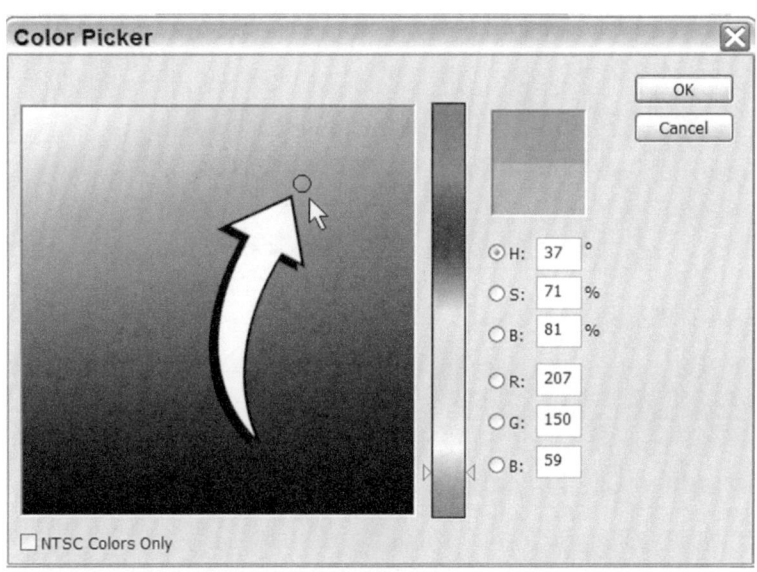

Double clicking on the color pane on an individual color group opens the Color Picker.

Move the selection circle to the preferred color.

Click OK

At this point you can set the opacity of the color, if working with detailed background buttons, it's best to go light on the opacity. The highlight will appear as more of a glow.

Click the arrow to open the pull down menu and select the desired opacity.

Continue until the color set is to your specifications.

Click Ok.

The color set is now ready to be applied to a menu.

If you've adjusted a color set that was currently being applied to a menu, the adjustments are applied to that menu. But do not confuse this for a global settings adjustment, as not all menus are changed when creating or changing a color set.

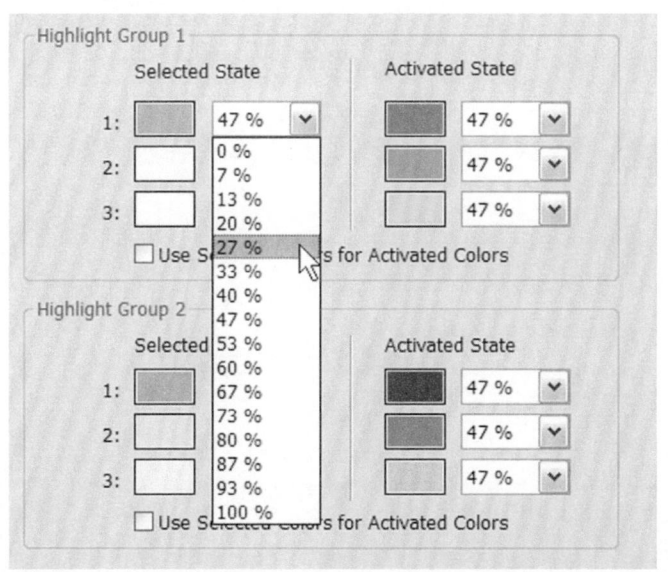

Understanding Color Sets and Subpicture Highlights

One of the most potentially confusing aspects of DVD menus is the idea of color sets and the =1, =2, =3 prefixes. Think of it as painting by numbers. The prefixes set which pixels on the screen will be colored by the subpicture. Just like a blank paint by numbers sheet.

Usually paint by numbers has a little key that says which colors go with each number. This is the Color Set. The Color Set can be changed at any time before building a project to disc.

Also keep in mind that for each color group there are three selection states. The normal (or unselected) selection state is usually transparent, but it can be any color or opacity you desire. Remember you control the paint by numbers color key, the DVD player paints what you tell it to, where you want it to.

If this still seems confusing, take some time to experiment with color sets and color groups. Not everybody gets it at first, but through trial and error it makes more sense.

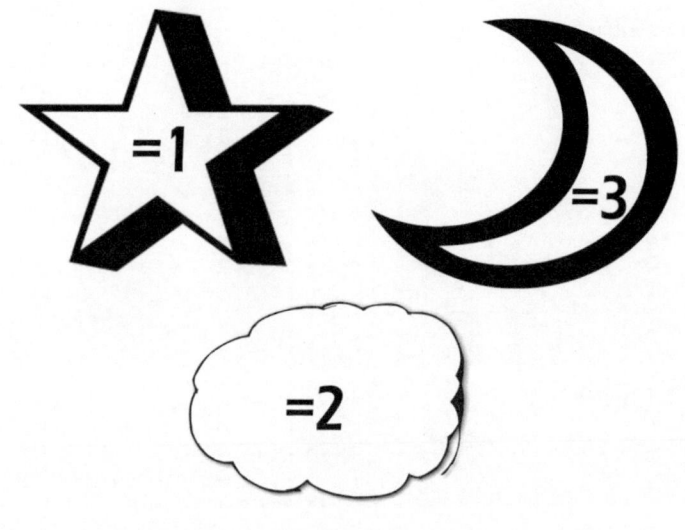

Color Set
=1-Yellow
=2-Grey
=3-Blue

Color Set
=1-Red
=2-Purple
=3-Orange

Color Set

NORMAL	SELECTED	ACTIVATED
=1-Transparent	=1-Yellow	=1-Red
=2-Transparent	=2-Grey	=2-Orange
=3-Transparent	=3-Blue	=3-White

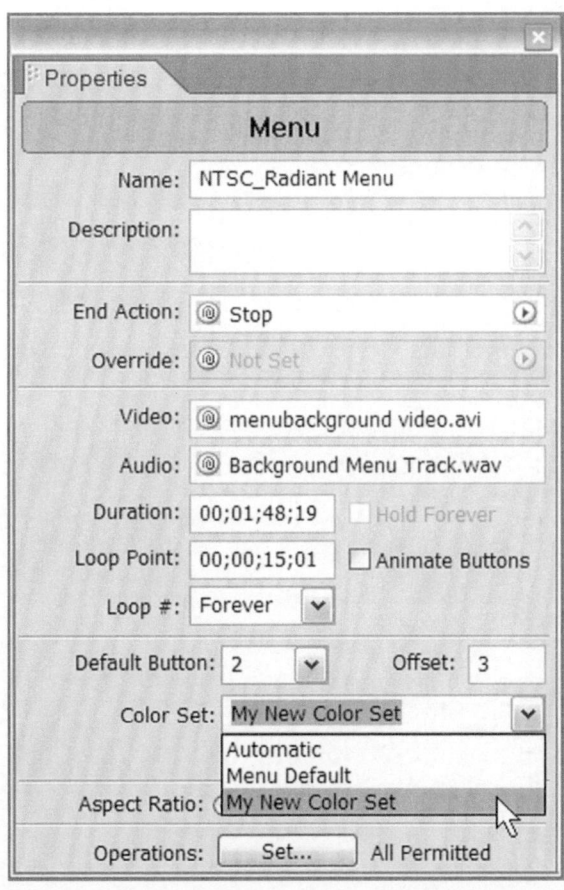

Change a Menu's Color Set

A menu's color is set to automatic by default, this automatic color set reads the original colors of the .psd file and creates a color set that best matches those colors. At any time you can change the automatic color set to menu default. If a new color set was created, it will be available.

To change a menu's color set:

Select the menu and open the Properties Palette

In the Color Set Field, click the arrow to reveal the choices

Select the desired color set.

The new color set is now applied to the menu's subpictures.

Use the Preview Window

The Preview Window is indispensable for checking a menu's links, navigation, end actions and appearance by simulating the controls of a DVD player. Plus you can set the menu in motion and see if the loop points are appropriate and clean up any gross flaws in design.

To Preview a menu:

Right click on the menu in the Menu Editor

Select Preview from Here

This opens the Preview Window. While the Preview Window is open, the rest of the workspace is locked and cannot be unlocked until the window is closed.

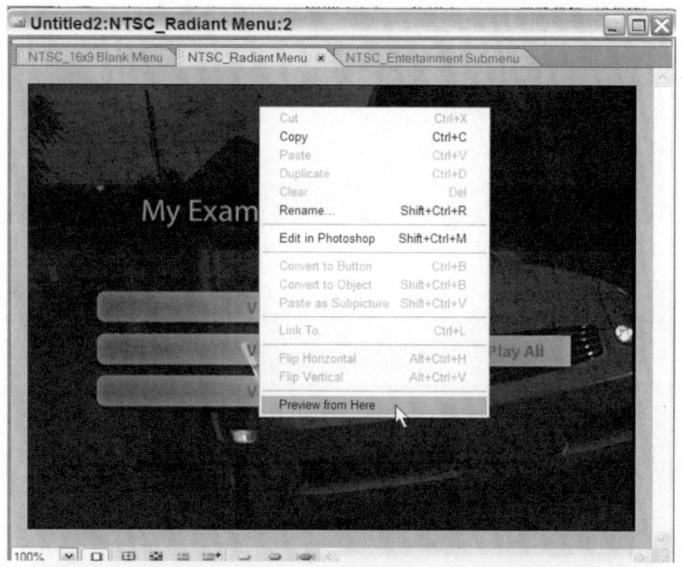

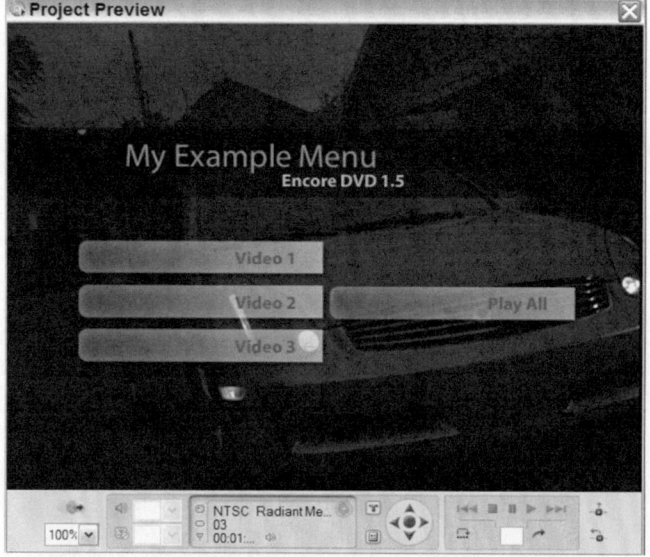

Photoshop users be advised that when a .psd menu is imported into Encore, it analyzes the color scheme used by Photoshop and tries to parse the colors of the =1 =2 =3 layers to DVD compliant subpicture colors. If you change the menu's color set in Encore, then use the Edit in Photoshop feature, the original colors used in the original menu will show up in Photoshop as if nothing had changed. Encore does not care what colors were used in Photoshop once a new color set is applied, nor will it update the colors when imported back into Photoshop. In other words, the colors of the =1 =2 =3 layers are irrelevant, only the color set in Encore matters.

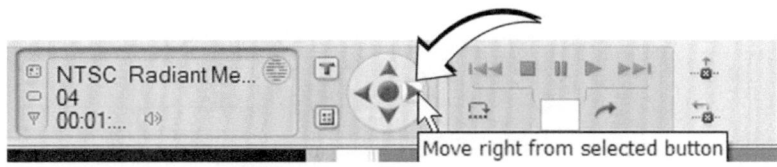

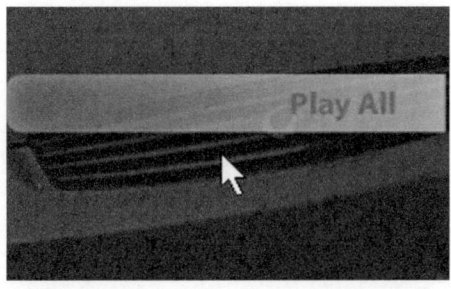

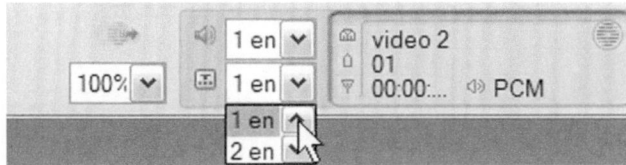

There are a few controls on the Preview Window that are easily recognizable such as the directional keypad simulating the DVD player remote control, the T button for the Title Button, and the M button for the Menu Button.

The available audio tracks and subtitle tracks can be changed, but more importantly as you navigate the menu you can see how your subtitle and audio submenu buttons change the DVD's settings.

Let's say you have your menu set to loop 1024 times, or your timeline is a little longer than you want to wait just to see the end action. Encore's Preview Window allows you to execute the End Action of whatever is being previewed. However if your menu is set to Loop Forever or Hold Forever, this option will not work.

Just about everyone who has set up motion thumbnails or background video of a menu, will come to the Preview Window and see "motionless" motion menu. Chances are you did everything right, but Encore needs to render the menu. In the main display panel, a red disk will appear if the preview needs to be rendered.

Simply press the Render Icon and Encore will render the preview, this could take a few minutes if the clip is rather long, or you have video thumbnails and a video background.

Rule of thumb: If Encore needs to adjust the video in any way, it will need to be rendered.

If graphics are in a menu with a video background, Encore needs to create a new background video stream with the graphics as part of the frames.

If the source video is AVI, it needs to be compressed to MPEG-2. Nine times out of ten, the preview must be rendered.

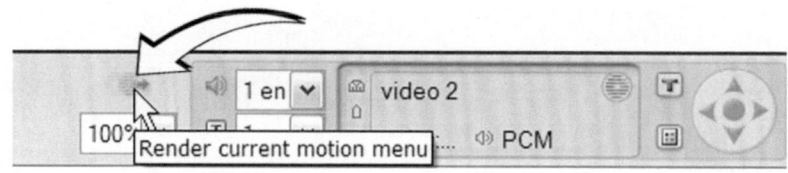

If your video thumbnails still won't work, chances are you didn't check the Animate Buttons box in the menu's Properties Palette.

You will notice a slight glitch or hang between menus and timelines. Don't worry this will not transfer to the final disc.

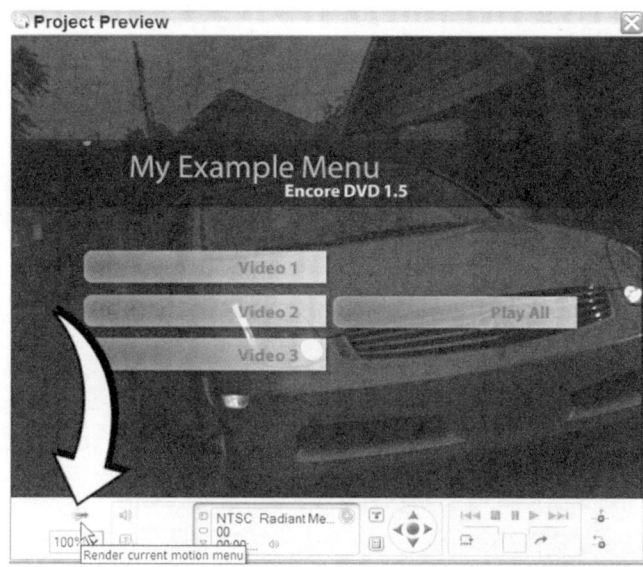

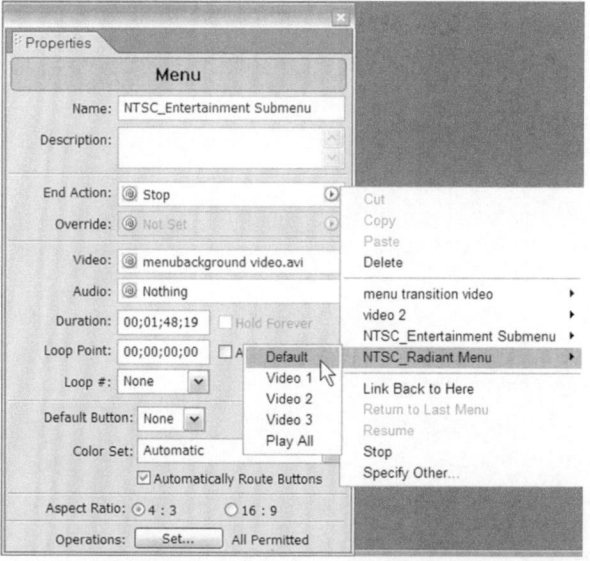

Set the End Action of a Menu

Setting the end action of a menu is not always necessary but is a convenient feature for presentation DVDs in a public setting. You can set a DVD menu to automatically play a movie or return to a specific menu if no buttons are pressed for a certain length of time. However, this option is not possible if the menu is set to Loop Forever or Hold Forever.

Note: Encore still makes having an end action available even though it is not possible in the Forever situations. You must set a duration for a still menu and uncheck Hold Forever. For looped menus, select a number of loops instead of Loop Forever.

To set an End Action for a menu:

Select the menu and open the Properties Palette.

In the End Action field, click the arrow and select the End Action destination from the list.

Sometimes the quick lists of items in the Link To, Override, and End Action Fields are missing certain timelines and menus. This is because Encore keeps a list of the 20 most recently used items. If you have not linked to this timeline or menu before, it will not show up in this list.

If the destination is not displayed on the list

Use the Pickwhip to link the End Action to an item that is in view.

Or use the Specify Other option in the drop down list.

Select the end action in the Specify Other Dialog and click OK.

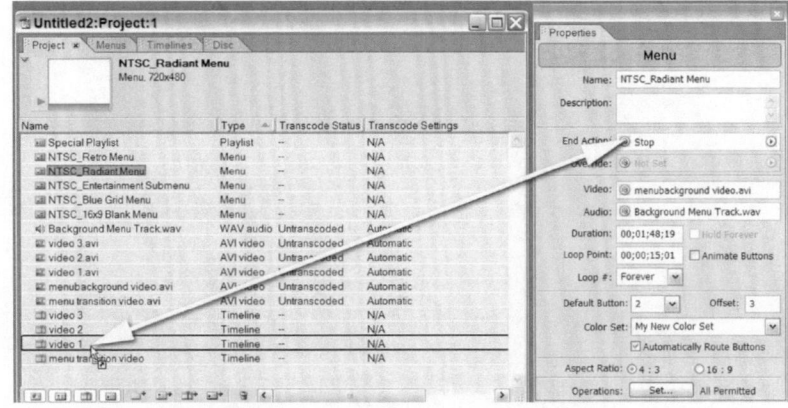

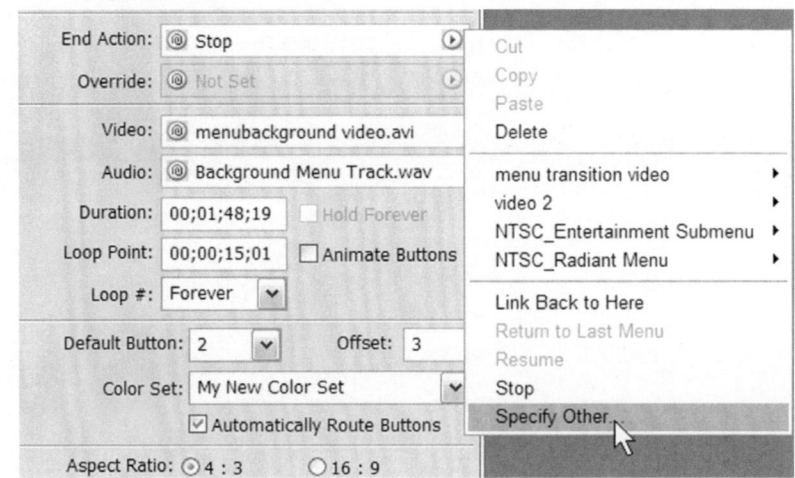

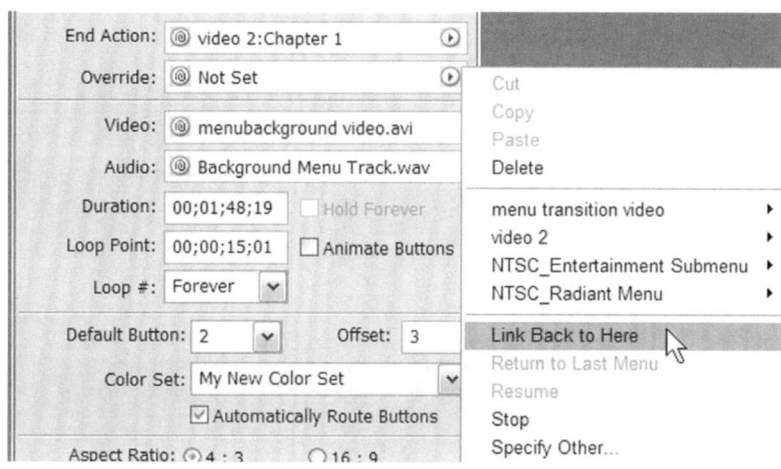

Set the Menu Override

Menu Override, like Menu End Action is not required by the menu. However, in order to use Override, the Menu End Action must be set. This Override allows more control over what happens when the DVD is left alone for a long period of time. You could set the menu to go to a feature timeline, then return to the stinger clip or introductory video instead of going straight back to the main menu.

To Set Menu Override:

Select the Menu, and Open the Properties Palette

In the Override Field click the Arrow to open the list of options.

If the item you want to override to is in the list, select it.

If not, go to Specify Other and use the Dialog to set the override.

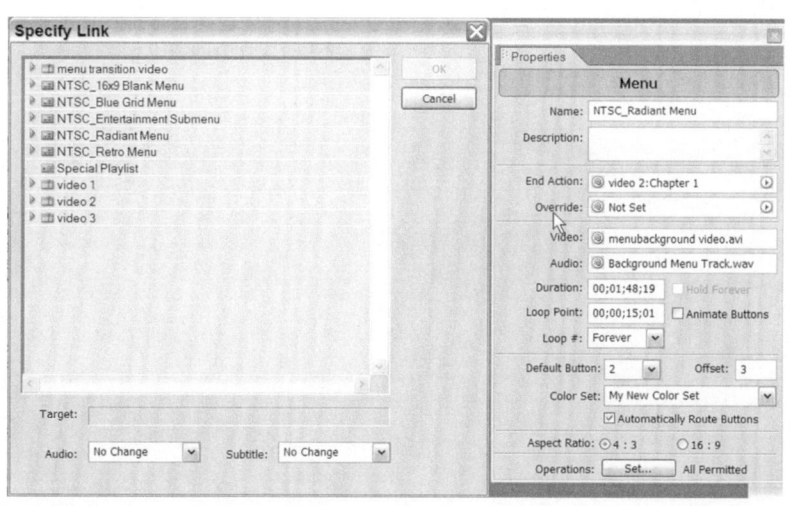

Chapter 8

Burn Baby Burn!

Burning the Project to Disk

Once the menus are built, the timelines are asssembled and everything is linked together, it's time to tie up all the loose ends. This can include adding DVD ROM content for use on a computer or setting up copy protection and region codes.

At this point you can save yourself a few dollars in blank DVDs and or a few hundred dollars in duplication costs by checking and rechecking your disc. Just because it works on your computer doesn't mean it will work on all set top players. And one seemingly insignificant detail can ruin the entire project.

Use the Disc Tab to Name a Disc

When you started your new project, the project name became the disc name. If you didn't give your project a name, and you burned the disc, the disc volume would be named Untitled. Not the best name for a disc. Check the Disc Tab to see if the name is suitable for the disc.

To Name a Disc:

In the Project Window, click on the Disc Tab

Click in the top field next to the disc

Enter a name for the disc

Now when the disc is inserted into computer that can read volume labels this will be the name displayed.

Set the First Play of a Disc (Intro Video or Menu)

By default the first menu or timeline created or imported into Encore is set as the First Play. This means when the DVD is inserted into a player this menu or timeline is played first. But don't rely on this! During the course of

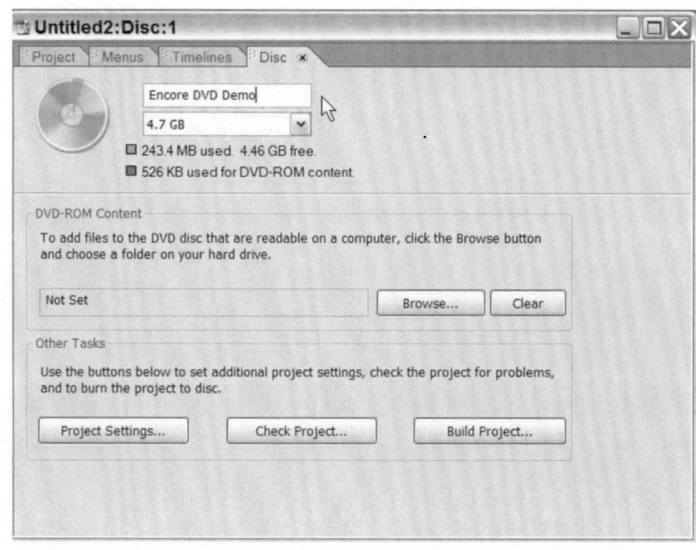

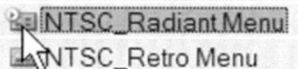

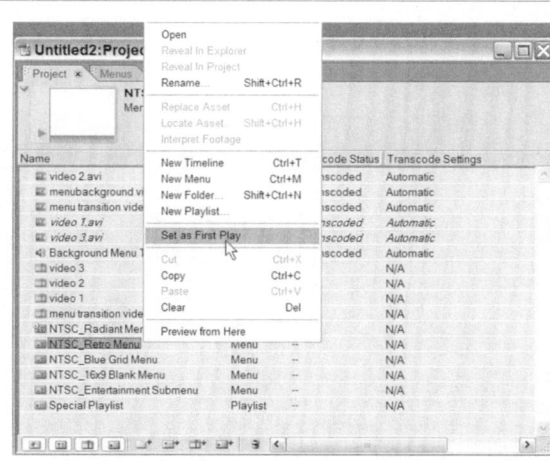

a project First Play might accidentally be assigned to a different timeline or menu. If the related timeline is deleted, the first play is not re-assigned. In this case, when the disc is inserted, nothing will happen. The disc will await instructions from the viewer.

To Set the First Play of a Disc:

In the Project Tab, right click on the Menu or Timeline that should be set as First Play

Select Set as First Play

Now when the disc is inserted, this menu or timeline will begin playing.

Add DVD-ROM Content to a Disc

A good number of people enjoy watching DVDs on their computers, and they have the advantage of viewing or using DVD ROM content. Among other things, DVD-ROM content can include PC software, sample files, screensavers, and any extra content related to the DVD. For instance, if the disc is a software training DVD, you might include an executable file and content for the software being trained on in the DVD.

First, organize all the DVD-ROM content you wish to use into one folder. Encore allows you to use one master folder for DVD ROM content.

Make sure your anti-virus software is up to date and that you scan the DVD ROM files throughly before adding the content to the DVD Folder. Once the media has been cleared, it's a good idea to disable the anti-virus software during the disk burn.

To add DVD-ROM Content to a project:

In the Disc Tab, Go to the DVD-ROM Content Section

Click Browse

Locate and Select the folder from your hard drive.

Click Ok

The file folder is now set. When the disc is built, these files will be included in the DVD Volume and will be accessible to computer users.

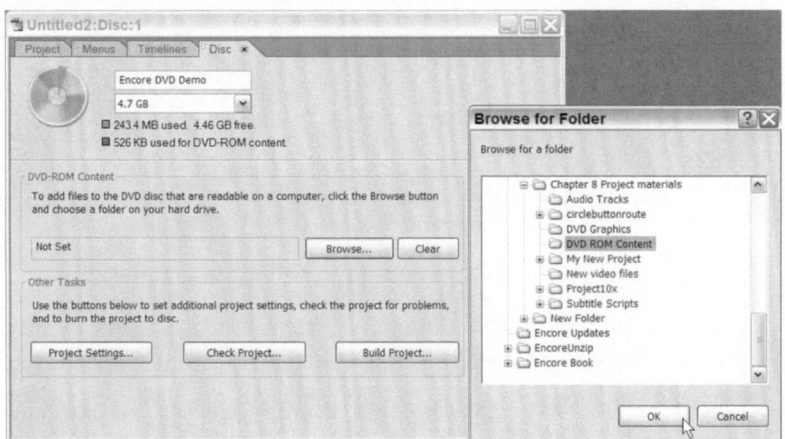

Check Links/Check Project

Nothing is worse than getting your DVD back from the replication house, popping it into your DVD player and finding one button or menu that just doesn't link. Every project should be double and triple checked on several different players to insure that the

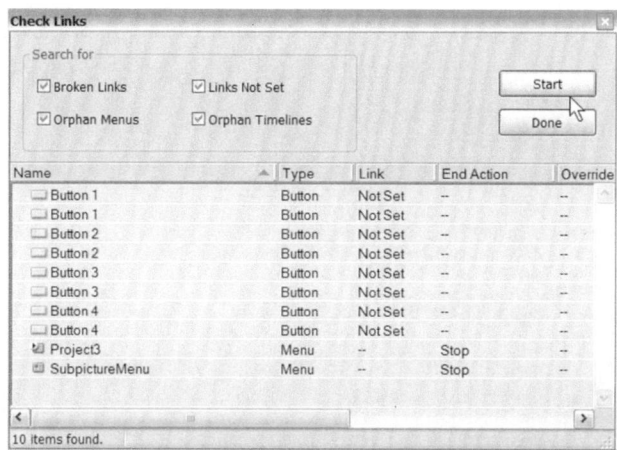

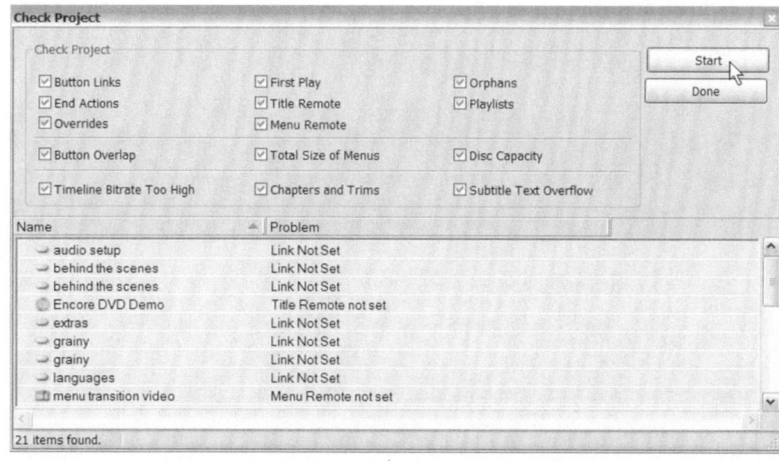

master copy is problem free.

Encore's Check Links feature scans the project and looks for:

Orphaned Buttons: Buttons that can't be navigated to..

Orphaned Menus: Menus that can't be navigated to..

Broken Links: Buttons that don't link to anything.

Orphaned Timelines: Timelines that have not been linked to.

Encore allows you to customize the search so you can look for just one or all of these snags

In Encore 1.5 the Check Links feature is now the Check Project feature. It has been expanded to include:

Overrides: Override property links that are not set or broken.

First Play: Whether the project's First Play property is not set.

Title/Menu Remote: Whether the project's Title/Menu Remote properties are not set.

Playlists: Playlists with broken or missing end actions, or empty playlists.

Button Overlap: Buttons whose overlap that may lead to browsing errors.

Total Size of Menus: Checks the size of all menus and warns if it exceeds the DVD limit of 1 GB.

Disc Capacity: Warns if project size is larger than the chosen disk media.

Timeline Bitrate too high: Bitrates that exceed the DVD-legal limit of 9 Mbps.

Chapters and Trims: Timelines in which chapter and trim locations were adjusted due to transcoding.

Subtitle Text Overflow: Subtitle text that is off screen because it has overflowed the text boundary.

Even the more organized DVD Authors accidentally drop a link from time to time. Always check your links to be sure they are correct.

To scan for broken or orphaned content:

Go to the Disc Tab in the Project Window

Click on Check Links

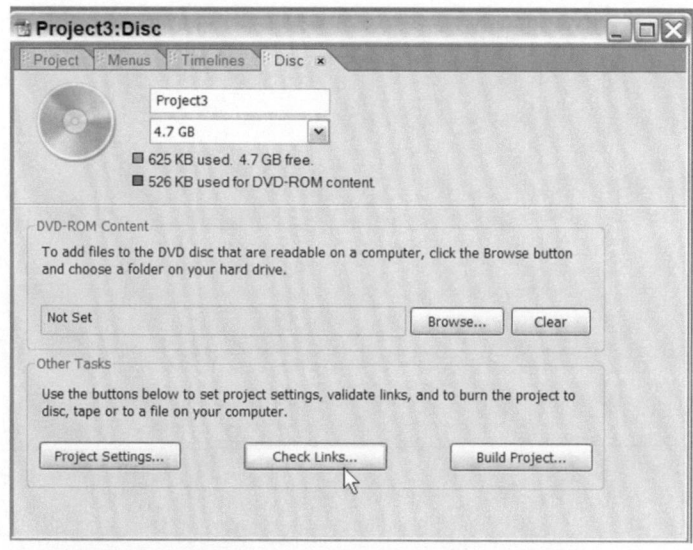

Check the boxes for the type of broken content you'd like to search for.

Click Start.

When the search is complete, the dialog will display all the content that displays troublesome navigation. You can click on the item in the window, and the appropriate window will open to allow you to fix the problem.

What's it Gonna Look Like? Preview an Entire Disc

Encore allows you to preview an entire disc before it is burned. This function uses the Preview Window to read the project like a disc. Instead of reading the particular timeline or menu in the window, the Preview command will read the project from first play. (Read Use the Preview Window in the previous chapter for more information.)

To preview an entire project:

With the project open, Go to File>Preview

Check every link and every asset to assure that all the menus work and all the timelines are displayed properly.

Menus and Timelines without end actions will show up. Sometimes you might want a timeline to stop playing, but Encore assumes you want all of your end actions to link to something else. If you didn't want an end action for a Timeline or Menu, then just ignore the report.

Encore 1.5: Encore now allows you to ignore any problems and build the disc anyway. This is not recommended unless you are sure the problem is not critical.

Set the Media Size and Type

DVD's come in various media sizes and the way Encore will create the disc is directly related to how much size it has. If a project will fit on a normal single-sided, single layer disc, the default setting is perfect. If you need a bigger disc for the project, then you will need to provide Encore with the media size you intend to use.

To set media size:

In the Project Window, open the Disc Tab

Click on Project Settings

In the field at the top, select the appropriate media size of the final disc

Choose One or Two Sided

If your project uses dual-layered, dual sided discs, then you must create four projects, one for each layer on the disc. Encore will set the layer break point at an appropriate chapter point. Remember, dual layered or dual sided discs cannot be burned, they must be stamped.

Once you have selected the appropri-

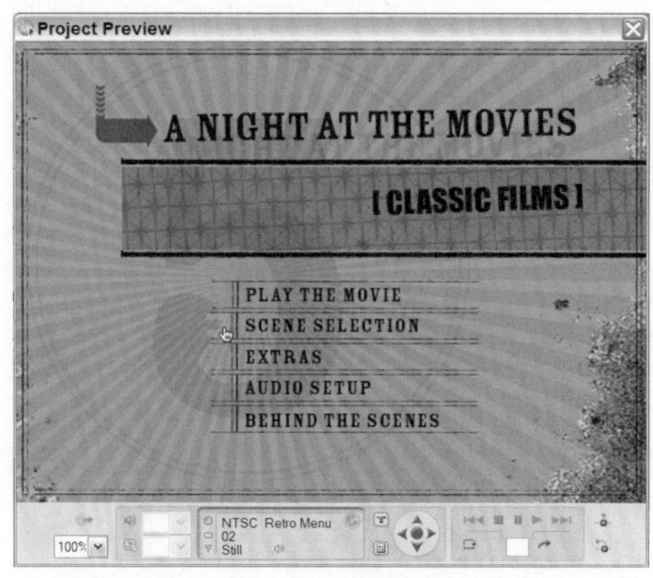

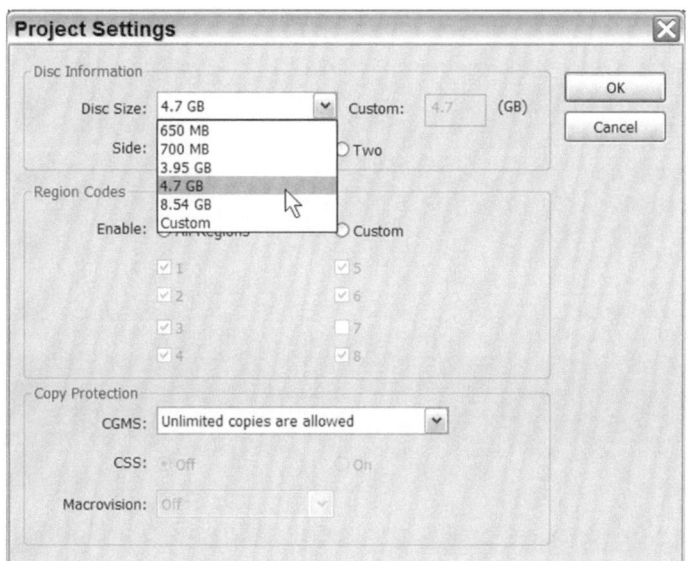

ate media, Encore will base its trans-coding and file structure for the size of the project.

Set Region Codes

Most professionaly produced DVD titles display a region code on the packaging of the disc. This region code specifies in which country the DVD can be played. DVD players are region specific and will only play DVDs coded for their region. This is a first level of copy protection, limiting the global distribution/piracy in other countries. This doesn't guarantee that DVD's cannot be played in another country but it does indeed help. Region coding only works for replicated discs, so discs burned on your DVD burner won't demonstrate this safety process.

1: U.S., Canada, U.S. Territories
2: Japan, Europe, South Africa, and Middle East (including Egypt)
3: Southeast Asia and East Asia (including Hong Kong)
4: Australia, New Zealand, Pacific Islands, Central America, Mexico, South America, and the Caribbean
5: Eastern Europe (Former Soviet

Encore provides a setting that allows a 600 - 700 megabyte project to be burned on a SVCD. The SVCD disc will function similar to a DVD but should only be used for very small projects. These SVCD's work best when played back in a computer and should not be relied upon for reliable set-top playback

Union), Indian subcontinent, Africa, North Korea, and Mongolia
6: China
7: Reserved
8: Special international venues (airplanes, cruise ships, etc.)}

By default, Encore specifies that the disc will play in all regions. Only adjust these settings if you have a need to specify region coding.

To set the Region Code of a project:

In the Project Window, go to the Disc Tab

Click on Project Settings

This opens the Project Settings Dialog. Here you can customize the region codes so discs can play in just one region, or perhaps in all but one region.

Click on Custom in the Enable row

Check all the desired regions, and uncheck the regions you wish to "block."

Once all the required regions are selected, click OK

Now when the disc is produced in a replication/stamping house, the disc

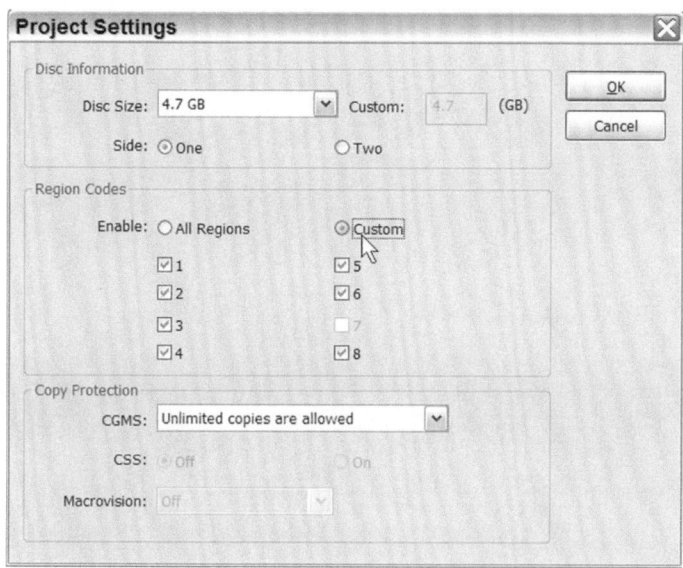

will only play in those regions specified.

Specify Copy Protection

In the quest to stop DVD piracy, multiple copy protection schemes have been invented. In reality no disc is safe from piracy. A determined "pirate" can circumvent all of these protections. Regardless, copy protection is still a deterrent and whether it is worth the extra time and expense will vary depending on many factors.

Copy Generation Management System(CGMS): A system that can allow the user to create a specified number of copies of the disc. A single copy can be created that cannot be duplicated as well. You can set it so that no copies can be made from this disc, or so that copies can be made only from this disc. Unlimited copying can also be enabled.

Content Scrambling System or CSS: Basically an encrypted code written onto a disc that prevents the DVD from functioning in a Non CSS compliant device. CSS compliant companies do not manufacture players that allow

If you do not want this disc to play in the United States or Canada you must first select another region then uncheck the region 1 box.

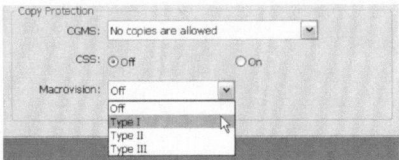

the copying of Video DVD content, and support the technology that makes it harder to copy from the device.

Note: Copy protection does not work for discs that will be burned by the computer. These forms of copy protection are only available on stamped or professionally replicated DVDs. A DLT is currently required for utilization of the CSS and Macrovision protection schemes.

Macrovision: Embeds a signal also known as a "flag" into the video and audio stream that interferes with the copying of a DVD to certain devices such as a VCR.

To set copy protection:

In the Project Window, select the Disc Tab

Click on Project Settings

Select all or none of the copy protection features available.

Click OK

Using any of the above copy-protection schemes requires a license from Macrovision. The replicator will report the number of discs replicated containing the protection flags to Macrovision, and Macrovision will bill the author/content owner for the licensing. A Macrovision license is required before the replicator is allowed to deliver the discs to the content owner. See www.macrovision.com for more information.

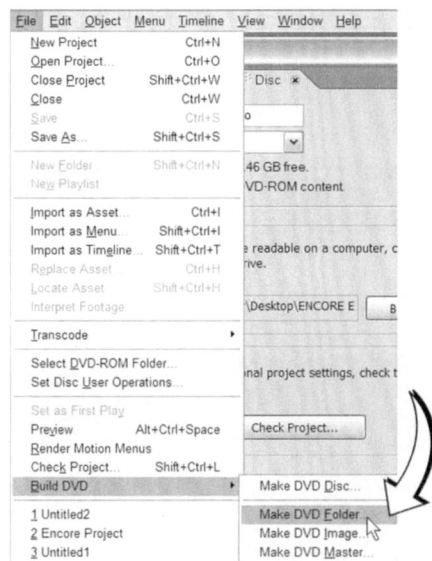

Write to the Hard Drive/ DVD Folder

At times it is best to write your DVD to the hard disc to give the project a final check in a different application (see sidebar.) By doing this, you create a DVD volume on your drive that can only be read by a computer.

To build a disc to the hard drive:

Go to File > Build DVD > Make DVD Folder

A dialogue will open providing options to save the project.

Click Save.

Encore 1.5 tip: 1.5 will allow you to save the project under a different file name when building a project. Click Save As and choose a new filename.

If there are any errors or playblack issues, Encore will give you a warning stating just that. You may view these errors or ignore them and continue. It is highly recommened that you view and fix these errors.

Now that the project is saved and all errors are fixed or accounted for, it is time to select the folder in which you wish to save the DVD information.

Choose a destination of the DVD folder and click Next

The Make DVD Folder Summary Dialog will appear and will await your command to build. Check the information in the summary.

Click Build

As the DVD is built to your hard disc it will show the progress towards the bottom of the dialogue box.

Preview a Disc with an External Software DVD Player

Many new DVD authors go through stacks of blank DVD's and hours of wasted time checking their projects by burning. This can be avoided by using the Preview option in Encore.

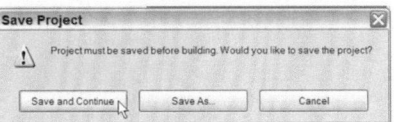

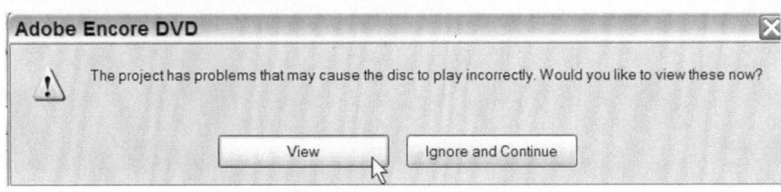

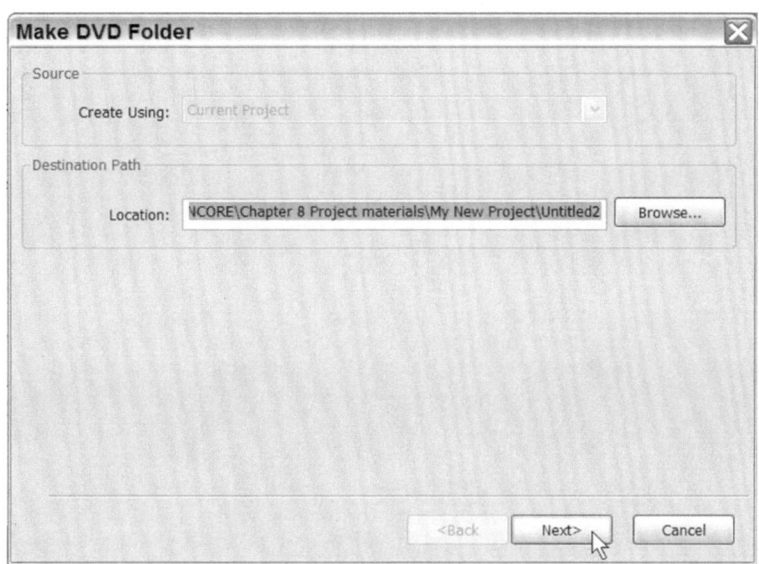

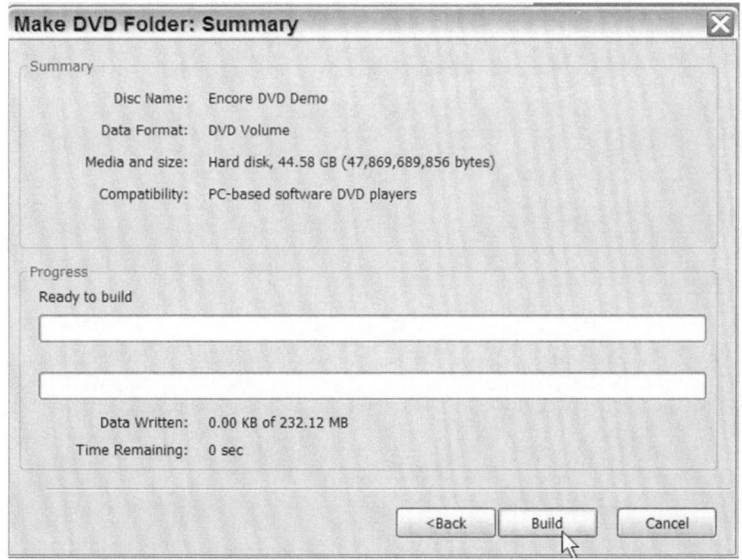

Encore's preview window is a great tool, however a slight lag or pause between menus and timelines doesn't give you an accurate feel for how the final disc will behave.

Encore allows you to write a DVD folder, or create an ISO disc image. If you have a software DVD player (WinDVD 5, for example) you can load the folder into the DVD player software and the player will treat the file as it would a DVD disc. (Check your DVD player software for instructions.)

When previewing the disc in the external DVD player application, make sure you are not running any other high priorty or video intensive applications. You want your DVD software to have almost full control over the hard drive and video card. This will give you an accurate playback.

Many software players are available that offer various capabilities including the ability to read DVD folders and/or disc images.

Make a DVD Image/ISO

Similar to a DVD folder, a disc image can be created on a hard drive. Once an image is created, it's ready to be burned to disc. Images are great because they work in many software DVD players and provide flawless playback and preview. They are also effective for archival and testing purposes.

To build a DVD disc image to the hard drive:

Go to File > Build DVD > Make DVD Image

Encore will need you to save the current project and a dialog will instruct you and let you save.

Click Save

If there are any errors or playblack issues, Encore will give you a warning stating just that. You may view these errors or ignore them and continue. It is highly recommened that you view and fix those errors.

Choose a destination of the DVD image and click Next

The Make DVD Image Summary Dialog will appear and will await your command to build. Check the information in the summary..

Click Build

As the DVD disc image is built to your hard disc it will show the progress at

**Encore 1.5 tip:
Now Encore will
allow you to save
the project under a
different file name
when building a
project. Click Save
As and choose a
new filename.**

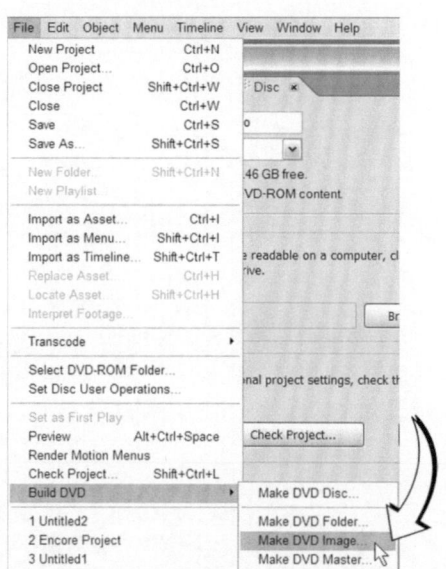

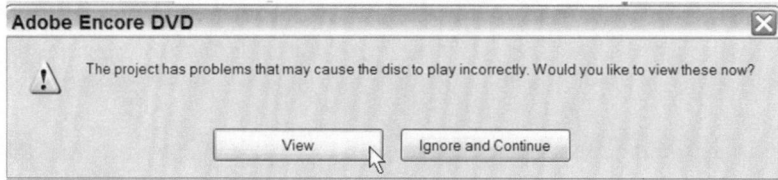

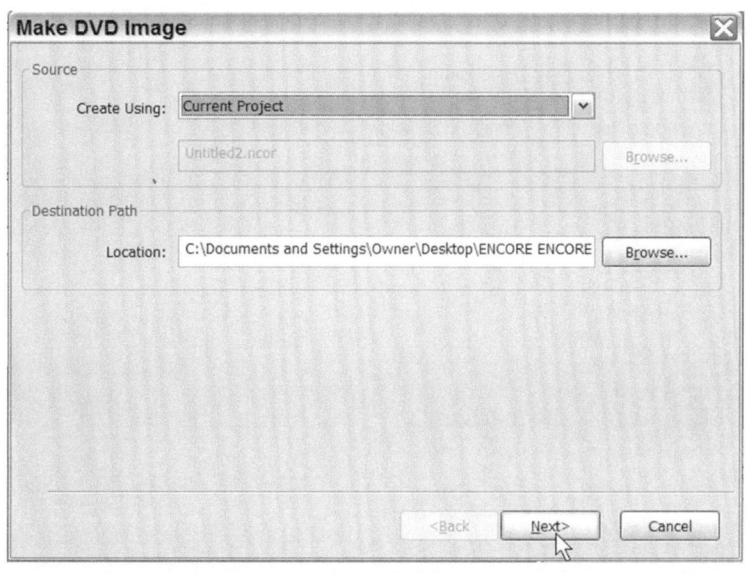

the bottom.

Make a DVD Master/Export to DLT

If you're planning to have your DVD replicated, then you must create a DVD Master. A DLT DVD Master is a versions of the DVD that replication houses use for stamping DVDs. Unlike burned DVD's, a DLT master may include codes for copy protection, region codes and/ or other advanced DVD features. DLT is a magnetic tape system, providing solid reliability and impressive data fidelity.

If you have a DLT tape drive Encore will recognize it when creating the DVD Master.

To export a Master:

Burnable DVD (DVDR) media can be submitted depending on the capabilities of the replication house, however DLT is typically preferable.

Make sure to throughly check your project for errors before writing a Master.

Go to File> Build DVD > Make DVD Master

Encore will need you to save the current project and a dialog will instruct you and let you save.

Encore 1.5 tip: Now Encore will allow you to save the project under a different file name when building a project. Click Save As and choose a new filename.

Click Save

If there are any errors or playblack issues, Encore will give you a warning stating just that. You may view these errors or ignore them and continue. It is highly recommened that you view and fix those errors.

Encore will now detect any devices and media that support Mastering. If it cannot detect your device, check your hardware documentation and load the most recent drivers.

Click Next.

Encore will check to see if the device and media are ready to build the project on to DLT. Once the check is complete a new dialog will open and give the specifics of the build and the progress.

Click Build.

Encore will now build and export the project to the Master tape.

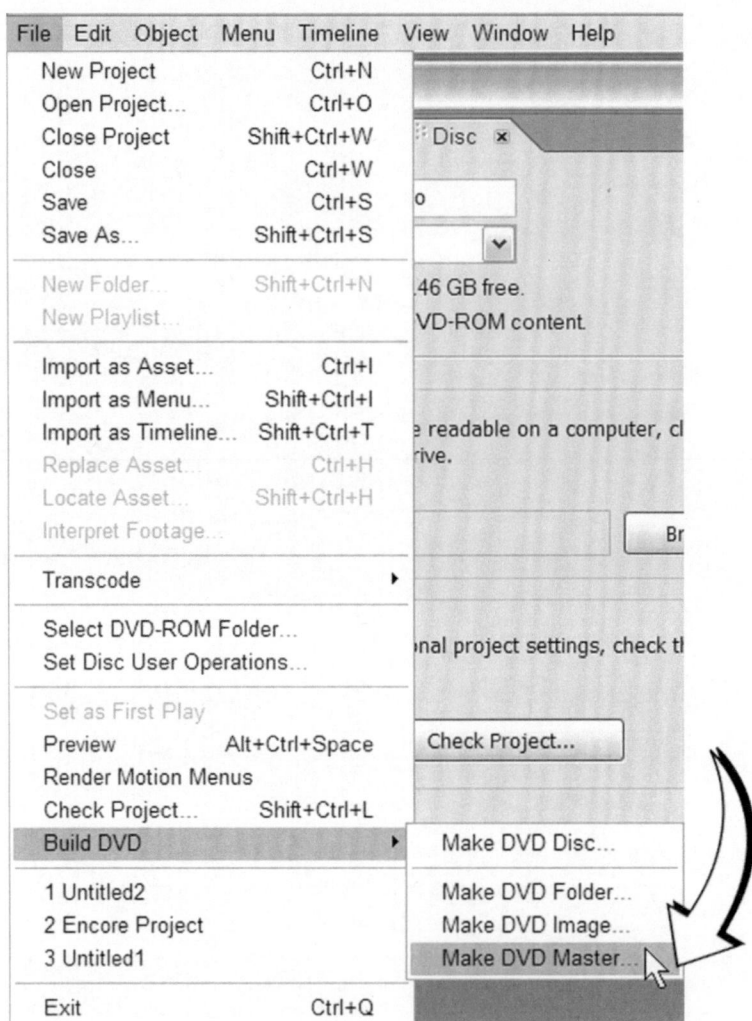

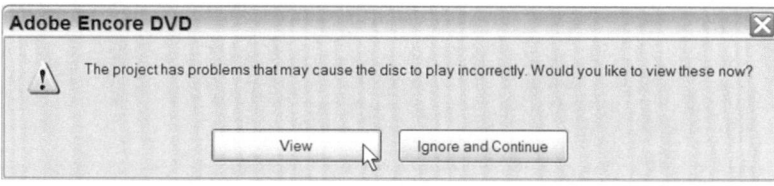

Burn to Disc

The majority of Encore users will likely burn their DVD's to a DVD disc. If the project is small enough, it might fit onto a typical writable CD. In either case you will need blank media in the drive, ready to be burned.

To burn a DVD disc:

Go to File > Build DVD > Make DVD Disc

Encore will need you to save the current project and a dialog will instruct you and let you save.

Click Save

Encore 1.5 tip: Now Encore will allow you to save the project under a different file name when building a project. Click Save As and choose a new filename.

Encore 1.5 tip: You can now choose to bypass all warnings and build the project without interruption. This will allow you to create the disc unattended.

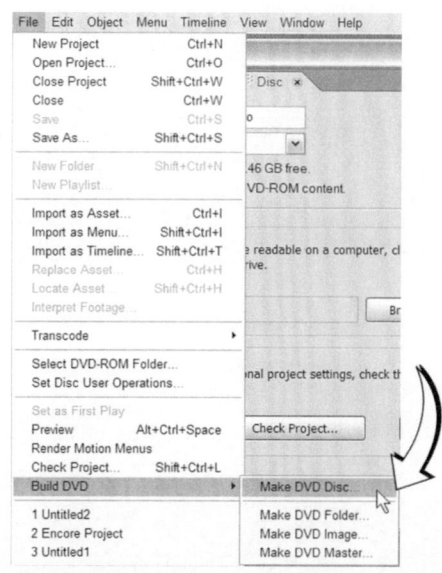

If there are any errors or playblack issues, Encore will give you a warning stating just that. You may view these errors or ignore them and continue. It is highly recommened that you view and fix those errors.

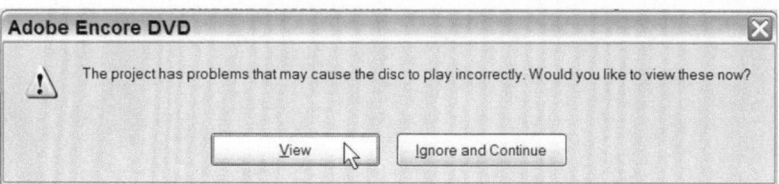

Now that the project is saved and all errors are fixed or accounted for, it is time to select set up the burn. You can chose to write the disc at the speeds indicated or set up the drive to do a test burn before writing the disc.

Choose the write speed and number of copies

The Make DVD Disc Summary Dialog will appear and will await your command to build. Check the information in the summary..

Click Build

As the DVD disc is burned it will show the progress at the bottom.

Check Player Compatibility

Just because a DVD plays in your computer doesn't necessarily mean it will play in every set top player in the world. In fact, recordable media sometimes doesn't play at all in older set top play-

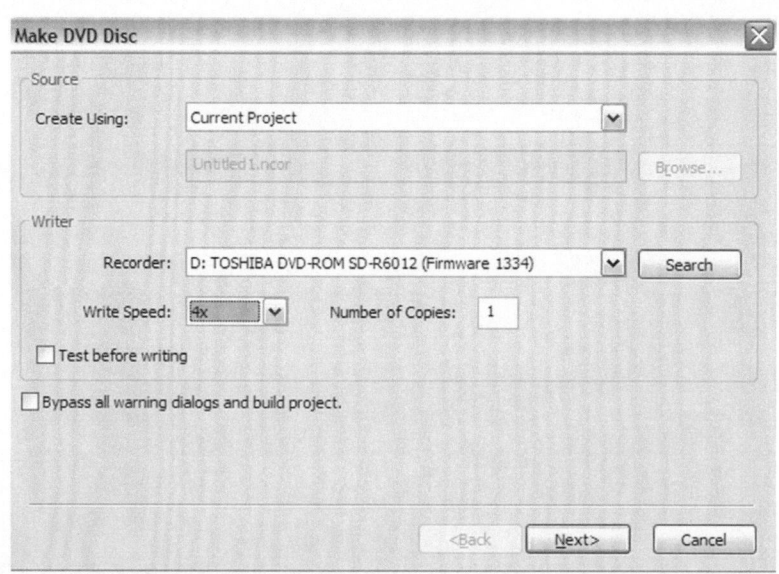

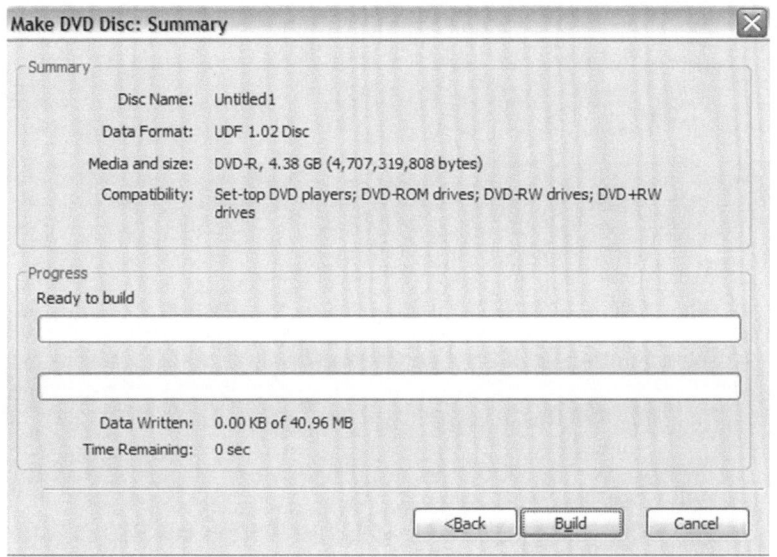

ers. The only way to see if your disc will play in set top players, is to check it in as many players as you can.

If your budget and scope require it, have the DVD replicated by a duplication house. This will all but guarantee that the DVD will be readable in every computer and set top player. It's costly, but if quality and a wide audience is your goal, there isn't a better alternative.

The best advice for assuring best compatability is often the hardest for some to swallow; buy quality recordable media. Spend the extra buck or two on the better DVD-R/DVD+R media. There is a significant difference between the high grade DVD-R/+R recordable media and the cheapest discs available.

While it is cost prohibitive, some authors still try to distribute rewritable DVD media. Not only does this cost a fortune, it's shooting yourself in the foot as far as compatibility. Keep your RW discs for data storage or for burning test projects.

DVD-R vs. DVD+R

There has been a lot of talk involving 2 rival DVD formats, DVD-R and DVD+R. DVD-R was the first blank DVD media recording standard. DVD+R was introduced later and is marketed as a better solution.

So which is better? Of course both sides say their format is superior, but from a DVD Author's standpoint it is comparing apples to apples. They perform comparably in terms of speed and reliability. For now, at least, there is no clear winner. DVD-R seems to have a slight compatibility advantage when it comes to older players. DVD+R appears to be technically superior and should eventually establish itself as a superior format.

Most importantly, make sure you choose the proper media format for your particular burner. If you use a DVD-R burner, then you should use DVD-R recordable media, and vice versa if you use a DVD+R burner. If you have a combo drive that can write both DVD-R/DVD+R then you have nothing to worry about.

Glossary

Some of these audio terms are relevant to Encore directly and other terms are related to the audio and video industry in general. Some of the terms are "new" language adapted from the analog world from which many features of Encore, Premiere, After Effects, and Photoshop are derived.

A/D Converter-Analog to Digital Converter Many A/Ds are also D/As, which convert digital back to analog for monitoring.

AC-3 Dolby's Audio Compression scheme, 3rd generation. Both stereo and 5.1 surround format files may be encoded to AC-3. Encore only supports the encoding of stereo audio, and import of 5.1 AC-3 files.

ACM Audio Compression Manager, developed by Microsoft as the standard interface for signal processing of audio data in the Windows environment, particularly geared towards the WAV file format. Some tools allow custom ACM processes.

ADC Another name for analog-to-digital converter.

AIFF Audio Interchange File Format. Can be used for storing audio in high- or low-resolution formats and sharing them between computer systems.

Aliasing The undesirable jagged or stair-stepped appearance of unfiltered angled lines in an image, graphic, or text.

In video, aliasing also refers to the visual-beating effect caused by sampling frequencies of an image being too low to reproduce correctly. Different video aliasing effects include raster scan aliasing (e.g., when sharp horizontal lines cause a flickering effect) and temporal aliasing (e.g., when wheel spokes appear to reverse direction). Contrast with antialiasing.

Alpha Channel The fourth channel of a 32-bit RGB image that contains transparency in the image. The other three channels are red, green, and blue.

Amplitude The height of a waveform measured from the middle, where silence would be indicated. If no waveform is drawn, then the audio section is silent; the measurement from center to the highest point in the graphical drawing is the value of the amplitude.

Acoustic amplitude is measured in decibels (dB) (see *decibels*). The louder the signal, the higher the amplitude, regardless of the measurement format (peak, RMS, Instant, etc.).

Anchor Point A bitstream location that serves as a random point. An example is a MPEG I-frame.

Antialiasing The manipulation of edges (i.e., those between areas with contrasting colors) in an image, graphic, or text to make the edges appear smoother. Antialiased edges appear blurred up close, but they smooth out at average viewing

distance. Antialiasing is critical when working with high-quality graphics for television display use. Opposite of *aliasing*.

Artifact Distortion to a picture or a sound signal. With digital video, artifacts can result from overloading the input device with too much signal or from excessive or improper compression.

Aspect Ratio Ratio of width to height in dimensions of an image. For example, the frame aspect ratio of NTSC video is 4:3, whereas widescreen frame sizes use the more elongated aspect ratio of 16:9 or 1.85.1.

Asset Any digital file that is part of the library or project is considered an asset.

Audition Adobe's new audio editing product.

ATSC Advanced Television Systems Committee determines voluntary technical standards of acquiring, authoring, distribution, and reception of high-definition television.

AVI Abbreviation for Audio-Video Interleaved; the format/ scheme created by Microsoft for synchronizing and compressing

analog audio and video signals. AVI is also the file format used by Video for Windows.

Attenuate An analog term, referring to decreasing the audio level. Usually described in decibels.

Audio File Audio stored in any digital format is an audio file. Not to be confused with audiophile, an audio affecionado.

B-frame In interframe compression schemes (e.g., MPEG), a highly compressed, bidirectional frame that records the change that occurred between the I-frame before and after it. B-frames enable MPEG-compressed video to be played in reverse. Contrast with I-frame and P-frame.

Balance The difference in level or apparent loudness between Right and Left in a stereo audio signal. See *Panning* for additional information.

Balanced Cable A cable that contains two conductors carrying audio, plus a shield for the ground that carries no audio. Professional mic cables are always balanced.

Bandwidth The range of frequencies in an audio file, EQ, or other signal or device that passes a signal. This term also refers to the datarate of a streaming file.

Bass Low frequencies in the overall spectrum of sound. Bass is approximated in the 0–300 Hz region of the frequency spectrum.

Bed Background music or sound effect laid under a voice over. Typical term in television and radio.

Bitmap A graphic image comprised of individual pixels, each of which has a value that define its relative brightness and color

Bit-Depth The number of bits in a sample. The greater the number of bits, the greater the resolution of the audio file, and therefore the more accurate the digital file will reproduce the original audio image.

Boost Raising the volume of an audio signal.

Brickwall When digital audio hits the 0dB threshold, bits are truncated and lost. This is known as "hitting the brickwall" because you can't recover the lost bits. Digital form of distortion.

Bright Descriptive term to describe high frequencies. If a sound is bright, then it contains a number of high frequencies. If the sound is not bright, it may

be considered dull (with few high frequencies). Sibilance is typically fairly bright, allowing breath and Ss, Ps, Ts, Ps, and other sibilant sounds to be heard.

Bumper Stock audio identifying the television, radio, or cable station, or perhaps designating a corporate audio ident, such as the famous Intel sound.

Capturing Refers to capturing source video for use on a computer. If analog, the captured video is converted to digital.

Channel Each component color that defines a computer graphic image—red, green, and blue—is carried in a separate channel, so each may be adjusted independently. Channels may also be added to a computer graphic file to define masks.

Chapter A new segment of an existing work, as the work is broken up into subject or scene specific sections. Chapter points are generated in the Encore Timeline.

Chorus (FX) A series of short, modulated delays with slight shifts in pitch to create the effect of multiple voices, stemming from

one voice. This effect allows a solo instrument to have the sound of an ensemble due to the slight differences in timing and pitch.

Clip A digitized or captured portion of video.

Clipping Distortion, given its name from when audio is "clipped off" after exceeding maximum levels. Can be caused at input, output, or processing stages. In the digital realm, clipping becomes brickwalling. Also: The cropping of peaks (overmodulation) of the white or the black portions of a video signal.

Codec Contraction of compression/decompression algorithm; used to encode and decode data such as sound and video files. Common codecs include those that convert analog video signals to compressed digital video files (e.g., MPEG), or that convert analog sound signals into digital sound files such as Windows WMA file format.

Compress (dynamic range) To reduce the amount of dynamic range of an audio signal, making the overall output more consistent. A compressor acts like an automated fader, bringing loud portions of an audio signal to a more quiet point, and raising the level of quiet sections to match louder transient peaks.

Compress (file size) Resampling, reducing a file size for streaming or sharing over the internet or intranet. Usually a lossy process, causing some loss of audio quality. REAL Media, MPEG, MJPEG, and Microsoft WMV/WMA are all examples of compressed media. Use Apple's Compressor to compress media.

Copyright Just as the word implies, the right to copy. Any composition is copyrighted when it's completed. No one has the right to copy the composition, video, or other art forms without the permission of the author of the work.

CTI Current Time Indicator.

Cue A specific piece of music composed to play at a specific moment in time. The moment the composition is to play is called a Cue Point. A list of Cue Points is called a Cue List, generally determined in the Spotting Session (see *Spotting*).

Cue also refers to set up a piece of media (audio or video) to play at a specific trigger, such as a DJ cueing up music or video to play at the press of a button.

Cut To remove, delete a section from a digital event. Also refers to a composition, typically in album form, with the composition being a "cut" of an overall album. Also refers to reducing frequencies in an equalizer, as in "cutting the bass" from a mix, meaning to reduce the amount of bass in a mix.

Cutoff Frequency The frequency that audio is deeply attenuated or reduced. Low-pass and high-pass filters both center around a cutoff frequency. The higher the cutoff, the less original audio is allowed to be heard.

DAW Digital Audio Workstation.

Decibel (dB) A device of measurement. Describes electrical power referenced to 1 milliwatt. So 0dBm is equal to 1 milliwatt, or 1m. dB may refer to dBu, dBv, dBm. To a listener, audio must be 6dB louder to appear to be twice as loud, while electronically, only 3dB of voltage difference are required for the same result. This is why a 200 -watt amplifier is not twice as loud as a 100-watt amplifier.

Deinterlace The process of removing artifacts that result from the nature of two-fields-per-frame (interlaced) video.

Destructive/Nondestructive Destructive editing alters the original file, and cannot be recovered. In the DAW and NLE worlds, destructive editing is often used to save disk space. With the cost of hard drives coming down, destructive editing is less prevalent than it was not long ago. Nondestructive editing does not affect the original file, regardless of what processes are applied.

Digitize Converting analog to digital audio or video. The moment analog information is stored on a hard drive by whatever means it arrives there, it becomes digitized.

Distortion See *clipping.* The point at which audio no longer maintains its original integrity, intentionally or not. Audio that exceeds physical or electronic limitations becomes distorted. Also used as an effect, particularly on guitars, violins, and other stringed instruments.

Dolby/Dolby Labs Founded in 1965, Dolby Laboratories is known for the technologies it has developed for improving audio sound recording and reproduction including their noise reduction systems (e.g., Dolby A, B, and C), Dolby Digital (AC-3).

Dull Opposite of bright. Sound that is dull lacks high frequencies. May be perceived as unexciting.

DV/DV25 Digital Video. The most common form of DV compression. DV25 uses a data rate of 25 megabits per second or 3.6 megabytes per second.

DVD Digital Versatile Disc, used for storing images, data, audio, and system backups. The standard for MPEG storage and display of moving images.

Dynamic Range The difference between loud and quiet passages in an audio performance. Sometimes referred to in terms of how loud audio is permitted to go without distortion or how quiet audio may go before noise is heard.

Dynamics Varying levels of amplitude that audio demonstrates throughout the project.

EDL Edit Decision List.

Effects (FX) Signal processors are referred to as effects, or FX. Reverbs, choruses, delays, phasers, and flangers are all referred to as FX.

End Action An instruction given to a playlist or video file, indicating what the DVD player should do following the end of a video's play. An end action might instruct the DVD to play the next video on the disc, return to a menu, or simply stop.

Envelope A graphic display of a volume, pan, or FX control, allowing automated control over the behavior of specific parameters in the mixing of sounds. Also referred to as the acoustical contour of a sound, its attack, decay, sustain, and release (ADSR)

.

Envelope Point A handle or node inserted on an envelope in Premiere or Audition, used to control various parameters of volume, pan, and automated FX functions.

Equalizer (EQ) A plugin that allows specific frequencies to be manipulated and controlled. Bass, midrange, treble frequencies are all broken down into specific bands and are controllable via sliders or dials, to cut or boost specific frequencies. This is one of the most important tools found in any DAW or NLE tool, as it allows specific contouring and shaping of audio events to help it fit more easily with other audio events.

Export Sending media from one application to another, such as exchanging audio from Audition to Premiere or Encore is an export process. See *Import*.

Fps Abbreviation for frames per second; the standard for measuring the rate of video playback speed. A rate of 30 fps is considered real-time speed and a rate of 24 fps is considered animation speed. At 12–15 fps, the human eye can detect individual frames causing video to appear jerky.

Fade A gradual decrease or increase of video or audio. Audio fades from audible to silent, video fades from visible to black. A fade may also be used to transition from one event to another (also called *crossfade*).

Field One complete vertical scan of a picture that has 262.5 lines. A complete television frame comprises two fields; the lines of field 1 are vertically interlaced with those of field 2 for 525 lines of resolution according to the NTSC standard.

FireWire An IEEE1394 high bandwidth/high speed interface created by Apple as an industry standard for file I/O, not limited to, but commonly related to video and audio. Also used as a hard drive interface.

Foley The art of creating ambient sound for film, synchronized with action on the screen. A Foley room used to record audio for film contains various surfaces and equipment to simulate or imitate sounds heard in the field recorded audio for film/video.

Frame Film moves at 24 frames per second, meaning that 24 individual pictures or "frames" are required for each second of film/video. An extracted still image or where the playhead parks in Premiere. is referred to as a frame. NTSC video moves at 29.97 frames per second, and PAL video moves at 25.00 frames per second.

Frequency In audio this refers to how fast a waveform or audio signal repeats itself. Measured in Hertz. Low frequencies are 20–50Hz, midrange frequencies are 250–2,000 Hz or 2KHz, and high frequencies are 2–20KHz.

Gain The amount that a sound is amplified from its original value; the change in its power point. See *Amplitude.*

GOP Group of Pictures.

Hz Abbreviation for Hertz. KiloHertz is abbreviated as KHz, and megahertz is abbreviated with MHz.

I/O Abbreviation for In/Out. Relating to Premiere or Audition, generally referring to hardware used to get audio in or out of a computer. See *AD Converter.*

I-frame In interframe compression schemes (e.g., MPEG), the key frame or reference video frame that acts as a point of comparison to P- and B-frames, and is not rebuilt from another frame. Opposite *B-frame* and *P-frame.*

Import To open a file in an application that originated in another application. Encore can import WAV, AIFF, MOV, and M2V files.

Interframe Compression A compression algorithm, such as MPEG, that reduces the amount of video information by storing only the differences between a frame and those before it.

Intraframe Compression Compression that reduces the amount of video information in each frame on a

frame-by-frame basis. Compare to *Interframe compression.*

KHz KiloHertz, abbreviated KHz. See *Hertz.*

Latency The processing time between audio's origin or trigger point and when the signal is actually heard. Latency above 10 milliseconds (ms) is unacceptable in a recording situation, because there is no way to properly match recorded audio with audio being recorded, resulting in out-of-time files.

Layback Importing, matching, and dubbing a finished score or soundtrack back to the video master. Exporting audio from Audition and importing to Premiere for final rendering, for instance, can be considered a layback.

Layer A part of a graphic document that is a subset of a larger document, that may be separated or uniquely managed. Photoshop documents in PSD form are layered.

Layover Recording audio from an analog source to a multitrack, DAW, or audio portion of an NLE.

Layout The manner in which a workspace or surface is defined and viewed. Encore permits single or split-window layouts.

Letterbox The aspect ratio of motion pictures is wider than those of standard televisions. To preserve the original aspect ratio of a motion picture, a motion picture includes black bars at the top and bottom of the screen when played on television.

Loop A segment or slice of audio that repeats without any indication of the end of the segment adjoining the beginning of the segment. Looped audio sequences are wonderful for seamless menu looping in Encore.

M&E Industry term for Music and Effects.

Master The finished product after a final mix has been created and the final mix components have been finalized with all EQ, compression, and volume settings. The final product on hard disk, tapes, or authored DVD is referred to as "The Master."

Media Another term for a file, related to audio, video, graphic, etc., in the digital environment.

Mic Abbreviation for microphone.

Midrange Audio found in the frequency bandwidths of 250–2,000Hz (2KHz).

Moire Visual distortion caused by the interference of similar frequencies, or the waving effect produced by the convergence of lines. See *Aliasing*.

Monitor Any device that allows audio or video to be seen or heard. Audio monitors are in the form of speakers or headphones, video monitors are in the form of a television, CRT, or LCD.

Mono A single channel of audio information as opposed to stereo audio containing two channels.

MP3 MPEG Audio Layer 3 compression format. Used to compress files for delivery over the internet or for playback on portable hardware devices to save space and bandwidth.

MPEG Abbreviation for Motion Picture Experts Group, a group that defined a standard for compression of video or audio media.

MPEG-2 MPEG-2 is an extension of the MPEG-1 compression standard designed to meet the requirements of television broadcast studios. MPEG-2 is the broadcast quality video found on DVDs and requires a hardware decoder (e.g., a DVD-ROM player) for playback.

Multimedia Media/files that contain audio, video, graphics, midi, animation, or text in any combination. Broadly used term to describe nearly any form of media.

Mute A software or hardware switch that prevents audio from being heard on a channel or channels. Audition/Premiere have a mute switch/button on every channel.

Near Field Monitors Small reference monitors/speakers within close proximity of the engineer/editor. Used in small rooms or for monitoring at low volume levels in larger rooms. Generally less fatiguing to the ear.

NLE Nonlinear editor.

Normalize A digital process for increasing the level of an entire audio file to a preset level without clipping.

NTSC National Television Standards Committee (sometimes humorously referred to as Never The Same Color).

One Shot An audio file that does not contain looping information, but is intended to play once, not necessarily in time.

Output Getting audio out of the computer to an analog speaker, digital output with SPDIF, AES/EBU, or other file format external to the computer.

P-frame In interframe compression schemes such as MPEG, the predictive video frame that exhibits the change that occurred compared to the I-frame before it. See *I-frame* and *B-frame*.

Pad Attenuation of the original audio level. See *Attenuation*.

PAL Phase Alternation Line. Most all countries use PAL outside of the U.S. and Japan (sometimes jokingly referred to as Picture At Last).

Pan Abbreviation for Panorama, or moving audio across the audio spectrum left to right, front to back, or combination of both. Each channel in Premiere or Audition contains a pan control that may be automated.

Peak Audio level's maximum point in a file.

Playback Listening/monitoring the recording after it's been laid to hard drive or tape. Reviewing the audio file as it's being composed. Also referred to as "previewing," which makes no sense, because you are not viewing the video or audio prior to any edit. You are listening or watching video postedit, making the term "preview" inaccurate.

Playhead Where the cursor lies within the DAW or NLE application as relevant to a timeline. cursor and playhead are generally interchangeable.

PlayList A set of instructions that tell a linked video how to behave, which audio it should use, when it should play, and what follows after its playback.

Plug-in DAW or NLE term referring to audio or video processors that may be used to supplement the application's audio or video editing tools.

Poster Frame Frame generated by video information in a video file, used as a button/frame in Encore to indicate contents of the video linked to the frame.

Preset Predetermined parameters of a plugin, template, or other predetermined setting for an application.

Preview Viewing or listening to media from an application. In Encore, preview is defined by watching video associated with a project and listening to audio loops/compositions assigned to the video, or listening to playback of a musical composition with or without video. See *Playback*.

Project A collection of audio and video files to be assembled for a final product.

.PSD PhotoShop document.

RAM Abbreviation for Random Access Memory.

Region A predetermined space/time on the timeline in any DAW or NLE application, controlling playback area/time. A segment of audio or video that may be separately managed for editing.

Render To blend all multimedia files together in one master file format. Akin to baking a cake from all it's individual ingredients.

RGB Abbreviation for Red, Green, Blue.

Roll-Off The point at which frequencies are filtered out. A low frequency roll-off will rapidly diminish frequencies beginning at the specified point. See *Attenuation*.

Rumble-Low frequencies too low to actually be clearly heard but taking up audio information space. Footsteps, vibrations, motors all create rumble. Many mixing/recording consoles incorporate rumble filters, set to approximately 60–75Hz, rolling low frequencies off at that point to clean up audio. See *Roll-off.*

Safe Title Area The area that comprises the 80 percent of the TV screen measured from the center of the screen outward in all directions. The safe title area is the area within which title credits—no matter how poorly adjusted a monitor or receiver may be—are legible. Encore displays safe title areas.

Sample Rate The interval and resolution at which audio is "photographed" or measured. Audio CDs are sampled at a rate of 44.1K and 16 bits. Audition is capable of much higher resolutions and sample rates.

Session A space of time dedicated to recording audio. Each time a new recorded file is created, it may be referred to as a session. Digidesign's ProTools uses this term for their basic document of assembled elements.

SFX Abbreviation for Sound Effects.

Sibilance The hissing sounds of the human voice, most noticed in Ss, Ps, Ts, etc. High frequencies, sometimes challenging to control. Use a DeEsser plugin or an EQ to control this phenomenon.

SMPTE Society of Motion Picture and Television Engineers. Also used as a timecode reference. **Solo** A button or switch that allows a single channel to be monitored. Mutes all other audio during playback when engaged. Audition offers a solo button on all tracks.

Source Audio Audio from the original program media. In a video file, this is on-location sound or audio related to the original source. It is often replaced or enhanced.

Spot Announcement for broadcast, e.g., a commercial. Also nickname of Douglas Spotted Eagle.

Spotting Identifying and documenting cues for music, effects, sounddesign, or other audio information should occur. See *Cue.*

Stereo Two-channel audio, consisting of similar or dissimilar audio spread across the left/right spectrum. Two separate

mono channels separated to one left and one right, would not be considered stereo, but rather dual mono. Stereo mixes in Audition or Premiere consist of placing elements on the multitrack timeline in representations of their occurrence across the left/right spectrum, and then mixed to a two-channel/stereo mix reflecting the positioning of audio elements.

Streamer Slug or graphic overlay on video playback, marking exact points that a cue is to take place. Functions as a visual hit point or cue. See *Cue.*

Subwoofer Speaker enclosure optimized to reproduce sounds from 20Hz to 125Hz.

S-video Short for Supervideo, a technology used for transmitting video signals over a cable by dividing the video information into separated signals: one for luma and one for chroma. (S-video is synonymous with Y/C video). S-video is a consumer form of component video used primarily with Hi8 and S-VHS equipment.

Sweet Spot The prime listening area between two speakers in a stereo environment or a 5.1 listening environment. This is the point that all audio channels are most precise, arriving at the same location at the same time. A relatively small area in most any listening environment.

Sweeten Polishing or improving an existing recording through adding other parts to the composition or audio elements. Processing of sound is also considered sweetening. Anything done to original audio in order to enhance its quality.

Sync Abbreviation for synchronize. A means of ensuring events consistently occur at the same time. Timecode is generally a common source to assure events being in sync.

T/C Abbreviation for timecode.

Temporal Compression A compression method that reduces the data contained within a single video frame by identifying similar areas between individual frames and eliminating the redundancy. See also *Codec*.

Timeline A component of Encore where graphic and video elements are placed to include them on the DVD. Timelines include chapter points and other elements.

Track An individual line containing audio loop elements.

Transfer rate How fast a disk drive or CD drive can transfer information to the CPU. May be a burst rate or sustained rate. High cache levels (8MB) or larger assist in providing information to the CPU at fast rates, important when building large composites in Premiere, lots of audio tracks in Audition, and deep menu structures in Encore.

Transient The difference between the lowest point of decay and highest point of attack in an audio file.

Transport Play, record, stop, rewind, fast forward, and record are all functions of the Transport in Encore. The Transport tools control position of playback and the playhead.

Treble The high end of the audio frequency spectrum, generally 2KHz and above.

Underscore Background music, not necessarily musically composed, to create an emotional atmosphere or environment. Similar to, and often called a music bed. See *Bed*.

USB Abbreviation for Universal Serial Bus.

Video File In Encore, this is relevant to QuickTime, AVI, or M2V files; data files that contain video information.

Volume The indicator for overall level of a loop, track, or master project output level.

Wave (.wav) The Microsoft designator for audio file formats, a common file type. Used by Windows applications as a file format.

Workspace The primary work surface in Encore, main window where most of the work is performed.